Assessment in Social Work

T0178017

Assessment in Social Work

Judith Milner

and

Patrick O'Byrne

Consultant editor: Jo Campling

Published by
PALGRAVE
Houndmills, Basingstoke, Hampshire RG21 6XS and
175 Fifth Avenue, New York, N. Y. 10010
Companies and representatives throughout the world

PALGRAVE is the new global academic imprint of
St. Martin's Press LLC Scholarly and Reference Division and
Palgrave Publishers Ltd (formerly Macmillan Press Ltd).

ISBN 0–333–65919–8 paperback

This book is printed on paper suitable for recycling and made from fully managed and sustained forest sources.

A catalogue record for this book is available from the British Library.

10   9   8   7
04   03   02   01

Printed in Malaysia

*To Huddersfield University Diploma in Social
Work students, past and present, whose contributions in
lectures and seminars helped us to develop our ideas
about assessment.*

Contents

List of Tables and Figures

Tables

Figures

Acknowledgements

There are many people who deserve our thanks for their help in the writing of this book. Not least are our colleagues, Pat Bastian, Eric Blyth, Christine Horrocks and Wendy Marshall, for their helpful comments on early drafts; Maxine Hamilton for her case example; Sue Hanson who translated our feeble efforts at word processing into a readable text with her usual cheerful efficiency; and Jo Campling for her support and guidance. We also wish to acknowledge the contribution of colleagues more generally. Our efforts have been greatly facilitated by the fact that we work in a stimulating social work department at the University of Huddersfield, which is well supported by agency partners and management. This has meant not only that we have benefited from a healthy exchange of ideas, but also that we have been well supported in our efforts in terms of time, advice and encouragement. We thank you all.

Last, but not least, we are grateful to Mary O'Byrne who tolerated Patrick's strange working hours during the preparation of the text with unfailing good humour, and to Rosie who bore with Judith's hours with stoic patience.

1

Introduction

Having practised as qualified social workers and worked in various agencies for more years than we care to remember, we have also taught social work students at the University of Huddersfield. The course module on assessment has always been the most particular challenge for us, and we have sought to develop competencies in the preparation of useful assessments that lead to planned intervention for the users of a range of services. In more recent years, we have been seeking new ways to bring clarity to this complex subject and also to address shifts in social work theory.

Probably the greatest of these shifts is the growing awareness of the uses of power, particularly the impact of powerlessness and oppression. At the same time, there has been a greater move towards constructionist thinking. Indeed, social constructionism has a great deal to say about power (see, for example, Burr, 1995; Parton, 1996). These writers also demonstrate that, as various ideas are being developed about postmodern approaches to social work and re-evaluating earlier theory, there is movement towards greater respect for service users' views. This involves entering much more into dialogue with service users, adopting a stance of uncertainty, and a willingness to listen to their accounts and co-construct more helpful accounts with them. Parton and Marshall (in press) describe the process as one of co-creating a sense of harmony with marginalised people, developing both reflexivity and action, rather than knowledge as such: in short, becoming aware of the socially constructed nature of social work itself.

Although there is no single definition of social constructionism, Burr (1995) provides a helpful explanation that takes the approach of listing the main things one would have to accept in order to be described as a constructionist. These include:

- taking a critical stance towards many taken-for-granted ways of understanding the world;

- viewing various ways of understanding the world as relative to periods in history and to culture;
- seeing knowledge not as being determined by the nature of things, but as constructed between people as they talk and interact;
- an awareness that social action is driven by the social constructions of the time;
- since the social world is made up of people's interactions, believing that there are no essential 'given' natures to be discovered;
- a questioning of realism and the idea of objective truth; and
- an awareness that the language we use determines the meaning of things, rather than vice versa; rather than being just a medium for expressing ideas, it actually determines thought to the extent that truth is the product of language: language constructs social reality.

From time to time through this book, we adopt a constructionist stance, particularly in our use of terms and phrases such as uncertainty, dialogue, language as crucial, partnership, participation, reinterpretation, people are essentially subjective, narrative, co-constructing meaning and reflexivity. Space does not permit a full analysis of this approach here, and the reader who needs such an analysis is recommended to use the work of the writers mentioned above. What we will be doing is drawing on this approach to present current ideas in such a way that they can be used in a practical framework. Here we are merely saying where many of our ideas on assessment are rooted, and we raise this to help the reader make sense of what may appear to be conflicting theories. For example, essentialist theory, as we outline in our presentation of Freudian theory in Chapter 7, does, we suggest, reflect no more than a particularly persistent social construction that is 'out of step' with other theories. Later theories such as behaviourism, cognitive psychology and solution-focused and narrative theory reflect much more recent social constructions that emphasise collaboration with service users, open-mindedness and uncertainty. Throughout, we stress the importance of assessment being rooted in usable theory in the sense that it leads to helpful action, as evaluated by both social workers and service users.

Having survived the experience of discovering how inadequate our earlier ideas were in terms of promoting anti-oppressive practice, we have been struck by the lack of any comprehensive framework for assessment in social work. There are, however, only too many linear, prescriptive and stylised assessment formats that come nowhere near meeting the complexities, uncertainties and ambiguities of current social work practice.

The lack of a conceptual framework was reflected in the literature, where it tended to be dismissed in a few pages of advice to the practitioner on the need to be objective and thorough. Closer examination of prescriptions on assessment activity revealed that techniques of assessment activity had developed from an unquestioned use of knowledge about the nature of people, which had been extensively borrowed from the disciplines of psychiatry and psychology and which was preoccupied with individual casework.

This did not seem to us to be a sound base for focusing on the task in hand, that is *social* work, especially in the new climate of social work following wide-ranging legislative changes. The new legislation defined assessment as a separate activity that was to be simple, speedy and informal, although the task was complicated by the need to provide value for money, involve the consumer and coordinate the efforts of a vast range of allied services. Social workers found themselves deluged with government advice on how to undertake assessments via a series of checklists for different sorts of service user.

There appeared to be no pool of wisdom on which social workers could depend in their efforts to meet the new demands and little evidence of the existence of well-developed skills in involving service users in the assessment process. The research into the effectiveness of social work assessments made depressing reading, especially when measured by service user satisfaction with assessment outcomes. Additionally, we found that, although most writers commented that assessment was a continuous process, there was little evidence that social workers did in fact re-evaluate their assessments. Indeed, there was a good deal of evidence that they sought to confirm rather than disconfirm their initial assessments, often shaping information to fit favoured theoretical models and concentrating on risks rather than needs. Most worrying of all was the realisation that a social worker's initial assessment took on the status of 'truth' and became the key determinant to future action and outcomes.

Therefore we attempt to examine the dominant concerns of social work in the new climate of empowerment, partnership, choice and value for money, and present an overarching framework for assessment work. Because social work assessments are essentially social studies of situations, we suggest that the tenets of sound qualitative research can be applied to this area. Our framework will emphasise the need for assessing social workers to make a clear statement of intent, be actively accountable for their values and take a systematic approach to data collection. At various points, for example in Chapter 3, the book will draw a parallel between good assessment work and participatory research. Everitt *et al.* (1992) also make this point and stress the value of the spirit of enquiry, making assumptions explicit, thinking through theoretical perspectives, clarifying hypotheses and testing them while engaging and listening to people's worlds and remaining conscious 'of the pervasiveness of ideology in the way we see the world' (p. 4). We suggest the development of multiple and testable hypotheses about the nature of people's problems and solutions and the making of decisions that lead to measurable outcomes and are subject to consumer feedback.

The development of multiple hypotheses means that social workers will be faced with the need to find their way through the thicket of concepts and theories that are current in social work, so we have provided a series of 'maps' that suggest ways in which social workers can find their way through the complex terrain of human situations. We do not suggest that there is any single correct way to analyse human situations but encourage social workers to be reflexive and develop a pragmatic truth that fits social work situations in a way which is most satisfying for service users. We see assessment as a journey for which social workers need to select the most appropriate map if they are to get to their destinations quickly and efficiently. We do not believe that assessment can be easily separated from intervention – change happens at all stages of the social work process – but we do think it dangerous to read a map while driving, so we recommend that social workers familiarise themselves with a range of maps before planning the assessment journey. Should they get lost on the way or should the service user not meet them at the destination, they will then need to consult the maps again. Uncertainty is, we suggest, the beginning of hopefulness.

As the values climate of social work assessments has changed, we suggest that there is little point in venturing into this difficult terrain without a weather forecast (Chapter 5). Any assessment must, therefore, be prefaced by a consideration of the power elements in social worker–service user relationships. Service user rights and responsibilities can best be understood in terms of equal opportunities and facilitated by social workers seeking to bridge the gaps between themselves and service users. Accommodating and being sensitive to all the 'isms' can seem a daunting task, but they can be conflated so that the task becomes more manageable and competition between various 'isms' reduced. We see gender issues as central in this process because men who suffer oppression because they are old, or disabled, or homosexual, or children, become 'unmanned'; black men become 'ultra-manned'; and most carers are women. We will argue that men need to be brought more clearly into the assessment process if it is to be both truly anti-oppressive and effective. This involves looking at not only the maleness of service users and their families, but also how male social workers can learn from women about caring.

Let us now introduce the structure of this book. Essentially, it presents a comprehensive framework for assessment that includes a set of maps to guide social workers towards helpful analyses, but first Chapter 2 considers carefully the contradictions of traditional assessment work, the problematic role of psychology and other social work knowledge and the impact of recent legislation.

Chapter 3 examines the evaluation of assessment and considers how far assessment can be viewed as a process rather than an event. Here our preferred framework is introduced fully, but, in order to prepare readers, we briefly mention in this introduction what that framework is and suggest that they will find this comprehensive framework useful irrespective of social workers' tasks and practice settings. We aim to demonstrate the breadth of the subject for which better analyses of situations can be arrived at by selecting from the six different 'maps'. Social workers will be able to select those maps that are more in line with their personal views of human difficulties and with their values (*their* constructions) and that are the most helpful for their individual practice. Map selection and the question of seeking the truth are dealt with in Chapter 4.

The framework has five stages, which we list briefly here:

1 *Preparation*: deciding who to see, what data will be relevant, what the purpose is and what the limits of the task are.
2 *Data collection*. People are met and engaged with, difference gaps are addressed, and empowerment and choice are safeguarded as we come to the task with respectful uncertainty and a research mentality.
3 *Weighing the data*. Current social and psychological theory and research findings that are part of every qualified worker's learning are drawn on to answer the questions 'Is there a problem?' and 'Is it serious?' (Existing theories are listed in Chapter 4; however, it is not the purpose of this book to discuss them at length.)
4 *Analysing the data*. One or more of the analytical maps are then used to interpret the data and to seek to gain an understanding of them in order to develop ideas for intervention. Six maps will be introduced in Chapter 4, each one being fully presented in

Chapters 5–10; we hope that their novel names will aid
understanding as well as recall.
5 *Utilising the analysis.* This is the stage in which judgments are
finalised. The difficulties of this stage are elaborated upon in
Chapter 11, where we acknowledge the stressful nature of this
stage of assessment, the issue of risk-taking and the importance
of language.

Because we devote six chapters to the analytical maps, it will be
clear that stage 4 is a major concern of ours. We hope that our presentation of these maps will encourage students and colleagues in practice
to draw on or select from these chapters to arrive at deeper and more
action-orientated analyses of situations and thereby create more useful
interventions. We are suggesting that this is best done from the humble
co-constructivist stance mentioned earlier. While practitioners need to
be clear about what they are doing, as Everitt *et al.* (1992, p. 33,
emphasis added) point out, 'it needs to be stated that *clarity is not the
same as certainty*. Certainty in theory leads to dogma and blinkered
practices. Clarity opens it up for scrutiny'.

We wish to stress the central importance of assessment for effective
social work, not only for planning interventions, but also for reviews,
for deciding when to end interventions and for the evaluation of interventions after they have ended. As will become clear in later chapters,
the search for a good assessment is not seen by us as a search for the
truth or a diagnosis but rather as a building of a more helpful set of
meanings and a more creative account that will assist service users in
moving on. Central to this is 'talk', reflective discussion that helps to
reframe difficulties and mobilise people's own potentialities.

Finally, we suggest that this book takes an approach that will be
helpful in promoting anti-oppressive practice, and that it will encourage practitioners to be 'concerned with developing knowledge in ways
which will enable service users... to become "knowers" (and have)
their understandings of their experiences of inequality acknowledged
as legitimate' (Everitt *et al.*, 1992, p. 3).

2

From Traditional Practice to Current Legislation

In this chapter, we outline some historical difficulties with assessment and its preoccupation with individual casework, searching for causal explanations in the past. Various pressures on social workers are considered, as are the consequences of the special role of psychology, notions of normality and the impact of recent legislation. Last, the issue of purpose is addressed.

The history of assessment

Traditionally, social work texts have expressed agreement that assessment is a key element in social work practice in that, without it, workers would be left to react to events and intervene in an unplanned way (see, for example, Davies, 1981; Coulshed, 1988; Reder *et al.*, 1993). But, having agreed on the centrality of assessment in the social work process, texts then dismiss the subject in a few pages. This could, perhaps, be due to persistent difficulties in defining the social work task itself and the subsequent skills:

> In default of any clearer definition, social work tends to be described in terms of the tasks which social workers undertake... This approach fits with the idea of social work minimising and individualising welfare services, but it does little to identify what the skills of a social worker actually are. (Curnock and Hardiker, 1979, p. viii)

However, this lack of definition of skills has not inhibited the publication of a steady flow of methods, 'how to do it' texts in which assessment has been treated as self-evident and unproblematic. Apart from some brief homilies on counterchecking facts and hypotheses and the necessity of reassessing wherever appropriate, most writers have made a list of information-yielding sources and then departed from the subject to other aspects of the social work process.

However, gathering information, sifting it carefully and coming to an 'objective' and 'accurate' conclusion is by no means as unproblematic as this inferred. Assessment has never been the scientific activity that many writers pretended. For example, Coulshed (1988) compared assessment with a social study, recommending that information be obtained from a long list of sources: clients, significant others, data in agencies, research findings, statistics and the worker's own knowledge. She concluded that:

> This social study avoids labels and is reached as a result of logical analysis of data which has been carefully and systematically collected. (Coulshed, 1988, p. 3)

She implied that editing needed to be done but made no suggestion on how this skill could be acquired, despite evidence that editing was not likely to be a straightforward task. For example, labelling theory suggested that there is a hierarchy of information, negative information being weighted more heavily than positive information and this tendency becoming more pronounced the longer a person was socialised into social work (Case and Lingerfelt, 1974). Similarly, Reder *et al.* (1993) found that social workers tended to treat information emerging after initial assessment both discretely and selectively if it failed to confirm the initial hypothesis.

The lack of clarity about the necessary skills involved in assessment meant that social workers became more preoccupied with the better explained methods of intervention. Methods then tended to influence the assessment, becoming a sort of 'practice theory' (Curnock and Hardiker, 1979), although this led to some strange recommendations in reports. Denney (1992), for example, found in his study of probation reports that many of the assessments seemed to contradict the form of work advocated. The most commonly used interventions were largely individual rather than social, although there have been some protests:

> If we are to maintain the integrity of 'community' care, 'social' service and 'social' work, we have to confront the constant tendency that we all have to *regress to the individualisation of individual problems*. (Smale and Tuson, 1993, p. 30)

Similarly, Barber (1991) also expressed dismay at the tendency towards 'reductionism' in which social work became equated with casework and individual solutions were found within the psychopathology of individuals and their interpersonal relations. He traces this development back to Mary Richmond's work in the USA, in which she identified two central themes: that clients and problems have to be individualised, and that successful casework requires careful diagnosis (Richmond, 1917). These themes, along with Freudian theorising, underpinned the vastly influential work of Hollis (1964). Yet Barber comments that, even earlier, C. Wright Mills was complaining about the limitations of such an approach:

> Present institutions train several kinds of persons – such as judges and social workers – to think in terms of situations. Their activities and mental outlook are set within the existing norms of society; in their professional work they tend to have an occupationally trained incapacity to rise above 'cases'. (Mills, 1943, p. 171)

Harrison (1995) refers to this as the 'forensic gaze', suggesting that it gives rise to 'placebo solutions'. He illustrates his point with the example of a refugee mother of five children (Mrs A), who lost half her family, struggled through a civil war, fought her way to England, studied in the evenings for a decent job and then popped out to the shop, leaving a 10-year-old in charge of the family. She was then 'threatened' with parenting skills training, a solution firmly embedded in the psychopathology of individuals and their interpersonal relations.

Why the preoccupation with individual casework? Barber (1991) complains that the problem with much casework theory is that the sole unit of concern and the focus of all analysis is the individual. The research by Sinclair *et al.* (1995) into assessments of young people accommodated by a local authority also expressed concern about the tendency of 'traditional' assessments to concentrate on searching for the origins of past problems. They comment:

> However it is defined, assessment was commonly associated with identifying a problem, the purpose of which was to find an appropriate resource or solution. (Sinclair *et al.*, 1995, p. 130)

Given that resources available to social workers have always been restricted, it is not surprising that they have been lured into locating the solution within the individual. There are several reasons why social workers find a broad, social assessment particularly difficult to undertake and present successfully to their managers. First, assessment of individual need is affected by expediency because there is pressure on workers to construct their assessments so that they fit into existing resource provision (Neill, 1989), although this is not quite what is envisaged in the original Department of Health guidance (1991). The pressures of expediency may mean that it is easier as a consequence to subsume some individual needs under more general family needs when faced with uncooperative family members, as the following example illustrates.

A hospital social worker was asked to assess Mrs B, an elderly, arthritic woman, for discharge home following her admission to hospital for treatment to bruises caused by her unmarried son who lived with her in her own home. At initial interview, the son was hostile to the social worker. Although he had beaten his mother severely, he gave a number of excuses for his behaviour – he was depressed following redundancy; he was embarrassed by his mother's requests to take her out in a wheelchair; she nagged him. At the same time, he was resistant to any social work attempts to change his behaviour and reluctant to see the social worker again. In order to minimise the risk of further assault, the social worker arranged respite care for the elderly woman, asked her not to make too many demands to be taken out in her wheelchair, and offered advice on how to deflect her son's anger. Expediency, related to the need to clear a hospital bed, a hostile family member for whom services were not well developed, and the lack of safety policies for social workers dealing with aggressive people, limited the assessment to the needs of the son rather than the original service user, utilising existing resources – however unsatisfactory these might have been. An assessment less influenced by resource limits, and intervention methods with which the social worker felt confident, would probably have pointed to the need for quite different resources and interventions to be developed. In other words, the social worker would have had to change the face of social work policy and practice:

> To empower the particular people they work with and respond to the unique circumstances that confront them on a day to day basis, professionals have to *reinvent* their practice and their perceptions of particular problems and solutions in each different social situation that they find themselves in. (Smale and Tuson, 1993, pp. 41–2)

The pressures of expediency are not, of course, limited to social work settings. For example, a midwife undertaking a 'booking in' interview with an expectant mother ignored her black eye because there was no section on the booking-in form for this sort of embarrassing information and no resources available within the hospital for dealing with this event, despite its obvious effects on the health of the woman and her unborn child.

Second, Barber (1991) also claims that the pressures of professional status affect and restrict social work assessments, the relatively low status of social workers compared with other professionals leading to 'social work's perennial infatuation with professional status' (1991, p. 25) and a resulting preoccupation with psychotherapy and family therapy as exalted activities among caseworkers. This means that there is a tendency for social workers to want to offer 'sessions' of therapy without necessarily undertaking a thorough assessment of its suitability. The recipient of the therapy may 'not always know, let alone agree with, the social worker's arguments and conclusions' (Davies, 1981, p. 69). Indeed, a psychotherapeutic approach might well dismiss any disagreement as client resistiveness. Additionally, these processes are aggravated by the pressure from agencies not to raise wider and seemingly intractable social issues, as the following example illustrates.

A child protection social worker raised the question of a local firm's exploitation of women workers at a case conference considering a single mother's alleged neglect of her young children while she undertook shift work in an effort to avoid the poverty trap of income support. The case conference was most unhappy with this information, with which it felt unable to deal other than by recommending the establishment of a crèche, which would not meet this woman's needs for quality childcare provision at unsociable hours in line with her shift requirements. The case conference preferred an assessment that sought the solution to the problem within the 'mothering'. This offered little to the woman's problem of competing demands on her as a worker and mother – what Edwards (1993) refers to as two 'greedy institutions'. Offering services around parenting skills did not address her very real needs to do with finance and social contact. Similarly, Bebington and Miles (cited in Department of Health, 1990a, p. 6) found that a combination of poverty and lack of available social support led to children being accommodated, and:

> Most people enter residential care because of the relationships they have, or do not have, in their social circumstances and not just because of their individual characteristics. (Smale and Tuson, 1993, p. 26)

When faced with the miseries of poverty, inadequate housing and poor employment conditions, it is easier to seek psychological explanations for events rather than explore complex interactions between the social and psychological dimensions of problems. The 'psychologising' of social problems in this way has been referred to as 'therapy to help you come to terms with your rats' by practitioners who are only too aware of the fate of an accurate assessment. Agency function rarely permits social workers to address major problems rooted in social deprivation, while, at the same time, holding them responsible for attempting to operationalise a care plan that is not founded on a realistic social assessment.

The role of psychology

While, so far, the thrust of this chapter has been to stress the need, to include the 'sociological' and decry the trend towards reducing social problems to the 'psychological', we believe that there is a rightful place for psychological explanations in assessments (the main theories being briefly outlined in Chapter 4). The real issue, however, is to avoid blaming or pathologising individuals by ascribing to them the cause of their difficulties that stem from injustice, disadvantage and deprivation.

Barber (1991) clearly argues that external difficulties cause and interact with internal difficulties. The 'social' frequently becomes 'psychological' and vice versa; the disempowered develop 'learned helplessness', for example, and resource improvement may not be a helpful solution on its own. While social workers need to draw attention to faults in the social system, they also need to bear in mind that many difficulties also have individual dimensions.

Many service users either 'lack the purchasing power to seek solutions to their problems or are constrained by the courts to submit to social work' (Barber, 1991, p. 29). Common to both instances is a lack of control over some of the important events in their lives, and therefore a 'psychology of empowerment' is useful. Powerlessness generates despair, listlessness and lethargy, people internalising the views of oppressors, blaming themselves and developing dysfunctional self-defeating thought processes and behaviours so that, in Freire's (1972) terms, 'the oppressor lives inside'.

Helpful assessments therefore retain a careful balance of the social and psychological as 'social work theories which seek to avoid or deny the need for individual change are likely to be as inadequate as approaches which reduce all human problems to the level of psychopathology' (Barber, 1991, p. 31). We will address this balance in later chapters, but here we turn to some serious problems with the 'psy complex' and how it has been developed in related social work knowledge.

What is normal?

As a developing activity over the last 50 years, social work has uncritically imported knowledge from other academic disciplines, most notably from psychology, and from other professional fields, in particular psychiatry. While it is common for professional disciplines not necessarily to own their knowledge, the dominant discourse in this area has had the effect of defining some people as 'normal' and others as 'pathological'.

When Rose (1985) developed the concept of the 'psy complex', he argued that, during and after the Second World War, the proliferation of clinics and nurseries for children made it possible to collect comparable information on a large number of subjects and that subsequent analyses led to the construction of norms. Developmental norms not only represented what was normal for children at any given age, but also enabled the normality of *any* individual child to be assessed by comparison with this norm.

Thus there came into existence a 'psychology' – a complex of discourses, practices, agents and techniques through which applied and clinical psychology could define 'normal' children and, by this definition, 'happy' families, 'good enough' parents and even social 'tranquility'. At the same time, psychology claimed an ability to deal with the problems posed for society by dysfunctional, abnormal conduct. However, Rose suggests that there has been a bit of fast footwork here, 'normal' (a value-laden term) being substituted for 'normative'. In theory, both words are adjectives meaning according to rule, establishing a standard or average. But abnormal, which is no more than a deviation from a standard or average, has come to mean undesirable.

That *normative* is regularly translated into *normal* is illustrated daily in television weather reports. Monthly totals of rainfall or sunshine are shown by comparison with previous seasons' averages. Although the previous averages will be altered by the addition of the current season's weather patterns, thus providing a new average, the old figure is regarded as a *normality* with which to contrast the current trends. The leap from normative to normal means, then, that there is some expectation of what sort of weather we can reasonably expect, and the weather forecaster is not infrequently heard to comment on how much sunshine we *should* have had – and, in the case of rain, how much we *ought not* to have had. By changing what is normative to what is normal, we then come to define the weather states that we regard as *desirable*. This does not matter very much in the case of the weather, but when we operate these processes in the case of human behaviour, it can be stigmatising to groups of people whose behaviour is only a variation of the normative, thus limiting the assessment process.

The most glaring example of this is found in a key theory underpinning social work assessment – attachment theory. Attachment theory is evoked at all levels of social work practice, providing an explanation for dysfunctional behaviour at any stage of the life span, including adult bereavement (Bowlby and Parkes, 1970; Parkes, 1972), loneliness (Weiss, 1973), marital disharmony (Weiss, 1982, 1991), poor relationships between elderly parents and their children (Cicirelli, 1989, 1991), dysfunctional family systems (Byng Hall, 1985; Marvin and Stewart, 1990), families and depression (Radke-Yarrow *et al.*, 1985), child abuse (Crittenden, 1988) and adult relationships generally (Feeney and Noller, 1996). The generic nature of the implications of attachment theory gives it enormous significance for assessment work.

While theory regarding the nature of the *process* of human attachments is not in contention, differing distributions of the various *forms* of attachment and the extent to which they can be used for generalisations are open to question.

Ainsworth *et al.* (1978) researched mother–toddler relationship styles by means of a 20-minute miniature drama known as a *strange situation*. They observed toddlers' behaviour in a sequence of three situations. First, the toddler was left with the mother in a small room with toys. The mother was then joined by an unfamiliar woman who played with the toddler while the mother briefly left the room. A second separation ensued, during which the toddler was left alone before the mother finally returned. The researchers were interested in the reunion behaviour between the mother and the toddler.

They found that the toddlers exhibited three basic relationship patterns. These were those with non-expressive, indifferent or hostile relationships, in which the toddlers devised a strategy whereby maximum closeness to the mother was obtained without fear of rebuff; those with strong, positive feelings towards the mother, where the toddler looked for the mother but played freely; and those with markedly ambivalent relationships, characterised by the toddler being clingy and angry. The researchers labelled these reactions as types A, B and C (for an overview, see Bretherton, 1992).

Type B was the normative response among the white, middle-class sample. Although the researchers reported that they did not impute that any one type of response was better than another, these attachment styles soon developed labels. Type A became known as the *avoidant* attachment style, type C became *ambivalent* and type B *secure*. There is a clear implication that the normative style, type B, is not only the *normal* style, but also the *desirable* style, and this has become translated into an explanation for later relationship development and self-esteem levels (Belsky and Nezworski, 1988) and even used as a predictor of potentially abusing parents:

> All children need secure attachments if they are to flourish and develop their potential. In any assessment of children, therefore, it is important to get to know the details of the current and past attachment figures in a child's life. (Department of Health, 1988, p. 38)

Yet this can by no means be reasonably implied by the theory. The research relates only to the behaviour of a small group of middle-class, white, American mothers and one child. Similar research in Germany (Grossman *et al.*, 1985) found that type A relationship styles were the dominant pattern (which would provide quite a challenge for community workers using attachment theory as their practice theory!). Similarly, the ambivalent classification – type C – was more frequent than anticipated in Israeli kibbutzim (Sagi *et al.*, 1985) and Japan (Myake *et al.*, 1985). There are obvious dangers in inferring desirable normality from what is merely normative within a specific cultural context. Also, the research only explains mother–child relationships, ignoring the influence of other attachments. For example, preschool teachers have been found to be nurturing towards insecurely attached children (Bretherton, 1992), highlighting the influence of significant others on attachments. Similarly, Harris (1991) found that a successful marriage acted as a substantial buffer against the depression arising from losing an early attachment figure. Wallerstein and Blakeslee (1996) likewise found that a good marriage can heal the scars of childhood – and that having loving parents who were happily married was far from a prerequisite for having a good marriage oneself:

> We have totally underestimated the amount of change that takes place in adulthood and have failed to grasp that the marital relationship is the central axis around which this change takes place. (Bayley, 1995, p. 5)

It is not only social workers who have adopted attachment theory uncritically – the UK as a whole seems to have internalised the tenets, as a survey of European attitudes shows (Family Policy Studies, 1994). In every country except the UK, bringing up and educating children was seen as the most important task of parenting; the British, however, saw providing love and affection as more important. Clearly, attachment theory is extensively overvalued in the UK, and a rigid adherence to it will seriously impair thorough assessment work.

By way of finding some way out of the trap, aware of the power of language, we have two opposing suggestions. First, avoid the word normal; in itself it implies desirability in some contexts and then oppresses the abnormal. In other contexts, it is a 'put down', as for example in 'Your essay was of normal standard'. Second, because most human characteristics can be set out in a bell curve of normal distribution, it is normal to have people at either side of the majority, some a long way from the average, so that we can say 'to be different is normal'. In our experience, it never hurts children or adolescents to be told this! They will often remark, 'You are the first person to tell me I **am** normal', and some will smile because they dread being different.

The existence of a 'psy complex' leads to an inevitable psychologising of the family and playing down of the social and cultural effects that will influence individual behaviour. The influence of psychoanalysis is strong here, although this was not obvious in the post-war period because of criticisms from new psychology about the theory of infantile sexuality, which meant that psychoanalysis did not gain much of a place in the state-funded sectors (Rose, 1985).

However, new psychology accepted much psychoanalytic theory regarding the importance of the unconscious and defence mechanisms, psychoanalysis retained its presence in literature and private counselling, and its therapies were deployed in state clinics for some children. This provided a new way for non-pyschiatric professions to conceptualise and actualise a specialised expertise and extend the scope of psychiatric normalisation to the private domain of family relations.

This was particularly influential in the expanded profession of social work in the 1950s and 60s, centering on dangerous and endangered children. This can be seen, for example, in the explanations provided by Bowlby (1964) for the production of disturbed children and adults; similarly, Young (1954) located the causes of illegitimacy within the unconscious desires of young women to seek a love object. The child guidance movement in particular became a programme for the production of healthy personalities by acting on the emotional interchange of family life, and children only achieved subjectivity through a kind of internal representation of the psychodynamic relations between family roles – in effect between mother and infant (son).

Therefore, social workers unfortunately became uniquely placed to link up the problems of *any one individual with the problems of them all,* to bring insight to family members and thus rectify the problem at its roots – in this case, in the family itself. During the formative years of social work practice, several types of socially desirable and undesirable behaviours were psychologised. Motherhood (rather than parenthood) and childhood were seen as 'desirable', while affectionless psychopathy and illegitimacy were seen as 'undesirable'. More recently, interventions have increasingly been aimed at children and pregnant women and less so at other adults. For example, the concept of psychopathy is now seen as inappropriate – probably because it does not respond to interventions. Indeed, most 'psychopaths' react vigorously against professional efforts. However, it has been maintained as a 'category' so that the most troublesome individuals can be contained (Ramon, 1986) and their potential dangerousnesss estimated (Home Office, 1995), while mothers (who are a softer target) are being increasingly subjected to surveillance, as is evidenced in trends within child protection work (Milner, 1996) and children's psychological needs have somehow become perceived as different from adults' psychological needs (Fox-Harding, 1991).

Within these dominant discourses, it is very difficult for social workers to make social rather than individual assessments, as the former would highlight what is currently well hidden, that is the moral issues involved in making judgments about what is and what is not desirable social behaviour. It is not surprising, therefore, that social workers tend to drift towards psychological reductionism, to analysing and working on the individual.

This was vividly illustrated for the authors in an assessment report prepared by one social work student. On the Diploma in Social Work course, the students undertake an assessment of another student's functioning for the assignment work on the assessment module. This particular student discovered that the subject of the assessment felt that s/he could achieve more if the tutors were more helpful and some of the lectures more interesting. The subject expressed no difficulties in studying or motivation. Rather than concluding that staff changes would help the subject, the assessment concluded that the subject needed some assistance to come to terms with his/her irrational thought patterns and suggested that a cognitive behavioural approach might prove useful. Even more surprisingly, the subject appeared to agree with these conclusions. No doubt, it is easier always to locate the difficulties in the least powerful individual, especially when social work explanations for 'dysfunctional' behaviour support this.

The effect on women

The least powerful adult with whom social workers most commonly deal is the mother. Despite client groupings around various specialisms such as mental health, disability, childcare, and so on, the bulk of carers are women and the bulk of social workers' clients are women (for an overview, see Braye and Preston-Shoot, 1995, p. 23). Not only is it easier to change a mother's behaviour towards her child than it is to change her partner's behaviour towards her, effect an improvement in her housing conditions or prevent employers from exploiting her labour, but also social workers are trained to focus on the subtleties of her relationships. Intuitive inferences regarding her psychic state and empathy with her emotional pain merely soften checklist assessment schedules, which allocate to her enormous responsibility for the well-being of her family.

For example, the Childhood Level of Living Scale (Polansky, 1981) lists 38 items that are the mother's responsibility, for example 'Mother expresses pride in daughter's femininity or son's masculinity', and 9 items which are the responsibility of both parents, for example 'Parents guard language in front of children', but no items which could be the responsibility of a father. Additionally, there is a Maternal Characteristics Scale with 35 items (for example 'Has shown defiance to authorities in word and deed'), but no paternal equivalent.

The impact of the new legislation

Traditionally, social work has become more and more bound up with psychologising the family, locating the roots of social problems within the family and solutions within the context of mother–child relationships. The sweeping reforms embodied in the new welfare and education legislation, with its emphasis on the family and its informal networks as an essentially private arena for the provision of care – a new view of the family as an independent economic unit – have clarified the distinction between assessment and intervention but added a new set of values for social workers.

Suddenly, the traditional social work values of confidentiality, individuality and respect have been hijacked by a political agenda that translates these values into a citizens' charter and talks of partnership, empowerment, multiagency cooperation, cultural/religious sensitivity and value for money. Also, not only have social work values become translated into everyday service users' rights, but social work practice has also been fundamentally changed by a greater reliance on voluntary agencies, related welfare agencies and service users' families themselves, all of whom may contribute to a care plan, emphasising the role of the social worker as assessor but reducing his/her role of helper, except as care manager:

> 'Assessment' has been heuristically separated from 'care planning', the former being focused on the identification of the objectives of care and the problems which are to be tackled, and the latter being focused on the actual selection of appropriate means to meet these needs, such as negotiating and coordinating services. (Challis and Davies, 1986, p. 43)

However broadly welcome the new legislation is to social workers, it has two major influences on assessment practices. First, by separating assessment from intervention and social workers from much 'hands-on' intervention, it removes them from the source of their practice theory. Second, it makes their values explicit. It does not increase resources, suggest new interventions or state how the people social workers traditionally 'individualised' are to be increasingly valued by society. While providing much-needed definitions of assessment, the new legislation has had the effect of leaving social workers in a vacuum between the old and new styles of working and/or encouraging a checklist mentality. Some of the blame for the vacuum, however, lies with agency management, whose role it is to equip staff for change; the law itself cannot directly govern practice.

New definitions of assessment

Although all the major pieces of legislation (the Education Reform Act 1988, the Education Act 1993, the Children Act 1989, the National Health Service and Community Care Act 1990, and the Criminal Justice Act 1991), emphasise assessment as a separate and important activity, with both the Children Act and the National Health Service and Community Care Act having the same ideological underpinnings, it is the latter which has most clearly spelled out precisely what is meant by assessment:

> there has clearly been detailed thinking on the purpose and nature of assessment activity and this is reflected in the impressive range of documents which have been produced by the SSI on this topic. (Sinclair *et al.*, 1995, p. 42)

If a social worker is able to adopt a discrete approach to each client group, he/she may well develop an expertise in a particular model of assessment, but there is no overarching framework. The following brief list of assessment definitions contained in the new legislation illustrates the complexities introduced:

Although assessment is a service in its own right it can be distinguished from the services that are arranged as a consequence. The needs-led approach pre-supposes a progressive separation of assessment from service provision. Assessment does not take place in a vacuum: account needs to be taken of the local authority's criteria for determining when services should be provided, the types of services they have decided to make available and the overall range of services provided by other agencies, including health authorities. (Department of Health, 1990a, 3.15)

Assessment arrangements should normally include an initial screening process to determine the appropriate form of assessment. Assessment: The process of objectively defining needs and determining eligibility for assistance against stated policy criteria. It is a participative process involving the applicant, their carers and other relevant agencies. (Department of Health, 1990a, Appendix B/1)

The PSR [pre-sentence report] should therefore be impartial, balanced and accurate... The purpose of the PSR is to provide a professional assessment of the nature and the causes of a person's offending behaviour and the action which can be taken to reduce re-offending. (Home Office, 1995, p. 7)

An initial investigation will clearly be needed in cases involving direct allegations or other reasonable grounds for suspecting abuse. The social worker must decide, in accordance with agency policy and in consultation with the professional network, whether or not a comprehensive assessment is needed at the next stage. (Department of Health, 1988, p. 20)

While Section 17 of the Children Act gives local authorities a general duty to safeguard and promote the welfare of children in need, there is little reference to the assessment of children 'in need' in the guidance accompanying the Children Act (Tunstill, 1993). As a consequence, women, who are most likely to be on the receiving end of assessments, are subject to a bewildering variety of formats depending on the location of the social worker within a specific specialisation with its own particular assessment definition. Take, for example, the following hypothetical scenario:

Mrs Edwards is a depressed black woman living in poor material circumstances with three children, two of whom have problems at school, and a partner who is due to be paroled from prison where he is serving a sentence for aggravated burglary. She has no near relatives, although she is a regular church-goer.

Mrs Edwards could find herself being subjected to several varied and contradictory assessment formats depending upon which part of the welfare services first came into contact with her. For example, her mental health needs might be assessed under the provisions of the NHS and Community Care Act 1990, but, equally, she may receive a risk assessment under the provisions of the Mental Health Act 1983. Similarly, the needs of her children may be assessed in terms of either Section 17 or the risks to them estimated under Section 8 of the Children Act 1989. Additionally, her children may be assessed under the provisions of either the Education Act 1981 or the Education Act 1993, depending largely on whether their special educational needs were determined to be worthy of specialist educational support or whether they fell into an exclusion from school category. Being black children, they would be particularly likely to be subject to racist assessments in either case (see, for example, Blyth and Milner, 1996). Mrs Edwards might well be assessed under the provisions of the Criminal Justice Act 1991 to determine whether she is able to reduce the risk of her partner re-offending. She is also entitled to an assessment of her own needs under the Carers (Recognition and Service) Act 1995. The only assessment from which she is safe is that proposed by the government White Paper on Adoption Law (Department of Health, 1993), although this is the only assessment which might lead to her obtaining a direct cash benefit. Should the reader consider this case example to be rather far fetched, we would ask them to read the Tyra Henry Report (London Borough of Lambeth, 1985) and consider the services that Beatrice Henry received.

New assessment complexities

Not only is our hypothetical woman likely to be bewildered by the complexities of welfare assessments, but so too are the hypothetical probation officer, approved social worker, child protection social worker, education welfare officer and community care manager. Despite their differing assessment briefs, they are all exhorted to underpin their efforts with the same principles; see Table 2.1 for a brief overview.

Table 2.1 Principles underpinning recent legislation

NHS/CC Act 1990	Children Act 1989	Criminal Justice Act 1991
1 Extend choice for service users	No extended choice	No extended choice
2 Partnership between users, carers and providers	Partnership with parents	Increased parental responsibility (binding-over)
3 Better joint working between agencies	Interdisciplinary case conferences	Risk assessment meetings
4 To be in charge of own life/decide on risks	Child to be consulted	No consultation necessary
5 Simple, speedy and informal assessment	Formal, comprehensive, prescribed	Formal, comprehensive, prescribed
6 Scope of assessment to be individually negotiated	Not individually negotiated	Not individually negotiated
7 Users' needs to be individually negotiated	Child's welfare paramount	Victim safety paramount
8 Requirement to find how many disabled people, keep a register and offer services	Register of 'at-risk children' but not children 'in need'	Register of potentially dangerous offenders
9 Cultural/religious sensitivity	Cultural/religious sensitivity	Cultural/religious sensitivity

As these principles are set out in most detail in guidance relating to the NHS and Community Care Act 1990, we will presume that the hypothetical Mrs Edwards' first assessment is undertaken by a care manager. This assessor is charged with aiding her empowerment through the rights of citizenship, the right to self-determination, dignity and individualisation. Her limited choices must be maximised and her individual aspirations and abilities realised (Department of Health, 1991, p. 23), and the 'assessment process should be as simple, speedy and informal as possible' (Department of Health, 1991, 3.3).

Additionally, Mrs Edwards should have extended choices as a potential service user and be involved in a participatory assessment process (Social Services Inspectorate, 1991). Baldwin (1993) argues that choice is defined as knowledge and experience of three or more options. Community care needs to be much more fully developed if these potential choices are to become reality. The current situation is that community care suffers from ambiguity, multiple definitions and being derived from economics rather than social welfare. While democratic user involvement has the potential to lead to empowerment, consumerist user involvement merely converts needs into markets (Baldwin, 1993). And our care manager has to work in an entirely participatory manner:

> Assessment is a participatory process. It necessarily involves establishing trust and understanding if meaningful information is to be obtained. The most effective way of achieving understanding may be to enable people to describe their situations in their own words, using their preferred language and at their own pace. Assessment should be a process of working alongside people. They should not be the passive recipients of a potentially humiliating service. (Social Services Inspectorate, 1991, p. 14)

After assessing Mrs Edwards' needs according to these principles, the care manager will come up against the reality that community care in the form of, say, respite or domiciliary care is in short supply and probably only available for 'deserving' or 'high-risk' cases. So this woman will have a high probability of facing child protection case conference scrutiny of her mothering as a means of converting her into a high enough risk case to obtain access to scarce resources (Denman and Thorpe, 1993; Milner, 1993), an experience which can hardly be anything but 'humiliating'. In this assessment arena, despite the parental partnership prescription of the Children Act 1989, the development of participation is restricted and ambiguous, and its focus limited and not always welcomed by families (Thoburn *et al.*, 1995).

The reality of providing resources in this scenario means that it is unlikely that 'Packages of care should be designed in line with individual needs and preferences' (Meredith, 1993, p. 41) or that 'Authorities are aware that assessment systems must centre on the needs of users and carers rather than the requirements of services' (Audit Commission, 1992, p. 36). This latter is particularly difficult to achieve in our scenario because of the prescription not to discriminate on the grounds of cultural needs (see, for example, Home Office, 1995, p. 5). Interventions and assessments for black people are particularly underdeveloped and inappropriate for these potential service users (see, for example, Ahmad, 1990; Denney, 1992).

Despite these potential problems for a community care manager, the Audit Commission (1992) expects an assessment to pull together the multiplicity of workers and assessment formats to create:

> a seamless service; agree distinction and responsibility between health and social care, liaison with housing agencies, independent organisations involved in planning. (Audit Commission, 1992, p. 64)

Assessing for a purpose

While no one would wish to deny the principles set out in the new legislation – indeed, it could be said that social workers have claimed a monopoly on caring values for far too long – it needs to be recognised that these principles are difficult to actualise in the absence of an over-arching assessment framework. They take differing levels of precedence according to the purpose of the assessment. Sinclair *et al.* (1995) find this helpful in childcare work:

> assessment is a term which can only have meaning when it is defined in terms of the purpose, the context and the manner in which it is undertaken. (Sinclair *et al.*, 1995, p. 36)

However, it is rarely possible to have a single purpose when dealing with families in trouble. Their real-life situations involve the assessing social worker in attempts to achieve a satisfactory balance between diverse needs, recognised risks and restricted resource provision. And there always exists the tendency to drift not only towards psychological reductionism as a placebo solution to inadequate resources, but also towards risk assessments as a response to continuous public castigation of social work efforts. Despite the principle that individuals should be allowed to assess the risks to themselves (Social Services Inspectorate, 1991), should an elderly person be found to have died alone at home it is likely that social work will be found culpable. However, the media are less inclined to blame social workers in this kind of situation than they are in child protection matters – an example of institutionalised ageism, perhaps?

A study of care provided for elderly people (Sinclair *et al.*, 1990, p. 176) found that:

> social workers were predominantly concerned with the degree to which clients were 'at risk'. So in order to assist decisions about staying at home or moving to residential care, workers examined depression, mental confusion, the client's failure to behave prudently, the effects of living alone whilst being physically ill or disabled, and environmental factors such as trip hazards or poor heating.

Risk predominates in the assessments of elderly people being discharged home from hospital. Clark *et al.* (1996) found that older people were less concerned about their safety than professional assessments indicated, being more concerned with coming to terms with their disabilities and retaining some control over their lives. This in no way follows the recommendations for comprehensive assessment outlined by Challis *et al.* (1990), which include physical and mental health, attitude and outlook, environmental and social circumstances, views of their most pressing problems and desired solutions, and identification of retained abilities and strengths. Of course, the drift towards a risk- rather than a needs-led assessment is even more apparent in assessments undertaken for the purposes proposed in the Education, Children and Criminal Justice Acts. Assessing for risk leads to a checklist mentality, which is, unfortunately, encouraged in assessment guidance contained in the Orange Book (Department of Health, 1998), National Standards (Home Office, 1995) and Code of Practice (Department of Education, 1994).

Sinclair *et al.* (1995) describe assessment as a preparation for decision making, and this provides a useful way of looking at assessment activity – how good are the decisions arising from it? The only way to estimate the effectiveness, or otherwise, of assessment activity is to assess its outcomes.

Summary

- Traditionally, assessment activity has not been well defined in the social work literature.
- Where there is an obvious psychological dimension, the balance between internal and external factors needs careful consideration.
- A preoccupation with individual casework has inhibited the development of 'social' assessments.
- 'Borrowed' knowledge from psychiatry and psychology has been the major influence on social work assessments.
- Assessments have tended to locate the problems of family dysfunction not only in individuals, but also in individual mothers.
- New legislation defines assessment as an activity separate from intervention.
- Assessment activity is defined differently in each new piece of legislation.
- Differing emphases on risk, needs and resources make it difficult for social workers to develop an overarching framework for all their assessments.

3

Outcome Evaluation and the Assessment Process

This chapter will first review assessment outcome and user satisfaction before discussing how assessment is a process rather than a one-off event and looking at Smale and Tuson's (1993) typology of assessments. Our assessment framework is then introduced and explained. The five stages of the assessment process are introduced and the issue of risk assessment is raised, as is the parallel with qualitative research.

User satisfaction

Research into service user satisfaction with outcomes has been uniformly depressing (see, for example, Mayer and Timms, 1970; Packman *et al.*, 1986). The clarification of assessment processes in government guidance should have gone some way to improving this situation, but the evidence, albeit mainly on children's satisfaction with care arrangements, does not indicate any marked user satisfaction. For example:

> Although overall the 'referred' assessments followed procedures which were more systematic, open and participatory, they were no more likely to lead to social work plans which were comprehensive or successfully implemented. Neither did the outcomes for the young people differ according to the nature of the assessment. (Sinclair *et al.*, 1995, p. 20)

These researchers noted particular deficiencies in social worker assessments: lack of expertise, inadequate evidence, gaps in information, preoccupation with past problems, overoptimism, service user dissatisfaction and the pathologising of black people. All of these would sound only too familiar to researchers of the most unsatisfactory outcomes for service users – child deaths (Reder *et al.*, 1993; Department of Health, 1994). The young people most rarely asked about their service user satisfaction are young carers, although there is a growing body of research that shows them to have low satisfaction levels as they are simply not receiving services (Blyth 1995; Dearden and Baker, 1995).

It is more difficult to measure adult service user satisfaction as much of the recent research focuses largely on the reporting of individual projects, although assessment outcomes are intended to inform planning about community care needs (Department of Health, 1990a). Also, as, in practice, the assessment holds the dual purpose of increasing service users' options *and* limiting the demands made on the service – what Payne (1991, p. 85) refers to as 'professional respectability to cost containment' – users will find it difficult to express their levels of (dis)satisfaction. The most frequently consulted service users – user groups – do appear dissatisfied with the consultation process. Barker (1994) reports that they are becoming increasingly overloaded and cynical, asking agencies to:

> stop asking us what we want, tell us what you think you can afford and involve us in shaping real plans to improve services. (Barker, 1994)

Assessment as process or event

Whatever the service user group, it seems generally accepted that assessment is more than a one-off event. For example:

> Assessment was conceived of as both an 'event' in the initial phase of early contact between the social worker and the elderly person, and also a 'process' whereby there was continual reassessment and monitoring. (Challis and Davies, 1986, p. 44)

However, outcomes research shows that this is largely a myth. Social workers almost invariably seek to confirm their original hypotheses (see, for example, Sinclair *et al.*, 1995; Kelly and Milner, 1996b).This poor practice can sustain prejudice and make anti-oppressive practice rather difficult to achieve (we will address this more fully in Chapter 5). Scott's Australian study of hospital and community child protection social workers (in press) provides the most detailed evidence of this tendency. As with Challis *et al.*'s study (1990), the social workers used a framework of assessment that gave salience to a narrower range of factors than that specified in agency guidelines, being influenced most heavily by risk factors. They tended not to consider situational and interpersonal conflicts, although, as discussed earlier, these are the main reasons for elderly people being admitted to residential care in this country. After risk factors, resource limitations had the most influence, with the result that needs factors were largely ignored.

To support a hypothesis developed at the initial assessment conducted within this constricting framework, Scott (in press) found that social workers sought confirming data rather than disconfirming data and that their reasoning was not supported by hypothesis development or exploration. Kelly and Milner (1996b) also found this tendency towards verification of an initial assessment, which meant not only that there was no re-evaluation of the assessment, but also that the social workers' range of options was reduced until they were left with no option but to close a case. They also found that social workers used self-justification to support the initial hypothesis. This most commonly took the form of persisting with the care plan on the grounds that it needed time to work – despite clear evidence that the plan was ineffective.

Sheldon (1995) similarly found that social workers used their interviewing techniques to 'shape' assessments data until they fitted a favourite theoretical model. Equally, he found that after one-off assessment, new information simply built up haphazardly on files, statements purporting to sum up problems and guide further actions being no more than lists of alleged factors loosely thrown together with little information on where they had come from or how they interacted.

While it is easy to sympathise with the resource and risk factors that constrain social work assessments, it is important to recognise that an initial assessment is the most influential determinant in the subsequent management of service user problems. Despite social worker complaints about feelings of powerlessness in the multiagency arena, their assessments provide the frame available to the case conference and influence its decisions. We will discuss this process in more detail later, but here we wish to make the point that there is no evidence that assessment is an on-going process that is improved by the involvement of a formal multiagency group. It is largely an important, single event in which the assessing social worker is the key player:

> Irrespective of whether cases were Referred or not, the district social worker held case responsibility and was therefore the key individual in the progress of the case and the outcomes following the assessment process. (Sinclair, 1995, pp. 27–8)

The only time a reassessment takes place seems to be when a new social worker takes over an on-going case. This must be confusing for service users (particularly if the assessment was participative), as well as demonstrating little faith in colleague's professional abilities.

Types of assessment

Smale and Tuson (1993) identify three different models of assessment, which appear to be closely linked to the salience given by social workers to risk, resources or needs factors:

1 *The questioning model.* Here, the social worker holds the expertise and follows a format of questions, listening to and *processing* answers. This process reflects the social workers' agenda and corresponds to the assessment style noted by Sheldon (1995) in which the data are 'shaped' to fit the social workers' theories about the nature of people. These theories are most likely to be psychodynamic in nature.
2 *The procedural model.* In this, the social worker fulfils agency function by gathering information to see whether the subject fits the criteria for services. Little judgment is required, and it is likely that checklists will be used.
3 *The exchange model.* All people are viewed as experts on their own problems, with an emphasis on exchanging information. The social workers follow or track what other people are saying rather than interpreting what they think is meant, seek to identify internal resources and potential, and consider how best to help service users mobilise their internal and external resources in order to reach goals defined by them on their terms.

Smale *et al.* (1994) make it plain that they consider the exchange model the desirable one: 'Routine, service-led "assessments" are the antithesis of an empowering approach to assessment and care management' (Smale *et al.*, 1994, p. 68). This, however, is not to say that there are not helpful questions that can deepen understanding, and these questions will flow from some theoretical map, as will be clear in later chapters.

We would suggest that the questioning model is most likely to be used when risk factors provide the main emphasis of the assessment, the procedural model fits assessment subject to resource constraints and the exchange model comes nearest to meeting a needs-led assessment. The questioning and procedural models are often found in combination, while the exchange model embraces the principles outlined in government guidance. It is the only model which has the clear potential to lead to re-evaluation.

Smale *et al.* (1994) provide a daunting list of the skills and values that would be involved in such endeavours. These include: joining with people yet developing a neutral perspective; adopting the central skills of authenticity, empathy and respect; empowering workers and service users so that essential decisions are located with the people who know most about the problems; reinventing practice, being creative; addressing social problems as a failure of a network of people; and testing the fallibility of existing theory and knowledge in each new situation. We hope that this book will provide some practical guidance, some useful tools and a choice of theoretical maps from which to develop more understanding, without causing workers overload and confusion.

There are obvious difficulties that must be addressed if assessing social workers are to balance risks, needs and resources within an exchange model. These three aspects cannot be totally separated – a major need is often the restoration of the person's own problem-solving potential and the mobilisation of his/her inner resources. There can never be a truly neutral perspective, although there can be explicitness. Service users prefer social workers to be explicit even where they do not agree with the perspective. Explicitness aids authenticity, but empathy and respect are more problematic than the social work literature admits. For example, a study of women social workers and women service users found that:

> commonality with service users, beyond the experience of intermittent empathic feelings was regarded as either impossible or deeply problematic. (White, 1995, p. 150)

It is difficult to show respect when social workers themselves are so little respected by service users and the general public. Neither social workers nor service users are likely to be empowered to the point where they will be entrusted with essential decisions. It is difficult to be creative and reinvent practice when you are subject to criticism much more frequently than praise and when your best efforts are undervalued.

Addressing social problems in terms of a malfunctioning of networks of people is perhaps the most useful starting point for improving social work assessments. Smale and Tuson (1993) consider it naïve to assume that local supportive networks exist 'in nature', and this is perhaps the major difficulty in actualising the values and principles outlined in government guidance. Jordan (1987) refers to effective informal supportive networks as welfare with a small 'w', and it is individuals who lack this sort of welfare who require Welfare with a capital 'W'. The purpose of social work, we propose, is, first, the provision of a formal network of Welfare and, second, the development of an informal network of welfare. This purpose would underpin all assessment work, subsuming the principles of empowerment, participation, cultural sensitivity, multiagency cooperation and value for money. We suggest an overarching framework below.

A framework for assessment

Although we recognise that it is extremely difficult to undertake a thorough assessment in a political climate that emphasises risk assessment at the same time as it limits resources and does not take need seriously, we do not think that social workers should accept these implicit constraints at the first point of assessment. It is rather like catching the first bus that comes along on the grounds that you haven't time to wait for the right bus or because you fear that, should another bus actually arrive, it might be full up. In any case, you will have a wasted journey, have used resources inappropriately and still not got to where you want to go. The difficulties have to be somehow surmounted if outcomes of assessments are to be more satisfactory.

We were struck by how the difficulties and deficiencies of social work assessments mirror early criticisms of social research efforts that attempted to move away from strictly quantitative, 'objective' research in order to achieve a better depth of understanding of human realities by using 'grounded' theory (Glaser and Strauss, 1969). Here, social researchers made no attempt to avoid the 'subjectivity' of the individuals and groups studied, allowing their subjects to tell their own stories, with themes and theories subsequently emerging from the data. This research method has obvious similarities with the exchange model of assessment proposed by Smale *et al.* (1994) in that it is founded on the basis of 'joining with people'.

This type of research suffers from the same problems as social work assessments in that no matter how one tries to allow the theory to flow from the data, researchers do (however unconsciously) hold theories about the nature of people, and there is always the danger that data will be 'shaped' to fit these theories:

Researchers cannot have 'empty heads' in the way that inductivism proposes; nor is it possible that theory is untainted by material experiences in the heads of theoreticians. (Stanley and Wise, 1991, p. 22)

However, this potential problem has been much better addressed by social researchers, and the qualitative methodologies developed have much to offer in the development of improved assessment processes (for an overview, see Robson, 1993).

Social work training devotes a great deal of time to the 'values' considered important in social work practice, but we have found that while students can talk intelligently about values, they find it difficult to demonstrate how they can be held accountable for their actualisation. They seem to think that appropriate action will necessarily flow if they have the 'right' attitude. For example, in our hypothetical scenario, we would expect social workers to be able to understand that Mrs Edwards, as a black woman, experiences double and perhaps conflicting oppression, and feel sympathy for this, but we would doubt that they could explain to her how this would actively affect their assessment. They would probably – and we would suggest fruitlessly – attempt to empathise with her. While empathy is necessary for joining with her, it is not sufficient.

Social researchers are much clearer about how they will be held accountable for their value stance because they will have prepared a statement of intent that is quite clear about relevant ethical issues – what they are, how they influence the research and how the researcher will 'behave' rather than just 'think' or 'feel'. For example, researchers in this field are very much aware of the sensitive nature of their research (Renzetti and Lee, 1993), particularly the fact that they are 'joining with people' who are less powerful than themselves – what Walford (1994) refers to as 'researching down'. Therefore they give careful thought to how they can protect their subjects from harm as a result of their endeavours *before* they begin the data collection phase. Social workers could give more consideration to the possibility that they may do harm as well as good. Their interviewing skills are so well developed that they may elicit disclosures that have little direct bearing on the referral they have received and which could also put service users at risk – particularly where there is potential violence in the family (see, for example, Dobash and Dobash, 1992, on the dangers of couple interviewing in domestic violence). It simply requires the social worker to decide what the boundaries are and clearly state the purpose of the assessment. Sainsbury (1970) maintained that the purpose of making assessments was primarily to represent the individual or family in its struggle for resources, but it should include drawing attention to any form of inequity that may be operating, as well as an understanding of the individual or family dynamics. He added that assessments need to include some consideration of why the situation is described as a problem and how far is the agency responsible for dealing with it. This recognition of the nature of one's agency function is part of every assessment and includes considering whether the user in question is able to use the help that the agency can give.

Additionally, it means thinking about possible interview schedules at an early stage and deciding how free-ranging any interviews can be. The 'open' interview proposed by the exchange model is recognised as particularly problematic in social research (Robson, 1993) and may leave vital areas unexplored. It is most likely that a semi-structured interview format will be the most appropriate one, and social work assessors could do well to consider the careful design of these in social research (see, for example, King, 1994).

In social research, this phase is accompanied by the drawing up of a plan to identify the key informants – the people, the documents and the agencies with the data needed for the assessment. This has the advantage of both broadening the range of data collected and setting limits on its potentially inexhaustible source (Coulshed, 1988). Social researchers also give thought at this stage to how data derived from verbal and written sources will be compared and evaluated (Jones, 1994), and how the data will be checked for authenticity (Forster, 1994). This process could be usefully incorporated into social work assessments to guard against the tendency of social workers to be heavily influenced by the first item of data collection and premature hypothesis development. Subsequent government guidance provides basic checklists to aid this process, but these checklists need to be more systematically used, developed and refined. Obvious gaps in data are rarely evident in written assessments.

Possible explanations will exist at this stage in both social research and social work assessments, but, in the former, they are more likely to be explicit and contain details of how they will be checked. Intuition may be accurate but should be testable. Even where there is only a single explanation, disproof is as important a consideration as proof. This means that when the data collection is complete, not only will themes emerge, but also data that do not 'fit' easily with these explanations will not be discarded. Interpretations can then be extended and multiple hypotheses developed. Utilising this approach in assessment activity would enable social workers to cope with the 'cognitive dissonance' that Scott (in press) noted was regularly avoided and fulfil

Smale *et al.*'s (1994) exhortations to reinvent practice and be creative
in each new situation. Social researchers are also more careful than social workers in
recording and handling data. Huberman and Miles (1994) refer to this
as the 'orderliness' of sound qualitative research via good data display.
This can take the form of verbatim transcripts, but, rather than remind
social workers of their experiences of verbatim recording during training, we suggest that other forms of data display would be equally effective. These include 'memos' (Field and Morse, 1985), flip charts and
working diagrams. Memos are particularly useful for storing data that
do not seem to 'fit', retaining them for later consideration, while flip
chart displays are useful in supervision sessions to ensure that discussion does not centre on one factor to the exclusion of others. Working
diagrams such as well-developed genograms and ecomaps are valuable
items of data display at this stage of the assessment.

Clear data display aids the next step of social research – the identification of emerging themes. These are noted in the first instance and
then 'collapsed' into categories (Burnard, 1991). Only after this process
has been carefully undertaken are decisions made about the priority of
emergent themes. The social researcher has to demonstrate how interpretation and analysis of data is as free from bias as possible. This is
done by what is known as 'reflexivity'.

Reflexivity is a broader and potentially more useful way of checking
assumptions than is the usual one-to-one supervision between line
manager and practitioner. The role of the line manager is a difficult one
as it involves facing both ways within agency structures, and it may not
encourage creativity (see, for example, the Department of Health (1991)
study of enquiry reports). Reflexivity involves checking one's interpretations of the data with people who do not necessarily have a vested
interest – colleagues and/or long-arm supervision – and, of course,
checking with informants. The aim is not to establish 'truth'; there will
be many truths and many realities that require various ways of knowing
and being in order to appreciate the full diversity of meanings and understandings that exist. More simply, what is needed is a clear formulation
of the situation that 'fits' with a range of other people's perceptions and
is 'testable in practice' (Sheldon, 1995, p. 114). The case conference (we
explain the problems of group pressures on consensus in detail in a later
chapter) is not the most effective forum for good reflexive practice, but
acquiring multiagency views separately and then attempting to make
sense of the possibly conflicting results will assist in getting more depth
to the assessment and a formulation of possible problems and solutions
that have broad agreement among key informants.

Reflexivity in a group of colleagues is enhanced if it is carried out in two stages. The first is the '*how to*' stage. This consists of the group listing hypotheses that flow from the heading 'In this situation it is really a question of *HOW TO...*'. For example, in assessing a situation in which a seriously abused and neglected child has been thriving well with foster parents for 4 years, but the birth mother wants the child, now 10 years old, to return to her, and the child wants to live with her and her abusive partner, it could be a question of how to:

- collect evidence to oppose the application;
- assess what support the birth mother would need to be able adequately and safely to mother the child;
- find ways of making the birth mother's home safe;
- use the law to remove the dangerous partner;
- find ways of maintaining residence with the foster parents *and* a relationship with the birth mother.

Only when the key worker decides (usually in consultation with a senior colleague) which of these (or other) directions to take does the second stage begin, namely that of '*GO AND...* '. This is a second brainstormed list of suggestions or options from which the worker can select, picking out what would be the most immediately useful to go and do. This process may well counter the 'groupthink' tendency discussed in Chapter 11.

The process of gaining depth of understanding of data begins with looking at the question 'In what ways is the problem a problem, and for whom?' It involves weighing up the situation, tentatively patterning the data, finding theoretical ideas that illuminate and help to interpret the story and make sense of it, then applying some of the theoretical maps to gain analyses, understandings or new accounts, drawing inferences (reasoning from the known to the unknown) and finally considering how to test the interpretations and recommendations. This process may go on after the meeting with the user(s) and it may be necessary to re-interview to check out ideas and share insights. Then there is the consideration of what resources are needed and what resources can be mobilised. This should always include the user's own internal and external resources and what intervention would be needed to mobilise these, so that, ideally, it is not just about meeting need now but meeting it in such a way that the individual's and family's resources are strengthened for coping for the future. Sainsbury (1970) adds that we should always consider whether it is necessary to intervene at all and whether there are any negative consequences from doing or not doing so.

By depth, we do not mean that social workers must know everything about their subject from cradle to grave. As we discussed earlier, a preoccupation with past events has been a positive hindrance in social work assessments – and it runs on the unrealistic assumption that social workers can change people completely. Rather 'depth' means reaching helpful explanations or analyses of what is happening and how things could be improved – being more rigorous and systematic. Thorough exploration of data from a number of sources means not only that social workers will have a wider range of alternatives, thus preventing 'stuckness', but also that we will become clearer about our practice theory. There is nothing wrong with *trying* to shape data to fit our existing theory as long as we actually know what it is and can explain it to people, we recognise when the data do *not* fit our theory, and we are prepared to revise and expand our theory and consider other analyses. This does not mean that we have to explain to service users that we are using, say, a social skills training or psychodynamic approach, but it does mean that we should be able to explain to service users what views we hold on how key social roles work and what explanations we have for their malfunctioning, being explicit about our views on the nature of people.

As distinct practice theories are difficult for many social workers clearly to articulate – students usually say that they are 'eclectic' – we will present an explanation of the main ones used in social work practice in subsequent chapters. We will not only outline the theories, but also include the advantages and disadvantages of each theory as an explanation of human behaviour. We do not offer them as prescriptive guides but rather regard them as a series of potentially useful maps to consult once one has identified the territory it is wished to cover.

If a social work assessment is undertaken with the same methodological rigour as sound qualitative research, it will necessarily include: a clear statement of intent, which also demonstrates how one can be held accountable for one's values; a systematic approach to data collection from an identified range of sources, which is carefully checked for authenticity and which identifies gaps in information; the development of more than one hypothesis about the nature of the problems and solutions; and a clear statement on how the final judgment can be tested in terms of demonstrable outcomes. The acid test of the assessment is satisfaction with subsequent decisions and action on the part of service users (empowerment in practice) and service providers. There should also be social workers' own satisfaction at not being 'stuck'. We present below the stages of such an assessment process in a linear model, although some parts of the sequence will overlap as re-evaluations will necessarily emerge during the process of checking the hypotheses.

The stages of assessment

1 *Preparation*
   - Make a list of key informants – people, documents, agencies. Keep this on file so that gaps in the information source are clearly visible.
   - Prepare a schedule for collecting data from *all* key informants. Adapt agency checklists for this purpose.
   - Decide on an interview schedule. If it is inappropriate to use an open interview format, make a list of essential questions to which answers are needed. Keep this on file, but give copies to the informants where this will be helpful.
   - Prepare a statement of intent that includes purpose, what one is able to do, limits and how one will be accountable for one's values. Although this may be given verbally to potential service users, keep a copy on file.
   - Make a note of early (tentative) explanations.

2 *Data collection*
   - Prepare a contents page for the file, listing the documents and where they can be found.
   - Store the data display on file, marking it clearly with details of who can have access to it. Store working diagrams, memos, etc. in a plastic folder at the back of the file.
   - Check verbal data for authenticity by repeating, summarising, and so on. Provide key informants with copies of on-going summaries for further checks.
   - Check written data for factual accuracy and mark unsubstantiated opinion clearly.
   - Consider widening the data sources if the accuracy is doubtful or there are obvious gaps.
   - Do not discount any data at this stage but note obvious incongruities or inconsistencies. Meyer (1993) has made suggestions for a generic check on what might be relevant.

We present our version of this, which could be adapted for particular agencies (Figure 3.1).

	Person	Partner	Family	School/ work	Home environment	Community	Society
Historic							
Physical state							
Behavioural							
Cognitive							
Affective							
Relational/ interactive							
Risk							

Figure 3.1 A data collection grid

For example, the community column might reflect a run-down neighbourhood, and the society column racism or a media campaign against a particular user group. It is always important that these 'social' columns, and not just the individual or 'psychological' parts of the grid, are considered.

We use the term 'data' simply to signify factual information. Because facts do not always speak for themselves and there is an element of subjective interpretation in most information-gathering, a distinction is sometimes drawn between 'data', which are unprocessed and raw, and 'information', which is interpreted and integrated into other knowledge. However, we favour data collection with as open a mind as possible, an awareness of biases if possible, and 'weighing' and 'analysis' as separate as possible, allowing for the spiral of theory and data discussed in the next chapter.

3 *Weighing the data*
   ● Consider how serious the situation is or how well the client is functioning in the circumstances.
   ● Identify persistent themes or patterns emerging from the data and list them.
   ● Cluster the themes and begin ranking them in order of priority.
   ● Check priority ranking with the key informants.
   ● Identify gaps in the data.
   ● Identify a group of people who will help with reflexivity.
   ● List the people to be consulted, noting their comments on file.

4 *Analysing the data*
   ● Identify theoretical perspectives and use them to gain depth of analysis (see Chapters 5–10).
   ● Develop hypotheses.
   ● Reach useful explanations for the situation.
   ● Make causal connections.
   ● Test the explanations for possible 'fit'.
   ● Check this with the key informants.
   ● Run a final check to guard against the selective use of information.
   ● Consult with the 'reflexive' group again, if necessary.
   ● Develop further explanations and list the ways in which they can be tested.

5 *Utilising the analysis*
   ● What help is needed by the user? By others?
   ● List the outcomes one hopes to achieve and the consequences one hopes to avoid.
   ● Clearly explain how these outcomes can be measured.
   ● Prepare an intervention plan.
   ● Establish an independent mechanism to monitor outcomes. This could include supervision, multiagency group or service users.
   ● Prepare a draft report that lists sources of information, analysis and initial judgment (see Chapter 11, which will also address risk).
   ● Obtain feedback on the report and revise it, noting any disagreements with one's judgment and the reasons for them.

   We have emphasised the need to develop more than one explanation for the data collected because this seems to provide the most effective counter-measure to the problem of 'shaping' the data noted earlier. Sheppard (1995) argues that this is one element in assessment that justifies the status of assessors as 'professionals', the others being the development of precision and clarity in the understanding of the use of concepts and theories, and becoming continually sensitive to disconfirming information (pp. 187–8). Additionally, a premature framing of the data has the effect of influencing the progress and outcome of a case regardless of the more usual checks such as supervision and interagency consultation. We will discuss framing effects in more detail in a later chapter but present an illustrative example here to show how developing multiple explanations improves the assessment process. A probation officer presented the following scenario at her local risk assessment case conference with a view to deciding whether or not the service user should be registered as a potentially dangerous offender:

Mr Y, a 44-year-old man, had collected his children for an access visit and taken them to his club, where he became drunk. He took the children home early and discovered his wife having a meal with another man. There was an argument and Mr Y left. After brooding about the incident, Mr Y drank further and then returned to the family home, armed with a knife. A fight ensued during which the new man friend suffered a punctured lung, the wife was cut and bruised, and the children became very distressed. Mr Y was arrested and bailed. Six weeks later, immediately after the preliminary divorce hearing, he once again got drunk and returned to the family home, where he shouted insults and threw a milk bottle through the window. He was charged with Section 20 wounding and was sentenced to 4 years' imprisonment for the wounding and 3 months for the criminal damage.

The probation officer put the following explanations to the risk assessment meeting:

1 This man constitutes a serious danger of re-offending because:

   • he has a history of offending (housebreaking, stealing, taking without owner's consent [TWOC], and drug offences);
   • taking a knife indicated premeditation;
   • the assault had serious consequences;
   • the man cannot accept that his marriage is over;
   • he has little consideration for the effects of his behaviour on the children, the 5-year-old having to undergo counselling following the fight;
   • his drinking is uncontrolled;

- he has little to do with his time since he was made redundant; and
- his wife reports previous domestic violence following drinking. He denies this or suggests that he must have had 'blackouts' after drinking.

(Sources of information: the offender, the wife and police records.)

2 This man's behaviour was a 'one-off', atypical offence with little likelihood of re-offence because:

- previous convictions were all in his youth, his middle years having been trouble free;
- his barrister recommended plea bargaining for a lesser charge but he insisted on pleading guilty to avoid his wife having to give evidence, thus showing real remorse;
- he now shows concern about the effects of his behaviour on the children and has negotiated with his wife to see them in the presence of relatives to reduce their distress;
- he now accepts that his marriage is over; and
- he has begun anger management and alcohol education programmes in prison, where he is reported to be cooperative.

(Sources of information: the offender and prison staff)

3 This man is likely to re-offend in particular circumstances because:

- it is easy to be remorseful and reformed in prison where there is no access to alcohol;
- he is likely to 'coast' through his sentence;
- he remains angry about his wife's new, much younger man;
- he is unrealistic about how he will avoid arguments in the future;
- there are potential problems over his accommodation on release from prison as housing away from his wife will remove him from sources of support such as relatives and friends, and he resents losing his own home; and
- anger management and alcohol education programmes are untested in real-life situations.

(Sources of information: the prison staff and probation officer.)

No one explanation was decided upon as the most likely 'truth' at the risk assessment meeting, but the ability of the probation officer to propose multiple explanations rather than having to defend a single one meant that the risk assessment meeting members could engage in a helpful discussion. They decided on:

1   What additional data were needed to check possible explanations, for example interviewing the wife away from the new man to check out previous domestic violence, seeking information about the children's emotional well-being, and making arrangements for this to be discussed at a further meeting.

2   What resources would be needed to reduce the potential for re-offending, for example what support relatives could realistically offer this man, what programmes needed to be established to continue and monitor the anger management and alcohol education courses begun in prison, what housing and employment facilities were available in the neighbourhood where the man would live on release from prison and how the marital property could be harmoniously divided.

The main advantage of the probation officer being able to hold more than one explanation meant that she could focus on all three areas of assessment – risk, resources and needs (in this instance, offender, victim(s) and circumstances) in a way which meant that she could develop a management plan appropriate for all the people involved, which was well resourced, with tangible outcomes and capable of being monitored.

In conclusion, we are arguing unashamedly for the making of high-quality assessment. This entails demanding, thoughtful work rooted in clear theory, and acknowledges useful assessment to be a complex on-going process. It would be highly understandable if social workers, faced with excessive workloads and many conflicting demands, regarded our framework as unrealistic, but the need in their case is for adequate resources in terms of staff and for supervisory support, rather than for short cuts or shallow work that can so easily backfire or make matters worse. Let us take time to ensure we catch the right bus!

Summary

- When measured by service user satisfaction, assessment outcomes are largely unsatisfactory.
- Assessment is usually a one-off event with little evidence of re-evaluation.

- Assessing social workers seek to confirm rather than disconfirm their initial hypotheses.
- Assessing social workers 'shape' data to fit their favourite theoretical models.
- Where risk is a factor, this predominates in assessments to the exclusion of need.
- A social worker's initial assessment is the key determinant to future action and outcomes.
- Social workers use a questioning, procedural or exchange model of assessment depending upon whether risks, resource allocation or needs are the main factors.
- Social work assessments could be improved if the tenets of sound qualitative research were adopted:
  - a clear statement of intent;
  - accountability of values;
  - a systematic approach to data collection;
  - the development of multiple and testable hypotheses;
  - decisions that lead to measurable outcomes; and
  - consumer feedback.
- Thorough assessments do not come cheaply; they need to be well resourced.

4

Selecting a Map

We have outlined the issues and the process of making assessments, and we have addressed data collection. Before considering in detail the theoretical maps that guide social workers' analyses of problematic situations, we will first explore the array of social work knowledge with a view to improving how we *weight* data (stage 3 of the process) and then decide which map(s) to select for the purposes of *analysis* (stage 4 of the process).

We aim to provide a way through the thicket of concepts and theories of which social workers become aware in seeking helpful explanations for the nature of people and society, and to locate some signposts. We identify the ideas that will be most useful in making judgments about data and map selection, and address how theoretical maps and data collection are not entirely separate. Additionally, we look at the debate about 'finding the truth'.

The theory thicket

Social workers are introduced to, and familiar with, a wide range of theory from the sociological (see, for an introduction, Haralambos and Holborn, 1990) to the psychological (see, for an introduction, Hayes, 1984). There exists a plethora of research findings concerning specific aspects of people's lives, including psychological research findings relating to such aspects as attachment and loss (Bowlby, 1964, 1982; Rutter, 1981; Murray Parkes, 1986; Howe, 1995), stages of human development (Bee and Mitchell, 1985; Sugarman, 1986), personality development theories (Schaffer, 1990), the hierarchy of human needs (Maslow, 1954), intellectual development (Piaget, 1977) and moral development (Kohlberg, 1968). Sociology offers theoretical insights into social strata, power and oppression (Haralambos and Holborn, 1990), while social psychology looks at, for example, groups and decision-making (Janis and Mann, 1977), and the dynamics of formal organisations (Morgan, 1986). The cycles of development in family life are studied (Carter and McGoldrick, 1980), as are deviance and crime (Walker, 1987), and mental illness (Olsen, 1984). On top of these, there is a knowledge of the law and rights (Brayne and Martin, 1993). So the question readers will probably ask is 'How do all these fit together?'

To answer these questions, we take the reader back to stage 3 of our initial overall framework – weighing the data. It is at this stage in the assessment process that the social worker makes judgments and evaluations on how well service users are doing in their particular circumstances. Are their strengths sufficient or are their limitations too great? Do their capacities and resources seem to be sufficient for coping? How does the difficulty or the particular situation compare with the norm? How much does it deviate from the culturally acceptable, the legal or the affordable? Are the risks acceptable? In other words, is there a problem? The making of these judgments is informed by a background knowledge of all the above theories and is also usually assisted by agency guidelines and procedures (for example, the *Looking After Children* pack, Department of Health, 1995b), and is underpinned by core social work values and skills, even though these are not often made explicit.

Agency practice will vary according to whether the dominant purpose of the work is the control of deviance, the empowerment of needy and oppressed people, or ensuring people's quality of life (Richards, 1987). However, how any worker uses theory is a matter of great uncertainty, which we hear most commonly expressed via metaphors such as 'once you learn to ride the bicycle, you do it without thinking'. It seems to us that in weighing up the gravity or need of a case, social workers' judgment is informed, and their beliefs bolstered, by the above-mentioned core theory. Most social workers would say this is useful and that they are using more than mere common sense.

The very existence of alternative and often competing theories of human behaviour and human problems does add considerable complexity to the task, but we hope in this chapter to provide some assistance in explicit theory selection. It is not, however, the intention of this book to elaborate on these areas of theory. We simply point to them as informing all social work activity and show some key sources where they can be studied. However, they do connect with the maps in that preference for a particular map will lead to more use of, or reliance on, particular aspects of core theory. One theory will fit better than another theory with individual social workers' views of people and difficulties, and with ideas on 'the nature of people' (Aggleton and Chalmers, 1986) implicit in any one chosen map.

We wish to emphasise that much of the theory can be used oppressively when social workers use it as if it were *the truth* for particular client situations. Most of it is culturally biased and presented as more 'certain' than it really is. For example, we rightly hesitate to describe any family as normal or abnormal, healthy or unhealthy, although we do need to have some idea of which families need help and which do not (Sainsbury, 1970). Theories help us to develop informed opinions when they increase our understanding of the likely relationships between events in people's lives, the impact of personal history and social background and present needs and behaviours, and when they add to our awareness of the sources of distress, be they external, such as oppression, or internal, such as guilt. They can help us to understand the values implicit in policies, human motivation and the importance to people of their roles in life and their expectations.

The trouble with certainty

We would like to think that theories can usefully help us to consider how some 'solutions' can make matters worse, how outcomes are often so uncertain that it is only at the end of our involvement that they can be verified, how all assessments are essentially tentative and how uncertainty can be a positive.

No assessment should be 'once and for all' – it is a continuing process that is improved as intervention proceeds. It is also revised when work is formally reviewed and needs to be reconsidered when termination is being planned. It remains in focus as effectiveness is evaluated after the work has finished. However, it is never to be believed in to the exclusion of other possibilities. Hence, we say that rather than seeking to 'prove' hypotheses, we seek to '*improve*' them – and proof will come only when the work is evaluated. Ideally, we need to develop competing hypotheses and look for evidence to disprove them because 'along with uncertainty comes hope for change', or at least because such an approach would remove the risk of grave inaccuracy. Over-reliance on theory conflicts with what Pozatek (1994, p. 397) calls 'the uncertainty principle' because the very act of observing changes what is being observed. This should prompt us to ask how we can tell that what we see is what was there before we saw it. Without realising this difficulty, workers can disseminate information and 'initiate and maintain a pathologising discourse' (Pozatek, 1994, p. 398) that is oppressive. The discussion of attachment theory in Chapter 2 shows an example of this. By way of contrast, the constructionist approach is to work with service users in a way that is respectful of the unique complexity of each person's life and his/her understanding of it. This shift in perspective is necessary to 'account for the unpredictability and randomness that are part of every day life' (Pozatek, 1994, p. 398) in any particular culture. Assessments by professionals all too often get accorded the status of truth and, unchallenged, the resulting beliefs become accepted as true.

This is not only oppressive to service users, but also limits what social workers think can happen. Pozatek (1994) reports seeing many interventions unhelpful to service users that involved a high degree of worker certainty. Understanding people's experience is as important as understanding their behaviour. This requires a collaborative approach to interpreting meaning, an awareness of the power of the prevailing discourse, a willingness to co-construct shared understandings of situations by dialogue with service users, and adopting a stance of uncertainty that pushes us to try harder to grasp a service user experience. Assessments have to be more like qualitative than quantitative studies, and be 'making sense' activities rather than ones clinging to naïve realist epistemologies. Influenced by postmodern perspectives, we believe that no single theory can fully tell the truth and that there is anyway a plurality of truths. Truth can only be interpreted (Parton and Marshall, in press) and certainty is illusory. We like the expression 'working truths'.

So we take an interpretist view, committed to understanding the *meanings* that service users use to make sense of their lives. This approach will be seen also in the next chapter when we discuss work with service users and the 'isms' of discrimination. However, although we do acknowledge the existence of reality that we can 'bump into', we maintain that assessments never fully reproduce it. What we see and hear is evidence or data, but we need reflexive checking of our assumptions and our plans for action in coming to an understanding of those data.

Therefore, while we need to be aware of what is known in the social sciences and use theory to check our own prejudices as we make the initial judgment in stage 3 of an assessment, we need to welcome uncertainty in work where 'the perturbing agent can only serve to trigger an effect: it is the living being [the service user] who determines the outcome of the interaction' (Maturana and Varela, 1987, cited in Pozatec, 1994, p. 397). What separates the social scientist from the mere technician is the 'capacity to shift from one perspective to another' (Mills, 1970). Parton and Marshall put it well when they say this demands that we can make our minds up about what to do but still remain open-minded. It will be clear to the reader that we are attracted to social constructionism in the way in which we view social and psychological theories; for an excellent introduction to this approach, we recommend Burr (1995).

Map selection

Stage 4 of the assessment framework involves analysis of the data, and this requires an application of one or more of the theoretical maps (derived from methods of intervention) in order to gain a useful depth of understanding that will guide intervention. In our experience, many assessment reports simply describe problems from various subjective perspectives and then give a common-sense summary of the situation, perhaps adding some suggestions for what should be done. When we ask workers how they arrived at their recommendation, they may say that this is what they always do in these cases, or that's the way it is done in the particular agency. The idea of selecting a theory to provide a particular analysis or explanation of how things have become as they are is felt to be only adding to the workers' difficulties and a rather academic exercise in any case, but it is crucial that our theoretical models are made explicit. We need to be aware also of the consequences of using a particular map, with its underpinning philosophy, as this may not accord with service user experiences.

There are many 'maps' from which to choose, but here we present five of those traditionally best known in social work and a more recent and less well-known one. None of the resulting analytic descriptions can reproduce reality; they can only propose helpful re-understandings:

> It is now widely accepted that any statement that postulates meaning is interpretive – that these statements are the outcome of an enquiry that is determined by our maps or analogies or, as Goffman puts it, by 'our interpretive frameworks'. (White and Epston, 1990, p. 5)

In considering the factors that influence theory selection in social work practice, it is our impression that *fit* with the original data or type of problem is the greatest influence in theory selection. For example, family therapy ideas 'fit' problems of family relationships, parenting problems 'fit' with notions of skills training, a task-centred approach has particular ways of looking at interpersonal interactions, and behavioural problems 'fit' with the behaviour modification approach. However, substance abuse could 'fit' equally with a behavioural approach or with a cognitive approach such as solution-focused work, and affective disorders such as depression 'fit' with a cognitive analysis of difficulties or psychodynamic interpretations. We need to get 'fit' not only between data and analytic maps, but also between our analyses *and those of service users themselves* – except when these are clearly in conflict with the needs or rights of others. The existence of adequate 'fit' between original data and intervention should not, however, be seen as necessarily prescriptive. In assessments of need or risk, notions about capacity for self-care 'fit' well in some situations, such as an older person living alone, but less well in situations such as a parent struggling to manage a child's temper tantrums. At the end of each of the following 'map' chapters, we will suggest some advantages and disadvantages that might be associated with that map and therefore possibly with its use in certain situations.

Perhaps the second greatest influence on assessment is the actual services that are available and the criteria for suitability of these, even when these only lead to fitting people in to the best (least bad) alternative (Wright *et al.*, 1994). The interventions that the worker can personally deliver and the worker's preferred explanation for problems influence theory selection. As the reader will discover, some maps claim to be useful for most situations, and most social workers will feel that they do not need to draw on all six maps.

An alternative way of selecting the most useful map would include the following features. Having engaged with a potential service user and begun to establish trust, thus generating a flow of information or data to which one has listened attentively, one could begin to ask 'Where is the problem/need/solution mainly located, outside the service user, within the service user, or between the user and others?' In other words, is it extrapersonal, intrapersonal or interpersonal? Frequently, a person's need/problem/solution is perceived by the individual or the family as being *both* internal and external (Sainsbury, 1970).

Where the problem or solution is considered to be mainly outside the service user, it is for the most part not the service user who is the main target for change but the social system. Then it may be a matter of advocacy, or a needs and risks assessment and a survey of appropriate resources, or possible systems analysis as a preparation for systemic change.

If it is felt to be inside the person, the assessing social worker needs to ask whether it consists of a habit, in which case behavioural ideas may fit best. If it is a feeling, a psychodynamic approach or a cognitive approach might be considered, while cognitive theory strongly suggests itself for a self-defeating pattern of thinking. If it is most likely to be found between the person and others, the selection of theory may depend on whether the 'other' is an individual, a family, an organisation or the community: if a person, task-centred theory or cognitive theories may help; if a family, ideas from family therapy theory may help; if the community, ideas from Chapter 5 may help, or a systems analysis (see Chapter 6).

Diagrammatically, the options could be presented as in Table 4.1.

Table 4.1 Social science theory

Extrapersonal	Intrapersonal	Interpersonal
Feminist or anti-oppressive ideas (Ch 5)	Behaviourism (habit) (Ch 8)	Task-centred or cognitive ideas (Chs 9 and 10)
OR	OR	OR
Resources, needs and risk assessment (Ch 3)	Pscychodynamic (feeling) (Ch 7)	Family therapy (Ch 6)
OR	OR	OR
Systems ideas (Ch 6)	Cognitive work (thought processes) (Chs 8–10)	Systems ideas (Ch 6)
	OR	
	Task- and solution-focused work (for combinations of behavioural, emotional and cognitive problems) (Chs 9 and 10)	

However, our attempt to set this out in diagrammatic form reveals the difficulty of appropriately matching theories to types of problem. This difficulty arises from the fact that more than one theoretical approach may be helpful in any one case and various theories can tackle some problems equally well, depending on the skills of the worker. For example, if a service user is depressed, psychodynamic theory may provide useful insights, but cognitive theory also has its own way of helping with this problem, claiming that feeling is the result of dysfunctional thinking. If the cause of the depression is interpersonal, family therapy could be indicated, whereas if the cause is external, tackling oppression and finding resources will be more important.

Also, social workers' own preferences and abilities have to be taken into account, as long as they can show that they are effective in achieving service user satisfaction. Some social workers and writers claim that one method of assessment and intervention can suit all situations, an example being de Shazer (1993), who suggests that there are no contraindications for solution-focused work.

Of course, various ways of working may take a longer or shorter time, and since our premise is that assessment is more helpful if it matches the intended intervention, busy workers will favour ideas from brief therapy. We feel that there is little point in doing a thorough Freudian analysis if there is neither the time nor the expertise to carry out the related intervention. Cost will be a further factor to consider. However, the 'bus' metaphor in Chapter 3 also applies; quickest and cheapest is not necessarily best.

In some situations, the theory will immediately suggest itself because the intervention will be 'ready made'. For example, if the problem is one of bed wetting, most social workers will suggest a reward system such as a star chart or a warning bell, both being based on behaviourist theory. So too is skills training for, perhaps, a man with underdeveloped fathering skills, and assertion training for those who have not learned to assert their needs appropriately and who may either be too aggressive or too passive. However, we cannot stress too strongly that assessors always need to look at the extrapersonal and the interpersonal before focusing on the intrapersonal because power is an ever-present issue. It is extremely rare in any case for any 'problem' to be entirely intrapersonal.

In practice, the selection of a theoretical framework is usually not a clear-cut matter. Finding the *best fit* will, especially for new social workers, often entail consideration of more than one map and trying them for fit and usefulness. In this process, one would be looking not only at aspects that fit well, but also at aspects that clash or misfit and then weighing up the positives and the negatives. By positives we mean those aspects of theory that shed light on the difficulty and how it might have started and, more importantly, on how it is maintained in existence and what might be helpful in its resolution. By adding together these positives and allowing for any negatives, social workers can compare different approaches for fit and usefulness. There is no reason why the service user should not be included in this process.

The spiral of data, theory and analysis

We now wish to address another aspect that can be confusing to assessing social workers: the overlap between theoretical analysis and data collection. This comes about because the particular theoretical approach that a social worker implicitly holds, or selects, influences the questions asked when reaching for depth of understanding. Furman and Ahola (1992) maintain that it is not the truth of a theory as established by research or some value system that matters but the usefulness of the questions that flow from it. They demonstrate this by using a totally fictitious theory and showing how it can lead to a useful analysis. The social worker begins by saying something like this:

> Come with me on an imaginary interview. In this interview I explain to people that in a dark, damp cave outside of town there lives a gremlin called The Haaja, whose sole purpose in life is to get people to have problems like yours. Any steps to change these problems upset him very much, because his whole life is dedicated to making people suffer these problems, in your case drug taking. Our job is to defeat the Haaja and our first step is to work out what he likes you to do and what he hates to see you doing.

So, in this interview, the theory being used to explain the problem is that such problems are caused by a gremlin called The Haaja. This being the case, the questions naturally include him. They lead to collecting new data that are linked to the theory – data about what the Haaja likes and dislikes. The questions could seek out a list of these likes and dislikes; for example, in a scenario where the subject is a drug user, The Haaja likes the subject to:

- associate with other users;
- not bother about getting a job;
- sleep during the day and 'hang out' at night;
- steal money to feed the habit;
- avoid treatment;
- ignore warning literature;
- squat;
- be anti-police; and
- not talk to the family about the drugs.

As the subject completes this list, s/he could be asked if it includes many of the things currently done. Then s/he could be asked to begin a list of dislikes the Haaja may have, such as:

- returning home;
- looking for a job;
- discussing the problem with the family;
- visiting a counselling service; or

- sleeping at night;

or anything else the Haaja would really hate, for example:

- reading about drugs; and
- trying to change his/her friends.

And which of these things could you start practising in order to begin to worry the Haaja? Note that the Haaja's likes and dislikes include both *interpersonal* and *extrapersonal* factors.It would not be difficult to include *intrapersonal* factors too.

These questions, driven by this fictitious map, can lead to a helpful analysis that helps the subject to see what might be done to start developing a solution for the difficulty. The subject may begin to see that many of the behaviours now engaged in are ensuring the continuance of the problem, or at least are helping to maintain it, and make its resolution less likely. However, our purpose in presenting this 'theory' is to show how the theory shapes the questioning, which, in turn, leads to sets of data being produced because our very questions construct their own answers:

> New narratives yield new vocabulary, syntax and meaning in our accounts [and] they define what constitute the data of these accounts (Bruner, 1986, p. 143).

In beginning an assessment, therefore, after having engaged with the subject, it is a matter of collecting initial data by listening to the stories of the potential service users and others. These data will point to a possible preferred theory in the mind of the worker, and the resulting questions will provide their own data (service users' answers or information). This will in turn lead to an explanation of this service user's particular situation, the explicit use of more than one theory clearly being an important safeguard against bias. Data collection does not stop dead at the end of a checklist so that inference-making can begin with the use of a theory; rather, these aspects spiral around each other as the theory is drawn on to generate new data of its own. This will be true of any theory that may be selected.

Interventive methods follow from the assessment, which is based on the data, including needs, risks and resources, and on the inferences made. This is not the same as the methods-led assessments referred to in Chapter 2, nor is it the same as jumping to conclusions too soon and making the data fit one's theory. As we stressed in the previous chapter, social workers should have more than one hypothesis, and both hypotheses and questions are generated by theory. There is always some 'theory' as we cannot empty our heads. Thompson (1995) discusses 'the fallacy of theoryless practice' and shows how complex actions cannot be divorced from thought. He is not just referring to 'book theory' but also to the informal theory that underlies people's explanations of events. It is only when we acknowledge what ideas influence our actions that we are in a position to question them. Without such reflection, we risk becoming dogmatic. In assessment, because social workers ought to know why they are asking particular questions, they need to know and make explicit what 'theory' is driving their questions.

Finding the truth

By now, the reader must be wondering how we can be placing equal value on different theories or even suggesting that a fictitious theory might be useful. Surely the truth about a situation is what counts? We do believe that there is such a thing as truth, certainly in the collection of accurate data or the identification of service users and the resources available to assist with their needs. However, we also believe that there are many, and often conflicting truths, about any one subject's situation, and a true analysis is more difficult. Since an analysis is a making sense of a set of facts, and it is possible to construct any number of accounts, we would argue that the most truthful analysis is the one that is the most helpful; the one that leads to the most useful understanding and to an intervention that achieves the service user's goals is the one that has the most truth. For instance, Pocock (1995) gives the example of a difficult child whose behaviour was first explained as 'innate badness', whereas a more helpful, and more true, explanation for all concerned was that he was angry over his parents' separation. In the current state of the social sciences, it is not possible to prove that any helpful analysis is more or less true than another, and we know of no one who expects that it will ever be possible to reach one analysis universally accepted as the most true. Neither is it likely that we will be able to reach a deeper level of meaning beneath surface appearances that will rule out all other meanings. For constructionism, it is unlikely in social work that there will be one version of events that is true in the sense of making all others false. This can be attacked as leading to a relativism that puts the very premise of constructionism in doubt (Burr, 1995), but its strength is that, if accounts can be said to be neither true nor false, meaning can easily be mobilised in the social world in the interest of particular disadvantaged groups. We know that the powerful are skilled at using discourses ideologically in their own interest.

Positivists felt that experts could acquire the necessary knowledge to explain and correct the world, to make continual progress and to know when they had found the truth of what was 'really' the matter. However, in this age of postmodernism, the subjective meanings of the individuals who are experiencing difficulties are being seen as central, and their 'stories' are being seen as mattering a great deal. Their attributions and explanations are part of the reality and even create that reality. Because there is a scepticism that we can locate 'the truth', what matters is the currently operating created 'truth' of this person and how a thematic map might help us to co-construct with the person a more helpful and empowering account. It is interesting that, later in his life, Freud shifted the emphasis from historical truth to 'narrative truth'. Essentialists feel that truth is something external to the person and something the person can regard objectively, whereas constructionists see it as essentially something that is created by the ideas, thoughts, constructs, beliefs, communications, words and language of the knower. We 'author' our lives, and if they are unsatisfactory we can 're-author' them. Language does not simply represent reality; it makes it.

This approach, that one story is as true as another, can be attacked as an exaggeration. After all, a cat is not a dog. There has to be some fit or correspondence between external reality and what we construe. Except when we are deluded, we can usually tell the difference between fact and fantasy. In our daily lives, we rely on those ideas that are 'object-adequate' (Pocock, 1995, p. 161), that fit with the hard realities which we 'bump into' daily. Some stories are more testable than others, and some stories come to dominate our understanding from time to time. Pocock (1995) takes the view that we can have more confidence in some stories so it is a matter of looking for the better story. A most useful theory represents the best story that can be written from a particular perspective to make sense of the uncertainties of life. Indeed, several stories can co-exist, offering different layers of perspective. What we need to locate is the 'pragmatic truth' (Pocock, 1995, p. 160), which will be the most useful in facilitating change in any particular situation as long as the outcome is both ethically sound and useful. It is important to hold to uncertainty, to develop more than one hypothesis and to compare alternative and competing understandings for usefulness.

In another sense, a theory can be seen as a story's plot, but we want to keep to the notion of map in this book. We hold to the postmodernist view and to the belief that the narrative can create the reality in human difficulties, but substitution of the term 'map' is meant in the narrative sense, as a plot for a story, or as an analogy that makes sense of a situation and gives direction. In social work, the situation is usually a 'stuck' one, where life has become like one episode of a miserable soap opera repeated over and over again. The best map is the one that fits that current situation best and is the most useful in facilitating progress – the most pragmatically 'true' and the most positive and empowering for the service user.

We maintain that social work's search for one cohesive theory is misplaced. Social workers need a selection of practice principles and values, coupled with a range of theoretical models and methods, as a foundation from which they can respond creatively to the infinite range of situations they will meet. This creativity will enable them to mix and match theoretical ideas, test values and techniques, and be eclectic – making deliberate and rigorous selection, and not merely jumbling ideas together – so that their responses to service users will be individualised rather than routine. Rather than being mere functionaries, applying a limited number of options for the resolution of problems, they will be thinking, reflecting, responsive professionals. In the words of Milton Erickson:

> Each person is a unique individual. Hence [work] should be formulated to meet the uniqueness of the individual's needs rather than tailoring the person to fit the Procrustean bed of a hypothetical theory of human behaviour. (Erickson, cited in Zeig, 1985, p. 8)

We must avoid being like Blaug's (1995) carpenter who, possessing a hammer, tended to see every problem as a nail. Each theoretical approach has its own usefulness or domain in which it is helpful in some particular way. No one map has been proven to be more effective than another in all situations, nor is it likely that such a map will be found. Many writers (see, for example, Pinsof, 1994) maintain that it is therefore a matter of linking together more than one fitting map to maximise usefulness and reduce deficit. Pocock (1995) supports this pluralist approach, which gives the worker more positions from which to be helpful by selecting 'a highly congruent better fitting set of ideas' (p. 162). A brief example from mediation work we recently engaged in illustrates how the truth can be altered to increase congruence.

A little girl was having severe tantrums over contact with her mother who, according to the father, had walked out and left them all. This father was distressed and angry, condemning his wife in the child's hearing. He repeatedly said of the child that she was 'disturbed' and 'It will take years to get her back to normal'. The mother was seeking contact with the child, but the child was refusing to cooperate. We worked with the couple, drawing on a divorce mediation map, and the father was able to agree that the child should be told that her mother had not left her; mother and father would be living in two houses in future but they both still loved her and would always be her only parents, and her father now wanted her to see her mother. To the father, we said, 'The child is not disturbed, she is playing a game, the game of being on her father's side and, as soon as she knows that seeing her mother is not disloyalty to her father, she will recover very quickly'. When they were seen a week later, the child was staying with her mother during the agreed times without difficulty. In this case, we had recounted a different plot from that developed by the family, using our knowledge of separating families and of mediation to develop a story that altered the meaning of the components of the problem and helped to bring about change.

Naming the maps

In the following chapters, we will be considering six theoretical approaches, which we have called maps of various kinds. We use the map metaphor derived from Bateson (1977) and subsequently developed by several writers in the family therapy field and by solution-focused writers such as Durrant (1993). This metaphor appeals to us because it helps to deal with the issue of truth.

Suppose one were travelling from a small town in Scotland to a village on the south coast of England. One could buy various maps that might be useful depending on one's mode of transport, on one's needs for the journey or on how well developed the roads or ways were. Assessing a potential service user can feel like entering uncharted (or multiply charted) territory as the worker searches for ways by which to 'arrive' at a 'conclusion'.

Our traveller from Scotland has quite a choice of maps. She could get a motorway map, which would show junctions and service stations. As she passes each of these, she will know how far she has travelled, whether it is in the right direction and what else she has to do to arrive at her destination. However, she may need a detailed road map to help her find her way when she is not on the motorway. If she wishes to walk, say to raise funds for a charity, she may prefer to take minor roads and footpaths, in which case another kind of map, such as an Ordnance Survey map, showing hills and valleys, might be more helpful to her. Likewise, if she were to travel by boat she would need a map of coastal waters. Perhaps maps also need to be understood by the person being met, or else the service user might not be waiting at the harbour! Maps should ideally have meaning and helpfulness for both parties and be in a language that both use.

Each of these maps could claim to be a map of Britain, and they all are true in what they represent. But none of them is truly Britain; the map is not the territory. On the other hand, if we consider the domain of 'the meaning of experience', we could say the map *is* the territory – that real meaning is simply that which we construct and narrate.

We regard theories of human situations as maps to the understanding of problems, all different, all offering a different construction, yet all potentially useful and equally true. It is crucial that, when faced with the often pressing needs of service users, we avoid taking the 'naïve realist' view and that we are reflexive about the effects of the lenses we use.

In Chapter 5, we offer the 'weather map' as a metaphor for anti-oppression perspectives, showing how both 'travellers' – social workers and service users – are affected by the winds and rain of the socio-political climate. In Chapter 6, we have called systemic theory a 'map of the world', in that it affords a glimpse of the overall situation and organises the vast territory of the extrapersonal in an accessible way. Because Freudian ideas relate mainly to getting below the surface of the person and their feelings, we have named Chapter 7 the 'map of the ocean'. On the other hand, behavioural work focuses on observable conduct and on the ups and downs of action, so we have named it the 'Ordnance Survey map' in Chapter 8. In Chapter 9, we have labelled task-centred work as the 'handy tourist map' for several reasons: it is popular with busy workers and offers relatively brief ways of working and an easily accessible guide to assessment that has a wide application. Finally, we have used the metaphor 'navigator's map' in Chapter 10 for the solution-focused approach because this is a map specially prepared for locating and getting to a particular goal, as navigator and service user fly towards the constructed solution. It will be clear that, at least in some instances, one map does not rule out another. Rather, they can complement each other, adding a further layer of understanding and providing further indicators towards possible interventions to bring about change.

As we address each of these maps in turn in subsequent chapters, we will offer case examples which we hope will further assist the reader in map selection. We hope in particular to show that several maps can apply in helping in any one situation and to some extent the choice that works best for one worker may be different from that which works best for another. In our view, social workers and service users should be encouraged to experiment and thus eventually devise their own most useful blend of ideas. The really important point is that professionals ought constantly to review their effectiveness and seek out ways of increasing usefulness to users. In this way, their array of maps can evolve over time in an atmosphere of research and evaluation, drawing especially on user feedback, but never claiming to have found the truth. This involves constantly checking for the advantages and limitations of each map, and for ways of making them more useful to the service users by helping to generate really helpful analyses of their difficulties.

Summary

- Social workers are informed by a wide range of social science theory in *weighing up* and *making judgments* about human difficulties.
- In developing a deeper *understanding* of difficulties, with a view to deciding on intervention, social workers can draw on a range of theoretical maps (based on the theories from which methods are derived).
- Differing hypotheses result from viewing situations with the aid of these maps. This is healthy since no one map can claim to lead to a single truth, and forming alternative understandings safeguards against bias.
- Pragmatic truth, that is that interpretation which is most helpful to both social workers and service users in developing solutions, is the most desirable, provided the work is firmly rooted in the values of respect and anti-oppressive practice (see Chapter 5).
- Social workers are encouraged to remain reflexive, to consider the consequences of using particular maps and to value service users' own 'theories' about their situation.
- While some maps are rooted in an essentialist approach (see Chapters 7 and 8), we include them as alternatives to be tested for usefulness and for 'fit' rather than to be applied 'correctly' as if they were able accurately to reproduce reality.
- Social workers need more than one map or tool in order to avoid being likened to a carpenter who only has a hammer.
- Having more than one map helps us to retain uncertainty and open-mindedness, which is the beginning of hopefulness.

5

The Weather Map:
Anti-oppressive Practice

The values climate

We are beginning our series of theoretical maps with a weather map on the grounds that there is little point in venturing into difficult terrain without a weather forecast. Although we have used the title 'weather map' for this chapter, perhaps climate might be a better word. In recent years, the values climate of social work has changed, bringing a greater emphasis on the understanding of oppression in all its forms. Because oppression, inequality and powerlessness account for much of the pressure, distress and stress of many service users, to ignore it in making assessments would be to add insult to injury and risk unfairly assuming that the people concerned are in some way to blame for their oppressive situations. Assessments need to take note of the barometer of oppression before venturing out on the journey of following various maps in the search for valid accounts of other people's lives and difficulties. There is no way in which social workers can avoid the issues and dilemmas (the climate) relating to injustice and power.

This chapter will address how these issues and dilemmas can be incorporated into a coherent anti-oppressive practice theory that will go some way to meeting the criticisms of social work assessments listed in previous chapters. The most commonly used methods of intervention, and the related theoretical maps, do not sit easily with the concept of empowerment, which has been largely 'grafted on' to existing theories. Despite their benevolent intentions, these theories 'essentially reflect the power relationships that exist between us all' (Dalrymple and Burke, 1995, p. 11). These existing power relationships are basically white, male, healthy, employed and Western dominated. McNay (1992) suggests that, while all oppressions are important, gender, race and class are more central to the profit base of our economy and therefore have a greater effect on how lives are lived and dominated (for example, by the exploitive division of labour). Clifford (1994) writes that the material basis of social divisions is a governing factor in understanding real lives, going on to suggest that good practice requires the participation of workers whose personal experience of oppression gives them a counter-hegemonic understanding of material as well as cultural and personal differences. By this, some sense of 'fit' is implied between the different levels of anti-oppressive theory – materialist social theory, strategic practice theory and working concepts – which Dalrymple and Burke (1995) maintain should respond to the reality of both service users' lives and social workers' lives. We will address the similarities and differences between service users and social workers, but this chapter will first address what the various forms of oppression have in common, in particular the abuse of power.

Power

Power is a significant element in every relationship and a main motivating influence. Indeed, all relationships, whether between one individual and another, between one group and another, or between rulers and subjects, can be said to be the result of power. In social work, power may be legitimately used to empower others in anti-oppressive practice or illegitimately used to oppress others in malpractice. Power is also an element in the competitiveness of life, of the struggle for resources, employment and education. Social workers, too, can experience a lack of power, and this can help them to understand service users better, but, crucially, the concern for social workers is when power is used to exclude and marginalise. In work with marginalised people, seeking to counteract negative images of self, negative life experiences, blocked opportunities and unrelenting physical and emotional distress, it is essential to take a three-track approach that links the personal with the cultural and structural. Thompson (1993) refers to this as the 'PCS model', P referring to personal/psychological and also to practice and prejudice, and C referring to cultural, commonalities, consensus and conformity. S refers to structural aspects, social forces or the socio-political dimension. Thompson describes P as being embedded in C and C in S, yet as all interacting with each other.

It is hopelessly optimistic, however, to think that empowerment can be actualised just by minor tinkering to social workers' preferred theories. Traditional family therapists and psychodynamic counsellors have not readily addressed the complaints of feminists and black people that their theories lack an appreciation of the impact of patriarchal power on women and the impact of racism on black people. Their adaptations have been largely cosmetic and have done little to make social workers more confident of what empowerment, partnership and choice actually consist of (see, for example, Macleod and Saroga, 1988; Cavanagh and Gee, 1996). It is naïve to underestimate the difficulties in operational-ising empowerment strategies – powerful people (and powerful theo-ries and methods of intervention) are resistive to yielding power: 'Power concedes nothing without demand... the limits of tyrants are precise by the endurance of those they oppress' (Douglas, quoted in Dalrymple and Burke, 1995, p. 14). Social workers are not in a position to *give* people power, and their aim to *help reduce* the powerlessness that individuals and groups experience is likely to be limited by other individuals' and groups' investment in power positions *and* in the complex nature of power.

There is an important psychological legacy left by powerlessness that includes lethargy, despair and listlessness – 'learned helpless-ness' – and, as Freire (1972) called it, a 'culture of silence' in which there is an apparent acceptance of servitude and dependence. The marginalised subscribe to the myth that they get what they deserve, and internalise, and are possessed by, feelings of alienation and worthless-ness. In a later chapter, we will address learned helplessness in more detail, but here we want to stress that approaches that help people come to terms with their situations need to be seriously examined in case they collude with such oppression.

Powerlessness is not necessarily expressed in terms of easily defined oppressed groups; it is much more diverse and complex. Indeed, Foucault questions the relevance of ideas about power as primarily repressive by counterposing the idea of power as productive (see, for example, Sawicki, 1991). Modern developments of power operate in subtle terms through self-regulation. For example, it is diffi-cult to see quite 'who' is oppressing mothers as the psychology under-pinning 'good enough' mothering has become internalised. Mothers operate within a 'discourse' that does not need the so-called experts of childrearing necessarily to be on hand for advice (for a fuller discus-sion, see Ingleby, 1985).

Similarly, children, a perhaps easily identifiable oppressed group, are not entirely powerless. Foucault considers resistance and power to be interrelated. Marshall (1996) discusses the relevance of the 'discourse' in which children place themselves as necessary for understanding the complexities of their power relationships. Thus, a child at school might be seen to be oppressed in terms of teacher discipline but may be acting in a children's discourse in which the teacher's power discourse is irrelevant. Marshall cites an example of a classroom incident involving young children and a female teacher in which two young boys temporarily positioned the teacher as a subordinate through the use of sexually explicit language. The teacher was unable to reassert control as the dichotomy between adult and child had been redefined as one between male and female, wherein the males are more powerful. The author concludes:

> Thus, through some discourses, children are able to enact strategies that gain power for themselves in relation to adults and can be experienced by adults as powerful. However, in the context of institutional adult authority these [strategies] may produce situations where children are excluded [from school] and can be seen as *powerfully powerless*. (Marshall, 1996, p. 104, emphasis added).

Appreciating that service users can be oppressed but, simultaneously, 'powerfully powerless' helps social workers to understand their own sense of frustration and powerlessness with children in care who truant, abscond or continue with the 'undesirable' behaviour that led them to enter the care system in the first place. These are not simply damaged and powerless children in a simple relationship with a powerful Welfare network, they are active participants in the various facets of their lives, exerting power often outside the linear relationship with the professionals in the Welfare network. Similarly, social workers will be familiar with service users who are the most easily identifiable as oppressed – poor, old, downtrodden, disadvantaged families – who exhibit resistance through the only power mechanism available to them, the people Dale *et al.* (1986) refer to as 'passive–resistant'. This form of resistance can be very powerful indeed. Cockburn (1991) suggests that we need to recognise power as multidimensional in that it is spread around and that almost all of us share in it a little. Similarly, she argues that power is not always negative in that it can mean capacity as well as domination.

The 'isms'

The very real difficulties in operating anti-oppressive practice are most clearly seen when we examine the inter-relatedness and complexities of the various 'isms', most notably race, gender, class, age, disability and sexual orientation. These not only interrelate but also compete. For example, if we take seriously that to 'separate racism and sexism is to deny the basic truth of black women's existence' (Dalrymple and Burke, 1995, p. 17), how do we seek to understand our hypothetical black woman discussed earlier? And is this complicated by the possibility that the assessing social worker may be black or white, male or female, heterosexual or homosexual, young or old, and thus have different personal experiences of oppression and power *vis-à-vis* not only the potential service user, but also their own institutional authority? Similarly, Wise (1995) cites an example of a young working-class woman, deserted by her violent husband, impoverished, isolated and unhappy, who deals with her despair by getting drunk and forgetting to come home to her young children. She argues that a feminist empowerment model would ignore the fact that the children are the most vulnerable people in this situation.

It is clear that some 'isms' are more powerful than others. Measured on a simple scale of 'isms' training, we would expect that social workers are more likely to have undergone race awareness than any other training. Although there should supposedly be no hierarchy of oppression, we suspect that anti-racism does take precedence in anti-oppressive training, even if not necessarily ever translated into effective anti-oppressive practice.

One reason for this situation could, perhaps, be that black men have much in common with the most easily identifiable powerful group in our society – white men. There are suggestions that masculine solidarity will make blackness the most important issue. As two white, male probation officers say, 'There is more that joins men across class and disability, and even race and sexual orientation, than divides them' (Cordery and Whitehead, 1992, p. 29). We return to the commonality of male experience later in this chapter but question here whether it sufficiently addresses the complexities of race and gender.

Remembering the differing 'discourses' mentioned earlier, black people, whether male or female, have to negotiate at least three different social contexts: *mainstream* (white) processes, in which they constitute a *minority* (racism), and within that minority context, they also have to negotiate *black cultural* agenda, which can be as diverse as Rastafarianism or Seventh Day Adventism. Their strategies for negotiating these different contexts (like the school children discussed earlier) will not always be displayed in power and oppression terms which social workers would recognise as appropriate to their positions as service users. For example, for black children, Boykim and Toms (1985) argue that 'the mainstream socialisation has to be negotiated *in lieu* of the minority and black cultural agenda'. These agendas clearly conflict with the mainstream one and, for that matter, also *with each other*. Blyth and Milner (1996) show that black boys' positioning of themselves in a racial and masculinist context in school may seem threatening to white male teachers who are concerned with the mainstream disciplinary context. Channer (1995), on the other hand, highlights the importance of religion, the cultural context, as the main issue in Black African Caribbean school achievement, while Hussain (1996) emphasises the importance of religion in transcultural fostering. These are power contexts that are largely ignored in most social work assessments yet are a source of strength for black people to alleviate their oppression in the other two contexts.

Ageism is a form of oppression that is easily underestimated, often being eventually added to all other oppressions, which increases the treatment of old people as non-persons. There is a dehumanisation inherent in old age as 'negative images of and attitudes towards older people, based solely on the characteristics of old age itself, result in discrimination' (Hughes and Mtezuka, 1992, p. 220).

However complex, unequal power relations are still at the root of social injustice and have replaced 'libido' as the core force in understanding human relationships. Those who benefit most from any relationship are those with the most power (McNay, 1992), so an assessment of, for example, mothering needs to look at a woman's lack of power and resources, rather than at her personality, or at least at the interaction between these two aspects. And if she is black, black culturalism mediates this through how racism compounds her powerlessness and through membership of community groups that can provide a source of strength and group solidarity.

What the various 'isms' have in common is the core value of equal opportunity. Any effective assessment needs to consider the impact of its absence and the absence of equal access to resources. Any fundamental solution to the problems of oppressed groups must include policies that address all elements of oppression.

These policies are difficult to formulate because of the complexities mentioned earlier and because of vested power interests, so social workers need to be aware that their efforts to develop anti-oppressive practice will not necessarily be well supported. For example, Thoburn *et al.* (1995) found that agency policies and procedures were as much a barrier to partnership initiatives in child protection work as were family characteristics. Additionally, assessments need to examine how oppression might be affecting the service user's functioning in the mainstream context. How can we overestimate the sheer grinding stress of experiencing daily injustice for any reason and of feeling devalued because of gender or colour? How can we overestimate the psychological effects of being hated, despised, regarded as only fit to service others and discriminated against in housing, education and jobs? The task is enormous but recognising this helps social workers to begin the first steps towards operationalising anti-oppressive practice. Below, we suggest ways in which this can be begun.

Dalrymple and Burke (1995, p. 120) propose that an ethical framework for assessment needs to include the following:

- Assessment should involve those being assessed.
- Openness and honesty should permeate the process.
- Assessment should involve the sharing of values and concerns.
- There should be acknowledgement of the structural context of the process.
- The process should be about questioning the basis of the reasons for proposed action, and all those involved should consider alternative courses of action.
- Assessment should incorporate the different perspectives of the people involved.

Negotiating perceptions

We have likened assessment to research, in which it is acknowledged that researchers' subjective views can critically affect outcomes. If assessment findings are to be considered valid, to have 'truth', the authors' assumptions and biases must be addressed. Likewise, if an assessment is to show a valid understanding of the subject, it must address the 'differences' gap between writer and subject, their mutual subjectivity, their different backgrounds and experiences of life. Social workers have needs too, and if these are not met they function less well. As Nice (1988) has suggested, social workers are taught and expect, like mothers with their families, to put the needs of others above their own. Recognising their own feelings lays upon them the charge that they are bad social workers. How we function can have an impact on how we see the functioning of others, so any meeting for assessment purposes involves the meeting of two complex subjective worlds.

Social workers also come from the world of the agency, and service users usually have ideas about those agencies that colour how they see social workers and affect the emotional impact they each have on the other. A social worker who overidentifies with agency procedures risks losing sight of the subjectivity and special needs of the user, while a social worker who overidentifies with agency policy risks unfairly rejecting individual need and failing to challenge and improve those policies. On the other hand, a social worker who overidentifies with service users risks failing in responsibility to the agency and in the fair assessment of priorities. To strike a balance between what the service user wants and what intervention the agency considers sufficient for satisfactory functioning requires recognition of our own values, feelings and biases, and the ability to engage in dialogue with the subjective world of service users in an open, reciprocal way (Sainsbury, 1970).

A conversation, what Friere (1972) refers to as a 'critical dialogue', can be developed in which experiences are shared and differences acknowledged. A shared narrative encourages the development of mutual understanding, deficits in mutual understanding can be acknowledged and a 'moral dialogue' ensue. Jordan (1990) makes the point that where this dialogue is not achieved and service users are perceived as uncooperative, the conclusions reached by assessors are greatly affected. For example, he says that a key factor in whether abused children are 'accommodated' is often whether the parents are cooperative, that is acknowledge the evidence of harm done, accept responsibility for their part in causing it and agree to measures to avoid its reoccurrence, including a programme for monitoring and/or changing their behaviour. Thus the outcome of the meeting between social worker and service user is crucially affected by whether their relationship is oppressively adversarial or anti-oppressively cooperative. In making assessments for services, too, there needs to be *negotiation* over issues of fairness, need and availability of resources as understood by both sides. For example, it is important to explore how an old person's need for day care relates not only to the carer's need for a respite break, but also to the availability or otherwise of culturally appropriate services.

Where there is a difference of gender, race or class between social worker and service user, there seems to be a tendency to focus unduly on deficit and/or risk rather than on *strengths* and seeking to establish how people's control over aspects of their lives can be increased. We all, social workers and service users alike, have unmet wants, and if these are ever to be met we must make our story visible and look at the stories of others, to see our situations not as 'no exit' places but as places capable of reform. In this way, we can gain an awareness of where our oppressions are located and of how structural as well as psychological obstacles operate, and have a sense of our ability to be agents of change and locators of resources. This requires the capacity to deal with self-blame, to attribute problems to unfair structures rather than people when that is the case, and to develop necessary supportive networks. Social workers need to identify service users' competencies and to affirm their experiences, so that self-confidence can grow. This requires asking for their stories; listening to and taking them seriously helps to build confidence and a sense of being valued. People also need the assertiveness to communicate their wants. Many women, particularly, suppress their own wants, so workers need to take extra care to seek them out. This is even more so with older women and especially where the social worker is male. Men and women often view satisfaction differently (McNay, 1992), and it is therefore often necessary to facilitate mutual listening by such means as circular questioning.

As it is neither possible nor necessarily desirable to provide, for example, every poor black female service user with a poor black female social worker, there will inevitably be large gaps between service users and social workers. This will be even more obvious when religious and cultural differences are considered. However, anti-oppressive practice dictates that workers *acknowledge* and seek to *bridge* these gaps. An openness about one's own culture and values and about one's lack of knowledge of the other person's beliefs is essential at the beginning of any involvement. This is then followed by an invitation to service users to help the social worker see life as they see it.

Social workers ought not to be too proud to ask the service user to help them understand how race or gender factors are affecting their situation. Without such a humble, 'one down' stance, male white social workers, for example, will rightly be seen by women and black service users as coming from another world (see, for example, Jordan, 1989; hooks, 1991, 1993). Written contracts (jointly drafted), advocacy, charters and published value statements also help to engage across the 'gap'. An illustrative example is the Hackney Social Services Department's excellent value statement/charter for social worker assessments (Sinclair *et al.*, 1995, pp. 309–10).

Social workers have been criticised for failing to acknowledge the strengths and coping strategies of minority groups. We suggest that one way in which this can be corrected is by respectfully asking the service users to share their story of struggle and survival in the face of social structural inequity, by asking not only about their wounds, but also about their capacity for self-nurturance, not only about their lack of a sense of entitlement and justice, but also about the strengths derived from their membership of their community group, and also any stresses that that membership might sometimes cause. This work involves social workers sharing some similarities and differences in their experiences of both power and oppression. For example, a white female social work student was assessing a black male social work student as part of an assessment exercise. In attempting to bridge the gap in the way outlined, the two students shared experiences of their early lives. To their surprise and delight, they found that they both felt dislocated from large extended families in tightly knit small communities that were collapsing under economic pressures. These communities were located in a white, Lancashire context for the woman and a black African Caribbean context for the man, but they had more commonalities than differences in their experience of oppression.

Bridging the gap is still an unclear area of practice, with agencies tending to stress the need for professional boundaries and workers finding it difficult to be truly empathic (White, 1995). While personal disclosures that are not necessary for a true engagement with the service user are inappropriate, if there is to be a moral dialogue leading to an appreciation of the other's world view and values, and an understanding of their perceptions and attributions, social workers have to acknowledge at least their lack of cultural sameness and their need to be helped by the other to understand. For example, in understanding an ultra-orthodox Jewish family's threat to 'sit-sheva' for a daughter who plans to marry outside her faith, it would be necessary for most non-Jewish social workers to invite the family to explain their profound distress, which is based on their considering their daughter dead. We are not saying that it is possible to close the enormous gaps of race, gender, class and ethnicity, only that we can acknowledge and reach across them, inviting the other person to reach across to us, and hopefully making real human contact that will be accepting, respectful and mutually empowering.

Black writers (see, for example, hooks, 1993) stress that black people need to tell their story, to set their own frame of reference, to have their values and spirituality appreciated, to be assertive, if they are to ensure continued growth despite centuries of being deliberately crushed (Spence, 1995). Our position as social workers who purport to empower service users demands that we be aware of our own social construction of knowledge and of the influences of our roles and agencies. Like researchers, social workers' values interact with the very essence of their work in constructing accounts of people's lives and in making judgments on the basis of these accounts. As social workers encourage people to give their own accounts of their lives, they also have to take account of their own lives (Clifford, 1994). They need to be aware of the consequences of their theoretical maps and to seek to move from a 'reproductive' approach towards an 'abductive' one in which collaborative accounts draw more on the concepts and meanings of service users. In their places of work, they also need to own up to their deficits of experiences and knowledge of particular groups, seek to establish community links with groups whose experience and insights are useful to their work, and work towards maximising the range of experience within their staff group.

Similarities and differences

Although we acknowledge that an understanding of the complexities and subtleties of power and oppression is difficult because of the dynamic nature of power, we think it necessary to identify commonalities of oppression and to conflate these so that the foundations of effective anti-oppressive practice can begin to emerge. As suggested earlier, there is more that joins men than separates them (Cordery and Whitehead, 1992). Cockburn (1991) maintains that there is a danger in the idea of 'multiple masculinities' in that it deflects attention from the consistency in men's domination of women and children at systemic and organisational levels: '"Troubled" masculinity may be, but male power is defending itself systematically and ferociously' (Cockburn, 1991, p. 216).

Masculinity does not fall from the heavens, says Connell (1983), but is constructed by masculinising practices, and there is evidence that the way in which men construct 'men-ness' affects masculinities as well as femininities. Not all men are dominant; not all dominate. Mackinnon (1987) says that men can be raped, feminised, even 'un-manned': 'they may even be de-gendered... For as women differ in their status, so do men in their power' (Mackinnon, cited in Evans, 1995, p. 150). For example, small boys and disabled, old and homosexual men are 'feminised' in that they are not considered 'real men' (see, for example, Marshall, 1981; Arber and Ginn, 1991; Mac an Ghaill, 1996). The process of construction of black masculinity is more complex and reversed, with black men being 'over-gendered' and exoticised, and their physicality unduly emphasised (see, for example, Westwood, 1990, 1996; Denney, 1992).

This construction of men as 'real men' or 'female men' or 'ultra-men' supports the claim of Sampson *et al.* (1991) that while gender is only one among many sources of power, it is central. As potentially oppressed groups of men are subject to these social constructions, it seems sensible to elevate anti-sexism to prominence in the hierarchy of oppression. There are three additional reasons why this would be a sensible first step in developing a framework for anti-oppressive practice.

First, social workers, accepting our recommendations about being social researchers, could then utilise feminist research methodology, which is derived from experience and reflexivity – not just that which has generated 'the knowledge' to date. While women and other 'minority' groups may be in a better position to see the power of men, it is by no means impossible for men themselves to look at the familiar from a different perspective (Edley and Wetherall, 1996).

Second, most carers are women yet suffer from 'powerless responsibility' (Rich, 1977) and must, therefore, be at the centre of anti-oppressive practice. Simultaneously, male social workers, in particular, need to examine their capacities for care as well as for control; Lloyd and Degenhardt (1996), for example, suggest ways in which male social work students can be provided with practice opportunities for both the practice and assessment of their caring capacities.

Third, elevating anti-sexism to prominence enables a core quality of anti-oppressive practice to emerge – womanliness. By womanliness, we mean the behaviour described by Gilligan (1982) in her description of three stages of women's moral development. First, she talks about women who care only for others, interested only in their personal responsibilities. Second, there is doing only for the self, which complements a traditional male sense of identity. However, she also describes a third stage, reached by some women, in which the woman becomes aware of her responsibility to care for *both* herself and others.

Gilligan (1982) emphasises that the state of failing to care for both oneself and others is a state of moral nihilism. How we manage this interdependence and reciprocity in relationships is at the core of what we mean by womanliness. We do not consider, however, that it need be the sole prerogative of woman, only that this quality has the potential for the development of a charter of human responsibility as well as a charter of human rights, and can ensure a balance between the two.

The commonality of oppression experienced by not being a 'real man' would not necessarily reduce the possibility of examining differences. For example, Hamner and Statham (1988) set out a feminist approach that looks at the similarities and differences between female social workers and female service users. Where two women are involved, the *commonalities* include the shared experiences of life in a male-dominated society, double workloads (paid and domestic), living with men, often as subordinates, and caring for dependants. They frequently include the experience of poverty, connected perhaps with being divorced, separated, a lone parent or restricted to part-time employment. In social service departments, many women service users' problems are clearly caused or aggravated by the men they live with. Many women's resources are overstretched or inadequate because of responsibilities for children or other dependants, poor housing, less access to education, health problems, transport problems and low pay. In addition, their situation and hardship is often compounded by a lack of facilities such as day care, nurseries and formal and informal support networks.

Society places different value on men's and women's behaviour, and the expectations of caring and of service weigh more heavily on women: women are expected to cope with everything! Self-esteem is greatly affected by how men perceive women and treat them as inferior. As Richards (1980) puts it, women suffer from systematic social injustice because of their sex. However, Evans (1995) holds that women can possess a superior and more accurate knowing derived from their experience of subordination, active parenting and nurturing responsibilities. We would argue that this is true also of 'un-manned' men such as disabled, elderly or homosexual men.

In making assessments, therefore, it may be helpful to ask some of the following questions of all potentially oppressed service users:

- What expectations do you feel you are not meeting?
- How do you feel you are coping?
- Do you expect too much of yourself?
- Are your burdens such that no one should be expected to do better than you?
- How good do you feel about who you are?
- How appreciated are you by others?
- Could your difficulties be more due to lack of resources than lack of ability?
- What traditional supports are lacking for you in this day and age?
- What particular strengths have helped you to keep going?
- Where could we start building a network of support?

Equally, *diversities* need to be acknowledged. Hamner and Statham (1988) suggest that how a particular woman's situation and problems differ from one's own should become part of assessment. Differences in status, power, role, lifestyle, race, culture, sexuality, education, work possibilities, access to community resources, degree of stigma and hope are elements of the differentiation of social worker from service user. This also applies to male and female social workers with male service users.

These differences create the gap we were discussing earlier, and a dialogue is required that will result in at least a touching of minds across the divide. In may be, for example, that one woman's experience of living with a man has been abject humiliation, and another's enrichment and growth; the latter needs to learn of the pain of the former, what self-nurturance was possible, and what strengths and strategies enabled survival or escape. It is worth pointing out here that, in some situations, the social worker gains all the opportunities for nurturance and self-growth in the relationship while the service user remains dependent (Milner, 1982).

In the case of black women, the extended family was historically a source of support, 'combating depression, stress and loneliness and thus reducing the impact of those factors on mental health' (Spence, 1995). The reduction of this support in the lives of many black women in Britain today has a devastating effect on their well-being; they push themselves so hard that they are exposed to excessive stress, and when they do achieve, they still may lack any real sense of entitlement. They often do not feel understood by social workers who must reach across to them, make humble human contact and invite them to 'put us in the picture'. Devore and Schlesinger (1991) make the useful point that while white workers need to be aware of service users' possible fear of racist or prejudiced treatment, black social workers need to avoid the 'stance that says "I've made it, why can't you"' (p. 191), expecting black service users to 'shape up' and not let the side down.

The gap between middle-class, (often) female social workers and white male members of the so-called 'underclass' can be just as wide. We are aware of a recent example of a man who noticed that his mother, aged 90 and suffering from a stroke, was being neglected by the nursing home. He found another home where he felt sure standards were better, but the home in which she was residing called in a social worker because they felt that the resident did not wish to move, despite the fact that she had told her son that she did. The social worker interviewed the mother and agreed she did want to move but failed to confirm this to the other home, who were waiting for this approval before they could receive the resident. In the meantime, due to this delay, the bed at the second home was taken by someone else. The man met with the social worker and her manager to complain, but he felt they were not interested in his problem, denied that his mother wanted to move and would not answer his questions about their earlier acknowledgement that she did so wish. He came away from the meeting having had no sense of engaging with the workers; he said he 'might as well be talking to folk from space; snobs who couldn't give a monkey's curse for my sort; wouldn't listen to me, so I gave 'em hell'.

Ignoring class differences between social workers and service users involves lack of respect. Blair's (1996) study of black pupils excluded from school showed that both pupils and their parents saw class as an important determinant of teachers' treatment of them. What emerged from the study was a 'complex picture of personal and institutional factors which highlighted the relationship between gender, "race", class and age' (Blair, 1996, p. 21).

The problem for male social workers

How can male social workers operate in a more womanly way, and how can they bridge the gap between themselves and potentially oppressed service users when making assessments? To consider the first question first, until society changes the ways in which boys are reared and educated to be men, it will be very difficult. Men will tend to be 'womb orientated' in their assessments of women and their difficulties, and they will tend to be 'incontinence orientated' in their assessment of men's sexuality and behaviour. By this, we mean that men will tend to be considered unable to control themselves and their feelings (see, for example, Fawcett *et al.*, 1996). We find this an odd paradox, that the all-powerful male should be seen as unable to control himself. Is it that women have less powerful feelings or that they have better control? We believe neither to be the case; there is no provable reason why men should not be required to exercise the same self-control as women. We would add that men also should learn how to reduce their power, because it is essentially not so much a question of being out of control as one of deliberately using violence and abusing power. Perhaps men could ask women how they manage to 'do' self-control. Pringle (1995) lists six themes in this regard:

● Men and boys must be assisted to acknowledge their capacity to be oppressive towards women.
● Men should link their oppressiveness to the structural oppressions in society.
● Social attitudes that reinforce men's oppressiveness, for example myths about 'real men', need to be counteracted.
● Reinforcement of attitudes by peer groups needs to be exposed.
● Strategies need to be developed for avoiding situations in which a man could be oppressive.
● Men need to be helped to consider the various forms of masculinity that they will use in various aspects of their lives.

It is not only feminist writers who recommend the use of a 'gender lens' for men as the growing body of literature on masculinity illustrates. For example, Hearn (1996, pp. 100–1) writes:

> For too long, men have been considered the taken-for-granted norm against which women have been judged to be different... the psychological and social construction of men has not been addressed... making sense of men necessitates placing them in a social context. This entails considering men's power relations to women, and the social development of boys and men... For most men this includes an acceptance of that basic power relation.

A frequent theme is that men must find different ways of being men, and this must include not being violent, abusive or oppressive, and include 'changing the internal gendering of agencies' (Hearn, 1996, p. 110).

On the other hand, while accepting that masculinity is a central issue, writings by practitioners who work with men (see, for example, Newburn and Mair, 1996) stress the need to engage with men, listening to their pressures and learning needs but avoiding collusion. This non anti-men masculinity focus does not fit easily with the dominant discourse, but practitioners argue that aggressive (male) confrontation does more harm than good, and men's stories report that men have real difficulties in knowing how to be men differently. Most of them do not see their own fathers as role models; many have themselves been abused by men and want closer relationships with their children but do not know how to achieve this. Many men have been brought up to give little weight to feelings and to think of moods as overpowering them. They may be afraid of their own anger exploding, and they need help to spot the cues leading to such outbursts and learn to extend their choices for self-control. Some men do respond to being helped to be safely loving, to address fears caused by homophobia and to appreciate that, in helping to liberate women, they liberate and empower themselves. Many men missed out on cuddles as children; they were 'toughened up' and told that big boys don't cry. In this way, they were prevented from learning the self-healing of hurts. Instead, they were pressed to provide, to go to war and kill or be killed, or be called 'sissy'. Many 'will have learned to narrow and limit [their] behaviour and attitudes according to expectations and experiences specific to [their] gender... [so] men need to develop male identities that broaden the notion of fatherhood, caring and other "less male" aspects' (Murphy, 1996, p. 71).

Nevertheless, many men will continue to be oppressive. We are not simply talking of individual men who are physically dangerous to women, children and weaker men. Following the development of pro-feminist literature, there has been a new men's movement that is anti-feminist in that it blames feminism for what it perceives as the demasculinisation of men. Cockburn (1991) argues that men's negative response to feminism is partly anger and partly distress; when men subordinate women (and other men), they become dependent on the subjects they have created. Attempts to remove the subordination causes enormous discomfort for men, which, at the very least, challenges old habits. For example, early research on the gender of the therapist (Hall, 1987) revealed marked differences between male and female therapists. Male therapists chose 'female' treatment goals such as the expression of feelings, while female therapists chose 'masculine' goals such as greater assertiveness and activity. Exhorting male social workers to 'get in touch' with their feelings yet emphasise assertion and action for others may well seem puzzling and contradictory to them.

Practising anti-oppressive assessment

In making assessments, social workers have two main aspects to keep in mind. We have addressed the first, namely how oppression is affecting the service user. The second is how social workers can start being empowering and avoid being oppressive. With regard to the latter, it may be better to ask 'In what ways *could* I be oppressive if I wanted?' and then think how to avoid doing those things. Do we, for example, assess the strengths of men but the needs of women? What assumptions do we regularly make about minority groups? In deciding who gets what, how are we influenced by the level of respect and gratitude shown by the service user? In the current political climate, are some of the attitudes of the early charity workers returning as we are given the task of rationing ever more limited resources? As Dalrymple and Burke (1995) state, we need to:

● work collaboratively;
● view users as competent;
● help users to see themselves as 'causal agents'; and
● develop people's confidence by affirming their experiences, seeking diverse solutions, since situations are so complex, building and using informal networks, and increasing access to resources and the ability to use them.

At all times, social workers must listen to the stories of people who are oppressed and who are different, retain awareness of the power differences, share similarities and differences, and negotiate in order to learn about service users' perceptions, experiences and resulting psychological consequences, including learned helplessness. We suggest that social workers begin by addressing and seeking to bridge the 'difference gap' by considering the following:

- Has the person been able or invited to tell their story of injustice?
- How can their experiences be validated?
- What awareness do they have of the impact of oppression?
- What beliefs do they have about their capabilities and about the possibility of escape from their plight?
- Do they blame themselves, or blame social inequity?
- How can they be empowered to take action?
- With whom could they collaborate – could a support network be mobilised?
- What resources do they have access to, and what other resources could be located?
- What would improve their sense of control over their life?
- How could they be engaged in a change process?
- How could services be more sensitive to their special needs?
- How could their potential and strength be released, so that they will be able to challenge unfairness and meet their needs?

To return to the metaphor of the climate of social work values, it is important to stress that anti-oppressive practice is not simply about empowering individuals within a linear social worker–service user relationship. There needs to be respect for all the people in each social work situation being assessed, and acknowledgement of their responsibilities towards each other at individual, family, agency and community levels. This is perhaps best exemplified by the extreme weather change in the Probation Service following the adoption of National Standards (Home Office, 1991). No longer can a probation officer focus on individualising an offender, which had the effect of placing the (usually) male offender at the centre of all probation activity – a very powerful position. Instead, the probation officer is now expected to assess the needs, risks and resources of all facets of each offending situation. This will encompass victim and community perspectives, as well as offender perspectives, also including, of course, the probation officer's rights.

Summary

- Power is a significant element in every relationship but is not necessarily negative.
- The 'isms' are best explored in terms of lack of equal opportunities.
- Anti-oppressive practice dictates that social workers acknowledge and seek to bridge the gaps between themselves and service users in order to facilitate a negotiating of perceptions.
- As men can be oppressed and 'un-manned', gender is central to power issues.
- Anti-oppressive practice not only involves developing better and more sympathetic ways of working with men, but also demands that male social workers consider how their maleness affects their orientation to problem situations and how they can learn from women.
- Assessments need to address the issues of how oppression is affecting service users *and* how the worker is part of this process.

6

A Map of the World: the Systems Approach

The diversity of the social work task

We suggested above that the function of social work is to provide a formal Welfare network for people in the absence of an informal welfare network. This makes it an extremely diverse activity covering almost every aspect of social life. Although this includes assessing and managing risk, meeting needs and allocating resources, these aspects are somewhat arbitrarily divided into specific settings, such as childcare, probation and education welfare, and specialisms such as marital and adoptive work. Social workers in these various settings and specialisms spend much of their time dealing with other agencies and organisations, all of which have differing mandates, purposes and relationships.

It can clearly become very confusing working out precisely what one is doing for whom and for what reason at any moment of time. More difficult still is knowing whether this is the most profitable thing to be doing and whether you are the most appropriate person to be doing it. A framework that would help a social worker to understand the purpose of each contact, the boundaries of the relationship, the benefits to be expected, and the identification of exactly who is the service user, who has sanctioned the work, and who and what will need to be influenced or changed, would obviously be most useful. Any map that attempted to provide such direction would of necessity have to be sufficiently general to embrace the boundless parameters of social work activity – a 'map of the world of practice'. Pincus and Minahan (1973) have produced the most commonly used framework of 'systems' for organising these complexities and giving social workers a sense of direction in their work. We will outline their approach in this chapter, listing the advantages and disadvantages of this approach to assessment. We will also include a brief section on family systems approaches, although these draw mainly on other theoretical maps.

A systems approach to assessment

Pincus and Minahan (1973) argue that individuals' social problems are mainly related to the interaction between themselves and resource systems in their lives, and they classify these resource systems into three types, presenting four interacting systems that map out the activities of the worker in any situation. They use the terms 'problem', 'client' and 'case', and our outline of the theory will also use these. This is partly for historical accuracy, but also because it is important to recognise that the theory is rooted in a value stance that sees these terms as unproblematic. This poses a problem for a social worker attempting to 'graft on' more recent value stances to do with empowerment, an aspect to which we will return later.

When faced with problems, or when attempting to avoid them in the first place, people usually turn to their 'resource systems' to find help in carrying out their life tasks. The three types of resource system identified by Pincus and Minahan are:

1 *Informal/natural systems.* These include family, friends, neighbours, co-workers, bartenders and many others. They provide emotional support, advice, information and practical help such as babysitting or small loans.

2 *Formal membership systems.* These include trade unions, recreational clubs, support groups, parent–teacher associations, cooperative associations and tenant associations, providing more specialised help than that available in informal systems.

3 *Public/societal systems.* These include housing organisations, hospitals and health professionals, social services departments, courts, day care centres, schools, places of work and the income maintenance agencies.

Many people's difficulties arise because of inadequacies in these systems or in their inability to use them, or because of breakdowns in the interactions between individuals and the system, including mishandled conflict, misunderstanding, bias, prejudice or a breakdown of relations in some other way. These result in social workers seeing people within these systems to assess what is the matter, perhaps to negotiate on behalf of the client or to mediate between client and system. Whatever the situation, consideration of a broad range of systems and the possibility that the problem can be caused not only by some factor internal to the person, but also by factors within these systems, helps the worker to maintain a broad view. This approach, however, requires a 'map' to guide the social worker through the resulting range of possibilities. This map takes into account not only the social workers, but also their employing agencies. Pincus and Minahan provide this in their four-part systemic framework (Figure 6.1).

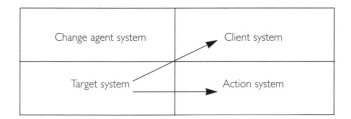

Figure 6.1 Pincus and Minahan's four systems

These four systems, and the relationship between them, will be explained in turn, but it may be useful to remember that they refer to distinct groups of people. In dealing with any particular case, this map helps the worker to sort out who resides in each system and whether they need to be moved to another system. We will return to this, with the aid of case examples, when we have defined the four systems.

The change agent system

The social worker who is primarily responsible for the work in a case is the main/central change agent, but she/he needs to appreciate fully who else occupies the system space in order to be more readily able to consider drawing on their participation. This anticipates the role of social worker as one of case management, as different from individual therapist, so the social work role in assessment is seen as central, with interventions then being allocated to a range of people.

For example, in the case of private counsellors offering a specific service, one person may be the sole change agent for the client, but for social workers who are employed by a service or agency this is not so. They will have co-workers and colleagues who operate in teams, such as in day centre work, or they will be able to draw on the services of social work assistants or ancillary staff, administrative assistants, supervisors and managers. In addition, they will have working understandings with staff in other agencies and contacts in related services who can be called on for assistance and advice. This means that the worker is neither alone nor expected to be skilled in all interventions so that, when faced with the variety of a full caseload, the social worker does not have to be a Saint George, slaying dragons single handed. In some services intra- and interagency co-working may be available or even the norm (see, for example, Blyth and Milner, 1990, on the advantages and disadvantages of interdisciplinary cooperation in child protection work). The worker is viewed as part of a system and therefore able, where necessary, to bring that whole system to bear on a problem.

However, some people within the change agent system may also be located in one of the other systems, as we shall see later.

The client system

In much practice, the term 'client' is highly ambiguous and is used very loosely to mean members of the public who have 'problems'. Many such people will not wish to be assisted by social workers even though they may be ordered, for example by a court, to cooperate with the worker, and will not view themselves as clients. Similarly, a parent may ask a worker for help in dealing with a difficult child, but who is the client – the parent or the child? Our initial reaction to this question is to say that the parent is the client, but the parent may not wish to be changed in any way, so is the person we are trying to change the client?

Various writers have defined 'client' in different ways, and we will see examples of this when we come to the work of William Reid (1978) and Steve de Shazer (1988). However, in the systemic map, Pincus and Minahan define a client very specifically as any person, family, group, community or organisation that requests, engages or sanctions the service of the worker, expects to benefit from the contact and has a contract or working agreement with the social worker. For the purposes of a systemic approach, any so-called client who lacks any of these qualities is only a potential client rather than a real one. When a community or service certifies a worker's competence and sanctions their intervention with a particular group of people, that sanction makes those people only potential clients, as in the case of a group of offenders on probation orders. Before they become real clients, the worker must secure the sanction of each individual by obtaining at least their permission to intervene in their lives, and also by establishing a working agreement with them from which they expect to benefit. Until this is achieved, they are targets for change, members of the next system to be described. Davies (1981) says that with unwilling clients, the state is both the employer and the client of the social worker and that the legally defined 'clientele' is really a target group.

When a potential client is unwilling to cooperate with the worker, it is important that the value of self-determination is respected and that such people are not treated as if they were willing clients. It is not only a legally defined clientele who will be unwilling clients; in most statutory agencies, the majority of service users are women who are unlikely to be clients in Pincus and Minahan's terms. This distinction needs to be accepted and unwilling clients worked with accordingly, so a systems approach to assessment gives priority to these differences, which should not be explained in terms of theory from another 'map', such as client resistance in psychodynamic terms.

We have referred to the use of the term 'client' earlier. The term has a history of ambiguity (for an overview, see Davies, 1981, Ch 6). Agencies may have their own language, replacing the words 'client' or 'potential client', some agencies employing the terms 'service user' and 'customer' interchangeably. We have heard of an agency that distinguishes between beneficiaries, mainly the community, and recipients, mainly those people immediately at the receiving end of social workers' efforts. This implies that the recipients need not benefit! So the language can become confusing. We hope that the Pincus and Minahan distinction is clear. For them, clients have to fulfil the criteria of engagement, benefit and contract set out above, otherwise they should be viewed as targets. While respecting the wishes and powerlessness of many of these people, social workers will frequently be working towards securing consent and sanction, and an agreement about goals and how to achieve them. This will require the use of negotiating skills, ethical persuasion and contracting (for an excellent discussion of reluctant clients, see Barber, 1991, Ch 4).

There is one further aspect of the client system to be considered, one which it shares with the other three systems. This aspect is that individuals are usually not only members of families but also members of communities or community groups and ethnic, racial or nationalist groups. The positive and negative consequences of such membership cannot be ignored, so knowledge of these groups is important. Pincus and Minahan say that a social worker taking up a new post should walk the streets of the district and look at the houses, shops and street life of the community in order fully to appreciate this. Devore and Schlesinger (1991) comment, however, that this walk provides only superficial knowledge of the lives of the people behind their own doors and fails to address how residents respond to their ethnicity in a variety of lifestyles and that there may be a huge gap between that lifestyle and the worker's own. As we stated in the previous chapter, unless this gap is addressed and workers strive to understand people's systems in terms of community and culture, useful assessments will be difficult to make.

The target system

'The people the change agent needs to change or influence' (Pincus and Minahan, 1973, p. 58) in order to achieve the goals are called the target system. The worker, usually in collaboration with the 'client(s)', will establish preliminary goals and then work out which people would need to be changed in some way. These targets may include the client, or people in the client system, because the service they have sanctioned may include helping them to make some personal change that they are resisting but which they agree is necessary if they are to achieve what they want. Or the change agent may assess that there are other changes to which the client has not yet agreed but which are mandated by others, for example the courts.

Frequently, however, people who are not in the client system will need to be changed in some way if the goals of the effort are to be achieved. The important point here is that *the client system is not always the system that needs to be changed'* (Pincus and Minahan, p. 59, emphasis added). Indeed, it rarely is the only part of the system requiring change as most 'problems' are related to interpersonal difficulties. For example, a client's problem may be due to unfair treatment or inadequate resources. Abusers and resource managers are common targets. The target system may react to persuasion in various ways. The people concerned may welcome the change effort that makes them part of the client system, fight against the attempted changes or remain indifferent. Many interventions by social workers will be directly with the target system, seeking to engage them or persuade them, or to ask them for help in achieving the goal. In some circumstances, the social worker may seek to increase leverage on a powerful member of the target system by invoking the law or the authority of other powerful people, such as elected representatives or the media.

So, one person may be a client in respect of one goal and a target in respect of another. For example, a social worker may be helping parents of a disabled child to get more resources and may at the same time be influencing them to change the way in which they are dealing with the child if this is aggravating the problems they are encountering. In other situations, the target system and the client system may consist of totally different people if the social worker does not consider that the client(s) themselves need to be personally changed in any way. Additionally, the target system may be people inside the worker's own agency, for example, a colleague who has to be persuaded to help, or the policy-makers who need to be influenced to change in some respect. If you are confused at this stage, do not be surprised. Any approach that aims to provide a system explaining all situations is bound to get very complicated. This is one of the main difficulties of attempting to be 'certain' in any assessment work.

In working with any situation, especially where there are several overlapping difficulties, many people may be in the target system. These include not only the obvious people, such as those who control resources, but people who are also members of the client system or the change agent system. Some of these may be potential clients who are targeted as the social worker considers it necessary to influence them to become real clients in respect to a certain goal:

> The relationships he maintains with these different target systems, the types of influences he brings to bear upon them, and the tasks he performs will be dictated to varying degrees by a number of factors; his goals; the separateness or overlapping of the client, target, and change agent systems; the perceptions the target systems have of his change efforts; and their reactions to these efforts. (Pincus and Minahan, 1973, p. 61).

The action system

The final system in this map is the action system. For the most part, social workers do not work alone in seeking to achieve goals. Those other people who work alongside, with or for the social worker, be they parents or friends of the client(s), teachers, district nurses, residential social workers or support groups, comprise the action system as long as they in some way take part in the change effort.

When first identified as potential recruits for the action system, they are members of the target system, but once they agree with the assessment, they become part of the action system. Some of them may also be part of the client system because they expect to benefit, as for example the partner of a person with a drink problem; others, for example colleagues of the social worker, may be also part of the change agent system. Because the social worker deals with several cases, there may be several action groups in existence, and it is likely that some people, for example, a social work assistant or a benefits worker who helps the worker on a regular basis, will be members of more than one action group, although others, for example a parent, will be members of only one. The two arrows in Figure 6.1 represent the activities of recruiting targets to the client system and the action system, a large part of social work practice. Yes, we know, a systems approach is both simple and confusing.

Having identified goals, the main task of the worker is to build an action system and maintain it in each case until the goals are reached. In this way, the worker does not personally carry out every task or provide all the support alone. Ideally, s/he will consider what work or support is required and will build a system of people who can best provide that intervention or support without the direct involvement of the social worker in either the formal or the informal welfare network. Social workers may be best equipped to carry out some of the tasks but seldom all of them, and the resources of families, communities and other agency workers are available to be mobilised. Frequently, after appropriate assessment and brief intervention by the worker, on-going support can best be provided by others, and the worker's task is then to merely provide whatever maintenance that system may need (case management).

Because the social worker is working with an action system, many of the dealings with the client(s) will be indirect. In other situations, such as assisting a couple with marital difficulties, the only people helping the worker in the change effort will be the spouses themselves, in which case they are also the client system. In other situations, members of the action system may assess needs, help to identify goals and influence various targets to change; some will be dealing with the client directly and some will not. In some cases, for example a residents' group in a local authority home, the members of the action system will all be inter-acting with each other, while in others they will not. In some situations, the action system will be virtually already in operation, for example in a family, yet in others it will need to be built from scratch. The systems approach helps to ease the strain of social workers by urging them to *do nothing* that can be done better by others in the action system, so that case management becomes a matter of maintaining action systems rather than being burdened with responsibility for personally carrying out every detailed task in each case, and assessment becomes a matter of first locating people correctly in the various systems.

The four systems in action

It may help the reader if we bring the four systems together in two case examples. We will take fairly straightforward examples for the sake of clarity; readers can then apply the same ideas to one of their own situations, taking a sheet of paper and dividing it into four boxes, and then filling in the names of those who are part of each of the four systems.

In our first example, the worker is employed by the local authority education department as an education social worker dealing with school issues affecting children and families at home, and attendance and behaviour issues that children and their families pose for schools. Grange Road School has a teacher, Miss Brown, who is responsible for the pastoral needs of the children, and she refers this case to the service, where it is allocated by a supervisor with an interest in the effects of divorce to a main grade social worker with an explicit preference for a systems approach.

Sally, aged 9, is not attending school regularly; she is late with her school work and appears to be unhappy in school. She lives with her mother, her father having left the family 2 years previously, although Sally visits him on alternate weekends. Her mother is poor, unemployed and feeling low since her husband left her. Sally has a friend living at the other end of her street. Many of Sally's absences coincide with history and geography lessons, which are taught by a Miss Adams.

The social worker elicits Sally's story, which describes interpersonal difficulties. Sally does not like Miss Adams because she asks her questions in class which she cannot answer and this makes her feel embarrassed. Sally is also worried that her Mum seems so unhappy, so she sometimes stays at home if Mum is not very well. She likes her father but not his new partner, so she does not enjoy her visits to him. Sally wishes that her mother were more happy, although she also agrees that she would be able to do better at school if she attended regularly. She agrees that the social worker can speak to her mother and the teachers.

The social worker meets Sally's mother, who confirms that she has not coped well with the divorce, which 'changed everything' for her. Note that Sally's story influences the construction of her mother's story as the questions related to Sally's story. She is concerned about Sally's education and welfare but she gets 'so low' that she sometimes needs Sally to stay with her during the day. Only part of this story sounds to be Sally's mother's own story. She already recognises that she needs to tell it within the framework of schooling Sally (see the discussion of Michael White's ideas on narrative in Chapter 10).

The social worker next meets Miss Adams, who is a very busy person because of her many additional responsibilities in the school. She does not know Sally very well because this is the first year she has worked with her and she is often absent. She has noticed that Sally sometimes does not seem to be paying attention and so she occasionally asks her a question to engage her. The worker explains that Sally has problems at home, but Miss Adams is rather defensive and agrees only to keep an eye on Sally and to meet the worker again in a week's time. As the social worker has not demonstrated an ability to 'bridge the gap' between the different realities of social work and teaching, Miss Adams does not feel free to give her full story.

The social worker now has some preliminary data and begins the analysis. The next question, then, is who, at this date, is in each system? We suggest a grid as in Figure 6.2.

CHANGE AGENT SYSTEM	CLIENT SYSTEM
Social worker Supervisor, who has a special interest in the effects of divorce	Sally, because she permits contact with Mum and teacher Mum, in so far as she wants help for Sally Miss Brown, for the same reason
TARGET SYSTEM	**ACTION SYSTEM**
Sally, in that the social worker wants to get her to go to school Mum, in that the social worker wants her to send Sally to school Dad, who might have some influence on Sally Miss Adams, for the same reason	The social worker

Figure 6.2 Systems – example a

It is obvious that the action system is not only extremely thin on the ground, but also totally dependent upon one person being able to 'do everything', so time spent assessing how this could be enlarged would be useful. The social worker should therefore set about building an action system that will consist of more than just herself. If Miss Adams' story can be persuaded to include other ways of engaging Sally's attention, she will be in the action system, and equally Miss Brown can become part of the action system even if it is in nothing more than her agreeing to look out for Sally and greet her in school. Should Sally's mum agree to assistance to address her 'low' feelings, she will become part of the client system, but may also become part of the action system should she be able to try to put Sally's need for education before her own need for companionship. Very quickly, through a systems assessment, more people with real power to act can be added to the action system.

Taking an entirely different case, the social worker is now in a team providing services for older people, supporting them in their own homes or helping them and their families to face moving into residential care or a nursing home.

Mrs Abbott, aged 88, lives alone. She is a widow and her only son lives 20 miles away and is unable to visit her regularly. She is no longer able to do her own shopping, suffers from memory loss and is occasionally incontinent. She has two caring neighbours who take turns buying her food, but they are concerned at the way she is deteriorating, especially since she recently had a fall and could not get up until they visited her. They contact the social work department requesting services for Mrs Abbott.

The social worker has met Mrs Abbott to consider her ability to cope with living alone, what services she requires or will accept, and who are the best people to provide it. Mrs Abbott is pleased to accept any help she can get to remain in her own home, apart from an alarm, but the social worker will need to persuade her manager to sanction payment for scarce resources. At this point, a systems analysis will look like Figure 6.3.

CHANGE AGENT SYSTEM	CLIENT SYSTEM
Social worker Service manager Home helps Aids and adaptations worker	Mrs Abbott, in so far as she wants help to stay at home The neighbours, in so far as they want to be relieved of some of their concerns
TARGET SYSTEM	**ACTION SYSTEM**
Mrs Abbott, in so far as she has not yet been persuaded to accept an alarm device to call for help should she fall Service manager, in so far as he has to be persuaded to pay for services Home help, who has yet to be engaged District nurse, for sanitary aids Mr Abbott (son), who manages Mrs A's finances, and will be asked to make contributions	The social worker The two neighbours who shop for Mrs Abbott

Figure 6.3 Systems – example b

As in the previous case, the systems assessment at this point shows that there is little action system except for the social worker and some involvement by two neighbours. Only when she has persuaded those in the target system to play their part in dealing with the problems will they then be part of the action system. Until that time, she has assumed the worries and responsibilities with the neighbours.

The advantages of a systems approach

So how does this classification of those with whom the social worker is involved help? It helps the worker to analyse a piece of work (a change effort) in a way that clarifies the purposes of various contacts and activities and the relationships that s/he has with the various parties involved. In the assessment, the various tasks that must be achieved during the social worker's involvement in order to build an action system are identified and the social worker gains a wider perspective of the whole situation, especially in terms of mobilising people and resources. Additionally, it saves social workers from feeling they have to do everything personally and directly, and highlights where resistance may be met and how individuals might best be persuaded to contribute to the effort. It also provides a perspective that locates where the worker should be positioned in each situation, how much more needs to be done and possibly in what order tasks can best be performed and by whom. By setting out a full target list and considering whether anyone else could be added to it, the social worker is prompted to look around widely and not limit his/her thinking. Reviewing the systems provides a useful checklist for evaluation and prevents social workers from concentrating on only one part of the situation, so reassessment is encouraged, with potential clients and potential action system members being drawn in. From this process, a plan of action easily follows, with revision of the membership of the four systems bringing the map up to date after each brief period of activity. This map helps the social worker to avoid assuming that the person who asks for help, or who is presenting the problem, is necessarily the main target for intervention. The system does not assume that any one size of action system is best; only after the purpose and goals are clear can the worker know whether the situation will require one-to-one direct work with the client, groupwork or a whole series of interventions with other people, including a large action system.

Traditionally, social workers have tended to concentrate on counselling skills and individual client–worker relationships, to the neglect of relationships with people who are not, or will not be, clients. Yet, increasingly, social workers need to develop networking skills or skills in thinking more widely when assessing situations and planning interventions. This 'map of the world' approach helps them to identify, analyse and compare the various systems into which those involved in any situation fit, what sort of involvement the worker needs to have with them and for what purpose. Another useful spin-off is that it helps social workers to realise that the agency for which they work may also be a target for change. This systemic approach helps social workers also to consider other possibilities, such as could the client be a target in some respects, is the real client someone other than the person who is labelled client, or are there others who, if they were influenced or changed in some way, would cause the problem to be resolved?

When things are nor progressing well, this approach invites the social worker to ask not whether the client is resistant but whether the action system is working smoothly, to think systemically about the possible causes of any dysfunction and to make the necessary changes. For example, if members of an action system, such as the staff in a children's home, are not working as a team, children will hear conflicting messages and individual therapy will be constantly undermined. Similarly, a children's home that adopts a 'token economy' approach can only work when and if the action system is consistent in how it rewards children; any assessment considering only the children and not the system would be inadequate. An increase in the number of problems is not necessarily due to any deterioration within the children but to a possible weakness in the action system.

A systems approach can also help workers as they constantly struggle to clarify value issues such as self-determination and empowerment. These values do not apply in the same way to all the four systems. Principles governing dealings with the client system do not apply in the same way to people in the target system whose behaviour may be contributing to the problem. The other person(s), perhaps a housing officer or landlord who is treating the client unfairly, does not require the same sort of empowerment or self-determination as does the victim of that treatment. Different means of persuasion may be justified, depending on whether that person is in the agency, target or client system. For example, a landlord who is seeking election to the town council may respond well to media pressure to improve a building. A violent man on probation may respond better to clear statements that the worker's responsibility towards other people for whom the man is a risk requires contact with those people and therefore this is done whether or not he agrees. We will return to these ideas later in this chapter when we address criticisms of the approach.

Finally, the systemic map fits any area of practice equally well, be it fieldwork, groupwork, residential work or community work. In all of these, social workers are involved in work that is not necessarily direct work with an identified client. The systems map aids assessment in that it locates, and fits into an action plan, all activities of the people in the welfare network. It helps social workers to look at the whole territory of social work and begin to order its complexities.

Disadvantages of a systems approach

The advantages of a systems approach in assessment work, in showing that the welfare of clients might be most effectively served if they were not the sole focus of change, in the ordering of thinking and in the re-evaluation necessary to draw more people into the action system, were seen as quite radical in the 1980s (Davies, 1981). Superficially, it seems that such an approach will lead easily into participation and empowerment efforts. However, practitioners have found that even a careful systems analysis does not *on its own* help them to achieve a depth of understanding of situations. This also requires the use of a more detailed map. Barber (1991) has greater difficulty with general systems theory; he (too) maintains that on its own it is inadequate, adding 'In seeking to be relevant to all presenting problems, generalist models are relevant to none' (Barber, 1991, p. 28). We do not go that far!

A serious disadvantage of a systems assessment, however, is that there is an assumption that the approach is somehow value-free and unbiased, in that the analysis will include all people and groups. The approach suggests how the data should be ordered but neglects the process of data collection in the first place. It also ignores the very real possibility that a social worker will use the theory in conjunction with existing notions about the nature of people. This is clearly demonstrated in our case examples. In both of these, women are represented more heavily than men, and they are constrained from revealing themselves as possibly unwilling members of either the client or action group by the way in which the stories are framed in the initial interview. The traditional social work tendency to 'victimise' the person with the problem remains. The men in the case examples are shadowy figures, a not unusual fact in social work practice (Milner, 1996), but, as with the women, this approach does nothing to examine the power effects surrounding their involvement. Viewing Mr Abbott solely in terms of his financial role hardly does much to encourage men to develop the caring capacities outlined in the previous chapter. And Sally's father is out of sight and out of mind, despite the supervisor's interest in the effects of divorce, which should indicate that the father will also have feelings on the matter. A systems approach *per se* does not help to bring these men into consideration as real people with a part to play in informal welfare networks.

Thus, while a systems approach seeks to introduce some rigour into assessments, it is capable of seducing social workers into a quick-fix solution. It does have several advantages, but when its generalist ambitions are reduced to more manageable proportions, as is the case in family systems approaches, the disadvantages become more obvious, as we will demonstrate in the following section.

Family systems

Moving away now from the Pincus and Minahan general systems approach, the term 'systemic' applies also to other approaches. The most obvious of these is family systems, that is looking on a family as a system made up of subsystems: marital, parental and sibling. Between the various subsystems are boundaries. These refer not so much to walls and doors as to secrets and alliances between subgroups in the system and between the family system and the supra-system (society). Boundaries may be more or less permeable to allow interaction and exchanges, or they may be more or less rigid, keeping in secrets and keeping out others. If the outer boundary of the family is rigid, it may keep out the eyes of society generally and perhaps make the family a more dangerous place if there is an abusive member. Systems approaches to assessments of families can consist of looking not only at individuals and their behaviour, how it affects others or what function it has in the system, but also at the structure or hierarchy within a family and, for example, the permeability of its boundaries, both external and internal. Where boundaries are too open or permeable, the system can be flooded with too many sensory impressions, the psychological contents of other individuals, with a lack of clarity about personal boundaries and identity, or even psychosis; the result is instability. Where the boundaries are too rigid or impermeable, impaired growth, development and creativity result; 'we get stability at the expense of extreme defensiveness' (Skynner, 1974, p. 290). For a detailed discussion of these ideas see, for example, Minuchin (1974), Barker (1981) and Masson and O'Byrne (1984).

In a systemic view of a family, whatever is happening in one subsystem will affect the others. For example, problems in the marital subsystem will affect the sibling subsystem, and behavioural problems in one member may be the result of a dysfunction elsewhere in the system. So it is not only the individual who has to be assessed but the whole system. Likewise, positive change in one part of the system can have a positive ripple effect elsewhere in the system, so it may be a matter of assessing where the most beneficial intervention could be made with the most effect, that is where is the best 'point of leverage' (Masson and O'Byrne, 1984, p. 7). Family systems ideas underpin some of the recent government guidance, such as the Orange Book (Department of Health, 1988). There are also models for making a family assessment. Here we refer briefly to two of the best known models and encourage the interested reader to consult specialist family therapy texts (see, for example, Barker, 1981; Masson and O'Byrne, 1984). The first model of family

assessment we wish to identify is that known as the McMaster Model of
Family Functioning (Epstein *et al.*, 1978). It considers six aspects of
how families function: problem-solving, communication, roles, affective responsiveness, affective involvement and behaviour control. The
McMaster model suggests various ways of considering family problems
under each of the above headings. For example, under 'problem-
solving' they distinguish between instrumental and affective problems
(if the latter are present, the former are usually also present, but not vice
versa), and they explore whether the family can identify the problem,
develop alternative plans for dealing with it, take appropriate action and
evaluate progress. Likewise, communication is divided into two kinds
according to whether it deals with instrumental or affective issues and
also whether it is clear or masked, direct or indirect. Roles, too, can be
instrumental or affective, both kinds being required. Behaviour control
can be assessed as rigid, flexible, *laissez-faire* or chaotic.

Minuchin (1974), on the other hand, takes a structural approach to
assessment and examines patterns of functioning, enmeshment or
disengagement, sources of support and of stress, the uses or benefits
of the symptom, family alliances and coalitions, boundaries and
power. Whatever model is used, most family social workers seek to
discover how problems are being maintained and also what it is about
the family that causes one or more members to develop symptoms or
difficult behaviour patterns. Haley (1976) sets out ways of engaging
('joining') a family in an assessment and offers a staged process for
managing the interview.

Other writers address family cohesion and family adaptability and
add such headings as task performance, values and norms when making
family assessments. Frequently, families are assessed in order to establish how they are meeting the needs of a child. The social worker
considers aspects that affect the growth of the child, physically,
emotionally and psychologically. Gorell Barnes (1984) has set out the
aspects of family functioning that need to be considered. These include
affectional bonds, provision of a secure base from which the child can
explore, provision of models with whom the child can identify, ability
to cope with stress without aggression or perpetual illness, the quality
of the interaction between the parents, the quality of discipline and good
communication networks, both internal and external. This model is
grounded in middle-class, white, English family norms and would not
be appropriate for families who gave a higher precedence to education,
for example, as we discussed in the earlier section on attachment theory.

There are many approaches to family assessment but they all have in
common the notion of system, and problems tend to be attributed to

dysfunctions in the system as a whole. When it comes to abuse of a family member, this systemic approach can imply that everyone in the system, including the victim, is equally to blame, if it is the system as a whole that is dysfunctioning.

There are two main criticisms of the family systems approach. First, it neglects the social context in which families live (see, for example, Justice and Justice, 1976; Violence Against Children Study Group, 1990). Second, feminist writers point out that it neglects or ignores the power of patriarchy (see, for example, Beecher, 1986; Walters, cited in Roys, 1987). More recent writers on family systems thinking (see, for example, Masson and O'Byrne, 1990) have taken this criticism on board, placing more emphasis on issues of patriarchy and male power in the assessment of family functioning.

We agree that systemic factors, although important, do not remove personal responsibility for unacceptable behaviour or individual abuse of power.

Summary

- By the 'map of the world', we mean a general systems theory, such as that of Pincus and Minahan, in which social workers can assess whether people are in one of the four proposed systems: change agent, client, target or action system.
- We recommend this as a starting point in any piece of work to help get one's bearings and to work out who is doing what for whom and for what purpose.
- The main disadvantage is that a general systems approach is so general that it is difficult to achieve depth of assessment.
- Family systems theory is mentioned very briefly as it provides a systemic way of viewing individual families and their members. Although it is a systemic approach, rather than being a map of the world, it is more akin to a map of one country.
- The systemic map of the world is never sufficient on its own and needs to be used in conjunction with one of the maps in the following chapters.
- It will be clear to the reader by now that these general maps alone cannot provide the sort of detail a traveller needs in order to find more specific answers in assessing a situation.
- Specific areas or aspects need to be 'blown up' through the use of other maps if social workers are to be able to see how to provide a thorough detailed analysis.

7

A Map of the Ocean:
Psychodynamic Approaches

The previous two chapters discussed rather general maps relating to social issues such as power and oppression; they also discussed systems and addressed values. We now present the first of four specific maps that contain the potential to 'blow up' the detail needed for arriving at thorough analyses to guide further action. This chapter presents, as does Chapter 8, a traditional psychological analysis of human behaviour, which may leave the reader wondering about the concerns expressed in Chapter 2 concerning the 'psy complex'. We did, however, stress that since external problems become internal and the internal affects the external, looking at nothing other than social aspects is as inadequate as looking at nothing other than psychological aspects; we need to consider both. Also, the ideas in the next chapters all need to be used alongside the ideas outlined in the previous two chapters.

Psychodynamic theory

In this chapter, we will be considering various ideas associated with the psychoanalytical approach to understanding the nature of people. We are selective in our sources, limiting ourselves to the work of Erikson (1948, 1977), Hollis (1964), Berne (1978) and Bowlby (1982), who have built on and developed Freudian theories in ways which have proved particularly attractive to social work. Our description of the theory will reflect a synthesis of many people's ideas and insights, their terms and their language.

The Freudian approach (Freud, 1937) has been labelled 'psychic determinism': viewing our actions as determined by inner forces that develop in early childhood. It places great store on a person's early childhood and on early parental relationships, the past influencing the present. Some Freudians go so far as to say it can even be tyrannical in its influence.

Therefore this approach can have a feel of digging down deep as an archaeologist would but, more so, it can have a feel of descending into the unconscious as if exploring in a submarine. Our chapter title comes from a comment by Hall (1954, p. 2) that the id is 'oceanic', in that it contains everything and recognises nothing outside of itself; if there is too much rough weather, it can turn nasty. We begin with a simplified diagrammatic presentation of the core ideas in this exploratory map (Figure 7.1). Bear in mind, however, that we are not discussing physical parts of a person but mental constructs that seek to explain people's functioning.

The mind		The world
Unconscious	Conscious	(Other people and the environment)
The superego The Parent (teaching)		
	The ego The Adult (thinking)	Reality
The id The Child (feeling)		

Figure 7.1 Mind and world

Although the id might not be capable of recognising anything outside itself, Freud certainly did recognise the outside world and its impact on the ego, so we have shown the world of reality on our version of this map and, as we shall show later, a large area of the map will deal with the interaction of the ego with reality.

Freud's earliest distinction was that between the conscious and unconscious mind, considering the latter as the greater part, consciousness being only the tip of the iceberg above the surface. In the 1920s, Freud developed the notions of ego, superego and id. While a large part of the ego, although by no means all of it, can be conscious, the vast majority of the superego and probably all of the id are unconscious. Freud also identified the 'pre-conscious' as that part of the unconscious that we can readily recall, that just under the surface.

The superego develops through a process of internalisation. The child internalises the values, rules, prohibitions and wishes of the parent and of authority figures, but the process is one that magnifies these rules and records them in the raw, without editing, and laden with amplified feelings. So it is not just what a parent says to a child but all the emotion, perhaps terror, that was felt at being blamed, abandoned or hurt in various ways: the small child who breaks a cup can feel that s/he has destroyed everything. Admonitions and rules go straight into memory, carrying the weight of total truth, never to be erased from the tape. The research of Penfield (1952) and the work of Berne (1964) have helped to shape this view of the superego, and Berne (1964) later referred to it as the Parent (using a capital P to indicate that this is an internalised parent) part of the person, the part that tells and teaches. Even though the telling is long lost from consciousness, the recording remains active in the unconscious, shouting loudly.

The superego may be restrictive or permissive (Caplan, 1961). People riddled with guilt can be said to have an over-restrictive superego and people with too little guilt an over-permissive or weak superego. Those with no internal rules, no conscience about hurting others, are labelled sociopaths. Caplan (1961) talks of the superego as the condemning and prohibiting part of the mind that says 'Do not…', or 'I must not…', and he distinguishes this from the ego-ideal, which says (of a desirable act),'So as not to let myself down, I ought to do it because that would fit my ideal me'. So, some people's conscience tells them they have to strive for great heights of achievement and set themselves high standards, be thrifty, and so on. Their parents may have reinforced these messages with great approval and with pleasure at the child's efforts. However, inconsistency on the part of parents would considerably weaken the message, and it is often said of delinquent youths that their parenting was inconsistent or contradictory. On the other hand, too rigid and dominating a superego could create difficulties by way of excessive guilt, leading to neurotic effects such as depression, phobias, obsessions, compulsions, neurotic anxiety and moral anxiety or shame. Reality anxiety (Hall, 1954), however, is seen as an ego reaction to the threat of loss.

The id is that aspect of the person which is primitive, the animal drive: it is the Child (again with a capital C in Berne's terms), full of feelings, capable of rage, operating on instinctual drives and urges, hungry to fill any voids that are felt. Like the superego, according to Harris (1970), the id is also shaped by early recordings of feelings of blame, fear and abandonment. Even those with a happy childhood will record Not OK feelings that can loom larger than all the OK feelings. We can all be said to have a Not OK Child in us. The child who feels unloved may seek to fill a sense of void by theft, sometimes impulsively, as in kleptomania. The id also feels hurt by rejection or oppression.

Berne (1978) distinguishes between two main drives of libido, which is sexual impulse, desire and attraction, and mortido, which is the killing instinct, hating, attacking and hitting out violently. He suggests some people are more prone to one rather than the other, although these are close relatives born of the need to survive and propagate. They explain something of what some people are looking for, so the id is described as being governed by the 'pleasure principle'; the lack of sufficient pleasure leaves it hurting, demanding and wanting irrationally, sometimes leading to a chaotic life of acting out, living for 'kicks' or sending out cries for help, such as the abused person who shoplifts to attract attention to his/her plight, behaving in a way that could be interpreted as asking to be caught.

The third area is the ego, the I and Me, the self. Berne labelled this as the Adult (with a capital A) part of the mind, which thinks, decides, plans and relates to the world of reality. It is governed by the 'reality principle', exploring and testing, born of curiosity. Allen (1974) maintains that, in Freudian theory, identifications are used in the process of sublimating id drives to more acceptable, higher goals and involve moulding the ego in the image of another. This powerful process, of central importance to the development of the ego, is quite resistant to insight: we like to believe that our self is totally original. This process is also close to the perhaps more familiar notion of role modelling. Children who lack a positive figure, especially of the same gender, struggle to develop socialised personalities.

The ego is placed between the superego and the id in Figure 7.1 because it acts as a referee between them, struggling to keep a balance between the gratification of needs and impulses and the sacrifice of this gratification to the demands of reality. This is what 'psychodynamic' means – an interaction and tension between the id and the superego in an attempt to keep a balanced ego, and a tension between the inner and outer realities of the ego. There is also tension between the ego and superego, with its possibly guilt-ridden prohibitions.

The ego lives under great pressure from three sides: the id, the superego and real threats in the world. Anna Freud (1936, 1968) itemised various mechanisms of defence used by the ego to help it cope with the instinctual drives of the id and, to a lesser extent, with the condemnations of the superego and the demands of reality.

The infantile ego experiences the onslaught of instinctual and external stimuli at the same time; if it wishes to preserve its existence it must defend itself on both sides simultaneously. (Anna Freud, 1936, p. 191)

She listed denial, repression, reaction formation, intellectualisation, displacement and sublimation as the main defences. Repression gets rid of instinctual derivatives, just as external stimuli are abolished by denial. Reaction formation secures the ego against the return of the repressed impulses, while by fantasies, in which reality is reversed, denial is sustained against attack from outside. The ego uses sublimation to direct instinctual impulses from their sexual goals to higher aims, and reaction formation is the ego further draining itself of the capacity for reversal (p. 190). The existence of neurotic symptoms itself indicates that the ego has been overpowered and some plan of defence has miscarried (p. 193).

The bringing to consciousness of repressed events is a crucial task in psychoanalysis. In some situations, such as a loss or a crisis, denial – 'This is not happening' – is often the first phase of grief and it is considered to be a normal healthy reaction. At the other extreme, however, when an ego finds no solution or escape, it can be thrown back on the very primitive mechanism of regression, returning to an earlier stage of development so that an adult may behave like a small child, perhaps engaging in wishful thinking or the use of magical or irrational symbolic means. More severe regression can lead to alienation from reality and a fragmentation of self, which is a splitting of one's self and of aspects of reality in a state of psychosis in order to cease to feel the tensions of the problem and thereby escape reality (Caplan, 1961). Projection is the process whereby an individual's drives or feelings are attributed to another person or persons. For example, someone who cannot tolerate the idea that they have urges to steal may attribute it to others in an irrational way.

The further extended list of defences show how post-Freudians have added to Anna Freud's defences, up to 44 such defences being mentioned in the literature. For example, Bibring *et al.* (*c.* 1960) suggest that there are dual aspects of defences: first, warding off anxiety in relation to unconscious conflict and, second, actively supporting adaptive functions of maturation, growth and mastery of the drives. They list 39 defences, two of which have two subdivisions and one of which has four subdivisions. These include asceticism, clowning, compliance, depersonalisation, eating or drinking, falling ill, identification, ritualization and whistling in the dark. Most people use several of these, at least from time to time, and they can be helpful or not depending on the degree of usage and the particular circumstances. There are so many unconscious defences attributed to people that we worry mildly should you decide to use a Freudian interpretation for understanding our motives in writing this book. It is important, however, to remember that defences can be helpful or unhelpful, particularly in a crisis when the ego is under great stress. For example, intellectualisation might helpfully involve making lists of tasks or thinking through the traumatic event. On the other hand, defences can be unhelpful when they lead to on-going denial of loss or projection of cause on to others. However, we sometimes think that projection is the curse of contemporary life in which no one accepts responsibility for anything. Part of the task of assessment in psychodynamic social work is to decide which defences are being used and whether they are a help or a hindrance, and, if the latter, to consider how they can best be confronted.

In translating psychodynamic ideas into social work practice, Coulshed (1988) writes that, in assessing people, we need to see whether the ego can tolerate self-scrutiny without becoming too anxious. In cases in which such scrutiny does not promise for change, we need to ask ourselves what level of support is needed to help the person cope with external pressures. Coulshed suggests that indications of such lack of promise might be anxiety, dependence, low intellectual capacity and distrust. She warns against 'laying bare' repressed feelings, or offering interpretations to that end, if the ego thereby risks being overwhelmed (Coulshed, 1988, p. 109). An immature, weak ego needs defences to be strengthened, rather than torn down; ego supporting is to be preferred to ego modifying in such cases.

Similarly, Hollis (1964) made a useful distinction between direct and indirect work. By direct work, she meant that 'psycho' work that directly addresses thoughts and feelings to relieve underlying inner stress, which may, for example, be due to excessive use of defences that limit a person's coping with reality. By indirect work, she meant manipulations of the outer world that address social or environmental issues, services and material provision. Such indirect work may be necessary in order to build trust, to provide a sense of being cared for, before direct work is tolerable. In dealing with children, direct work on painful issues may be facilitated by discussion of fairy tales and parallel stories about animal families through which a child can tell of painful events in a less threatening way.

The use of this approach emphasises a thorough and lengthy assessment during which the therapeutic relationship is established, but brief work has also been considered possible in some situations. We recently met an example of a family in which a boy was not doing well at school and his father was 'in a state', trying to cope with his anger at the teachers while trying to maintain his son's enthusiasm for education. The social worker asked the father whether he had been keen on education when he was at school. He said he had not, and he had a very negative experience of teachers. When it was suggested that perhaps he was still addressing his own past school issues, rather than his son's, this insight helped him to rehearse his meeting with the school so that when it took place he was better able to focus on his son's situation, behaviour and needs in a rational and helpful manner.

Wasserman (1974) points out that it takes a strong ego to be able to mourn, suffer, verbalise anger and even be depressed. So the absence of depression in some situations, while it might appear to be adaptive, might in fact be due to an over-defended ego and therefore be maladaptive. A dramatic fictional example of this is the mother in the film *Ordinary People*. In assessing people, social workers have to look not only at their behaviour, but also at their situation and consider the stresses that may be operating, the degree to which the ego is pressed upon and the stresses with which the ego can or cannot cope. So, ego functioning is not only influenced by internal pressures from the superego and the id, but very much also by external stimuli. Social, cultural and economic factors, injustice and oppression, do not remain outside the person: 'much of what is now inside a person was once outside' (Hamilton, 1941). Since casework is mostly concerned with efforts to influence adaptive capacities (Austin, 1948), our assessments are more likely to be useful if they focus on the interface of the ego with the world: how the ego is learning, controlling and balancing with self-reliance and pride. This will mean that a social worker will not be concerned about intensive psychoanalytic techniques of free association, the recovery of the repressed, or the interpretation of dreams and breaking through resistance. Rather than a blank screen approach, she will offer a relationship, listening and reflecting with the client, joining the resistance (Strean, 1968), so that they can get going with the problem-solving that needs to be done. This does not in every case require the reliving of past traumas.

On the other hand, Fraiberg (1980), whose work is based on that of Bowlby (1964), gives detailed descriptions of situations in which repressed feelings need to be faced. She quotes a mother who cannot feel for her child because she cannot let herself recall the horror of being abandoned by her own mother. Lawrence (1992) suggests this is more likely to apply to a mother with a female child rather than a male child, so the difficulty is handed on from female to female. In this approach, women and mothers seem to attract more than their fair share of attention!

One also needs to understand the process of transference in order to keep the therapeutic relationship reality focused, seeking to lessen threat, repetitive themes and dependency, and addressing ambivalence (Wasserman, 1974). Although transference is not strictly a defence, more an example of the past manifesting itself in the present, it is a process that takes place when a person transfers feelings relating to one person, for example a parent, onto the social worker. Thus the social worker needs to consider whether the client is really referring to the social worker or perhaps to some early parental figure.

Understanding defence mechanisms may help us to understand what seems to be puzzling behaviour in another, but we should be very cautious not to attach them as labels to people or to believe that they are true – in our view they are simply useful hypotheses. Flirt with them by all means, but do not marry them. Many present-day researchers, for example, say that there is no long-term memory before the age of 3 and no evidence of the repression of events before that age being possible. They would say therefore that any so-called memories from before the age of 3 are false.

We would now like to consider the *functions* of ego, another area that can offer useful possibilities for assessment, particularly of the strength of the ego. It is the function of the ego to provide stability, equilibrium and predictability in such a way that, once we get to know someone, we can say that in certain circumstances s/he is liable to react in a certain way that is 'true to character'. This makes for sound relationships. Bowlby (1982) explains this in terms of the child making stable internal representations that will depend upon attachment styles developed in infancy but persisting into adult ways of relating. (Note that the prediction of others behaviour that makes people feel in control of social situations is explained in different ways in the psychological literature. See, for example, the discussion on attribution theory in Chapter 11.) The ego also manages cognitions, perceptions, planning and problem-solving. It makes judgments and decisions, adapts to reality and controls impulses, for example not hitting out at someone being offensive who is bigger than oneself! The ego is responsible for personal growth, coping with stress, using skills and tolerating frustration, loss, pain and sadness. It is the ego that neutralises pressures from the superego and urges from the id. It produces self-assertion, the ability to verbalise feelings rather than act them out, and finally directs our striving, our attempts to achieve and to care. To do all this, the ego needs to be flexible, adaptable, resilient, reality based, stable in the face of pressure and tolerant of anxiety and loss.

The ego, therefore, has a massive task to perform, which can make it feel overwhelmed and in need of defences. We all need some defences at times, but many clients may particularly need us to strengthen or support their egos, not by breaking through defences with interpretations but by respecting and working with defences, acknowledging the threats they face and discussing the implications and confusion of their ambivalent feelings, or considering their unfinished emotional business, providing support perhaps through a corrective relationship that provides an emotional re-education, so that the client can move on to be an independent coping person.

The term 'coping', however, has particular connotations for feminist writers, who read it to mean putting on a front of coping by splitting off unwanted feelings, getting on with life without a fuss. Women often have no other choice; they dread failing to cope and are likely to suffer serious consequences if they do. For example, women tolerate much domestic violence rather than risk losing their children and put up with accusations that they have failed as mothers to protect their children (Kelly, 1994). Worse still, a black woman is stereotyped as being expected to cope with 'all kinds of hardship and material and emotional deprivation, as though she had no feelings or needs at all' (Lawrence, 1992). Thus we need to consider how reality is structurally more difficult for some people due to the oppressions of society, sexism and racism and other forms of discrimination:

> Following the early work of Richmond, psychosocial casework does promote indirect or environmental interventions as well as direct clinical work, but even today it retains a narrow understanding of what constitutes 'the environment', resulting in social interventions which usually seek little more than to mobilise or modify existing community resources. (Barber, 1991, pp. 16–17)

The terms 'independence' and 'separation', so central in psychodynamic explanations of 'healthy' personality development, have difficult connotations in that, because society is fundamentally patriarchal, women are more likely to have feelings of vulnerability, weakness, helplessness and dependency (Miller, 1973) or, on the other hand, to have learned from their mothers that they must orientate themselves 'towards meeting the needs of others' and 'to be a carer and not to expect to be cared for' (Lawrence, 1992). For an alternative view of ego development, see Mead (1934).

Transactional analysis

Harris (1970), and later Berne (1978), developed the idea of transactional analysis in order to look at the relationship between *any* two people, not just parents and their children. They describe the transactions as taking place between the Parent, or the Adult or the Child of one person and the Parent, or the Adult or the Child of another. This is shown diagrammatically in Figure 7.2.

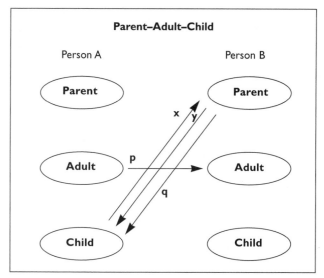

Figure 7.2 Parent–Adult–Child

If person A is being irresponsible, sulky or childish, this behaviour is likely to provoke the Parent of person B. This transacting is shown by the lines x and y. This is a complementary reaction from B; it is expected and appropriate. Other obviously complementary interactions are Parent–Parent, Adult–Adult and Child–Child. However, if the transactions are crossed, there can be trouble, for example if A's Adult addresses B's Adult but B's response is from B's Parent (telling A off, perhaps), as shown by lines p and q.

For Berne (1978), the transaction, 'the unit of social intercourse', is the key unit of study. Transactions will vary depending, for example, on whether the client is relating to her social worker, to a partner, to a friend or to her own children. In some situations, she may find that she may need to be helped to practise using her reasonable, reasoning, grown-up Adult more. If practice makes no difference, she may need to be encouraged to get in touch with feelings from the past, which, because they are presently out of consciousness, are dominant in certain circumstances. Events and people in our lives can 'hook' our Parent or our Child, which can appear to 'take over' for a while.

Parent–Adult–Child contamination is another interesting idea from Harris (1970). Parent contamination (of the Adult) is when the Adult is

holding to unreasonable, taught ideas, such as a strong prejudice
against a certain group. This may be accompanied by a 'blocked-off'
Child, making it difficult for the person to play or have fun. Child contamination of the Adult is when feelings from the Child are being inappropriately externalised/exhibited in the Adult, for example as
delusions. This may be accompanied by a 'blocked-off' Parent, leaving
a risk of a weakened conscience, a low sense of guilt or responsibility,
and a lack of social control, remorse or embarrassment.

Harris (1970) further expands the Parent–Adult–Child metaphor to
describe a manic person as one whose Parent is applauding the Child,
and a depressed person as one whose Parent is 'beating on the Child'
(p. 105). In both of these, there is Parent–Child contamination, and
Harris suggests that such people are probably brought up 'under the
shadow of great inconsistency' (p. 105).

Transactional analysis explanations of relationships

It may help here to 'recap' and show an ego gram of a particular service
user, Miss O, aged 70, based on the work of Berne (1978) (Figure 7.3).

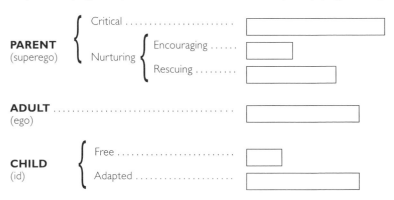

Figure 7.3 An ego gram

This can be seen as a graph of the family 'within' Miss O, who had
had become quite depressed when relatives were 'nasty' towards her
because she would not give them a loan. It is based on conversations
with her, listening to her memories of her responsibilities as the eldest
child, her impressions of her parents as strict and stern, and her assessment of herself as being afraid to have fun but planning little decep-
tions to help her cope. Her Parent (the capital indicates that this is the
internalised version of a real parent) is therefore represented as highly

critical and not very nurturing. What nurturing there is is more rescu-
ing than encouraging. Her Child, on the other hand, is not very free,
being fearful of the critical Parent. It is, however, fairly well adapted,
meaning that it has found a good deal of (possibly 'naughty') ways of
making do. Meanwhile, her Adult (ego) is reasonably strong, but she
still has some growing to do. The critical Parent and the adapted Child
are both very difficult to manage. Much depends on what level of stress
is caused by the world, especially the world of relationships. If this
proves to be too bleak and stormy a place, this ego will need quite a lot
of support and luck.

Psychodynamic explanations of personality development

Psychodynamic theory sees people as developing in a sequence of
stages, each one dependent upon the successful negotiation of the
earlier one for its own success. Freud was interested in the early stages
of child development, particularly sexual development, while Bowlby
(1982) focused more on the social and emotional interactions of this
period. Erikson (1948) extended Freud's developmental outline across
the life span, including social as well as sexual and emotional influences. Table 7.1 attempts to set out the main concepts.

   In psychodynamic social work, this theory suggests that it may be
useful to explore whether, and how well, these stages have been negotiated or whether aspects of some stages are still presenting difficulties
in the present. It is also important to bear in mind, however, that matu-
rational crises can be compounded by situational crises.

   While Freudian personality theory has as many feminist adherents as
it has critics (see, for example, Baker Miller, 1973; Barr, 1987; Pearson,
1988), Erikson's life span developmental outline has proved more resistive to feminist revision. The criticisms remain acute whether they are
specific, such as Gilligan's (1982) analysis of moral development,
which suggests that while boys may develop from identity to intimacy,
the process is reversed for girls, or more general (Rorbaugh, 1981;
O'Hagan and Dillenburger, 1995). This is probably because the entire
text is riddled with sexist and racist terms. For example, Erikson (1948)
refers to 'the non male form of the female genitalia' and he describes
black identity as three different forms of 'nigger' identity. Certainly,
social work students love Erikson, but we harbour suspicions that this
is because his outline is seductively simple and, all too often, his is the
one book to be found on agency shelves when it comes time to write up
accounts of practice in theoretical terms.

Table 7.1 Stages of human development

AGE	STAGES	
	Freudian	Eriksonian
Birth to 1	Oral (hunger)	Trust vs Mistrust Level of confidence in reality in being able to form attachment, and have needs met
2 to 3	Anal (excretion, muscular control, retention/letting go)	Autonomy vs Shame and Doubt Who is in control of holding and letting go. If parent is over-controlling, child learns shame and doubt
4 to 6	Phallic/Oedipal Male child loves mother; has castration fears Female child loves father; has penis envy; jealous of mother Stage passes as desires are seen to be impossible and child identifies with same sex parent	Initiative vs Guilt Planning to act independently, avoiding if possible guilt about relationships
5 to c. 12	Latency period	Industry vs Inferiority Focus on conscious memory and learning skills, testing others, finding identity
c. 12	Genital – beginning with puberty	Identity vs Role Confusion
	Young adult	Intimacy vs Isolation Seeking satisfactory sexual relationships
	Adult	Generativity vs Stagnation
	Maturity to Old Age	Integrity vs Despair Seeking to accept the past and one's achievements, the mix of good and bad times, and valuing the resulting self

Bocock (1983) provides a useful discussion on the links between Freudian psychology and the sociology of areas such as deviance, the family, gender and sexuality. As social systems are made up of personality systems, sociologists such as Talcott Parsons have been interested in how one influences the other. The process of socialisation and the acquiring of values are easily linked to ego development, and perhaps the failure of great social revolutions has been rooted in individual psychology; perhaps the workers of the world did not unite because of personal values linked to nationalism and identity. Freudian theorists also offer some insights into the irrationality of politics.

Advantages of a psychodynamic approach to assessment

Whatever criticisms exist of this approach (and there are many, as we will shortly discuss), it remains a particularly useful way of attempting to understand seemingly irrational behaviour. This is pertinent when clients' difficulties appear to reside inside themselves rather than at the interface of the client and structural inequalities. Even the most severe critic is likely to admit that the notion of defence mechanisms is a useful consideration in the assessment of men who have difficulty expressing their emotions and that transactional analysis provides a simple and accessible way of looking at clients' interpersonal relationships. It acknowledges the influence of past events and helps to create a healthy suspicion about surface behaviour.

Insight can empower people to understand what is going on within themselves and between themselves and the outside world. Supporters of this model suggest that it is useful for situations in which long-term work with a neurotic person is indicated. Cases of compulsions, hysteria, excessive dependence and people unable to face an emotion (loss, for example) may also fit this approach.

It has also influenced a listening, accepting attitude in social workers that avoids over-directiveness and is useful in informing the earliest stages of assessment: deciding on the interview format and helping to 'blow up' specific parts of the analysis. All maps lead to a set of questions that can be considered by an assessor, although these are not directly put to the subject. This map suggests the following questions, but we feel that rather than developing an interrogation, they ought to considered as directing a conversation, using the values of exchange and narrative, so that the answers to them emerge:

- Which developmental stage is reflected in the behaviour?
- Is the superego (conscience) overly rigid or overly permissive?
- Is there anxiety? How severe is it?
- How dependent or independent is the person?
- Are there signs of ego breakdown?
- What ego defence mechanisms are being employed, or are implicit, in the person's behaviour?
- Which ego defences need supporting or strengthening?
- Or are they strong enough to allow some insight work?
- What threat is the person experiencing?
- What ambivalences are present?
- Are there some repetitive themes?
- Which ego coping functions are working or not working for this person?

- What are transactions with others like?
- What 'contamination' is there?
- Does the person know what they should do and yet repeatedly not do it?
- Has the person had a figure with whom they have been able to identify?
- Have I considered the gender difference implications, especially in terms of coping and independence?

Disadvantages of a psychodynamic approach to assessments

As discussed in Chapter 1, psychodynamic theory has had a huge influence on traditional *social* work practice but is fundamentaly flawed as theory for social work because the sole focus of concern and the focus of all analysis is the individual, even when social factors have been identified and targeted. This leaves no scope for genuine psychological empowerment (see, for example, Ingleby, 1985; Barber, 1991). As it is based on a pathological, medical model, the social worker is the expert and an exchange model of interviewing is rarely feasible.

Because it is based on middle-class, white, male assumptions about the nature of families, differences and difficulties due to membership of an oppressed group are ignored in any analysis: the 'isms' can not be included because of the very nature of the theory. For example, homosexuality is explained as a matter of inadequate Oedipal development with weak fathers and dominant mothers in the case of male homosexuality (for an overview, see, Kline, 1972), and fear of mutilation via pregnancy in lesbianism (Jones, 1932). By posing the notion that gay people are not 'proper' men and women, the theory effectively ungenders them. It is particularly insulting to women in general, overlooking power differences, although, as noted earlier, many feminist writers have managed to accommodate a psychoanalytic point of view (Miller, 1973).

The therapeutic implications of ventilation and reflective discussion in the psychodynamic approach also rest on white, middle-class norms regarding the desirability of self-growth and self-awareness. While this is considered to be appropriate for some ethnic minority groups, such as Jewish and Italian people (Devore and Schlesinger, 1991), it is not considered appropriate in many other cultures. Tinkering with the theory to incorporate ethnic sensibilities is never enough to surmount the hurdle posed by attempting to translate the effects of racism into an individual psychological problem requiring psychotherapy.

The biggest problem for social workers using the psychodynamic map to inform their assessments lies, probably, in childcare work. We do not consider it an overstatement to say that psychodynamic analyses of children's problems have proved at best trite and at worst dangerous. In the former situation, we refer to those superficial assessments that attempt to locate a teenager's abuse by a man in her early attachment experiences with her mother, usually couched in vague terms to do with self-esteem and resulting in largely ineffective but probably harmless interventions, such as counselling sessions. However, the theory is dangerous in so far as it translates men's sexual desires for children into children's sexual desires for their parents. The issue in child abuse work is not necessarily one of 'unresolved mistrust' for the child in Erikson's terms or 'promiscuity' in Fraiberg's terms (1980) but one of abuse by an adult (O'Hagan and Dillenburger, 1995). And, in making children culpable for their own abuse, the theory implies that their mothers must have been negligent (see, for example, Ward, 1984).

As a theory informing assessment work, it will do little to help social workers meet with men or develop methods for working appropriately with them. However, many of Freud's ideas are common currency (Payne, 1991), and these ideas are not only deeply embedded in social work practice, but also involve very strong feelings: people either love them or hate them. No prizes for guessing our opinions on the subject but, if you are an adherent, remember exactly all the ideas that come with the package.

Summary

- The psychodynamic approach offers a considerable analysis of a person's *individual* problems, thus 'blowing up' small pieces of a situation to achieve depth of understanding. This does not necessarily give much direction for planning interventions.
- Ego psychology and transactional analysis ideas are more user friendly for busy social workers than is psychoanalysis *per se*.
- Psychosocial casework promotes indirect interventions, but the environment is usually construed in a narrow way.
- The idea of defence mechanisms contributes to an understanding and assessment of seemingly irrational behaviour.
- Psychodynamic theory has had an enormous influence on social work practice but is fundamentally flawed as a theory for *social* work as it largely ignores issues of oppression to do with sexuality, gender, race and class.

8

An Ordnance Survey Map: Behavioural Approaches

We now turn to a less essentialist psychological perspective in that there is less a sense of a 'given' reality within people and more a sense that people learn to be what they are and can learn to be different.

Behaviour modification theory

The approach outlined in this chapter assumes that as problem behaviour is learned, behavioural disorders can be changed through the application of learning theory principles. Behavioural social work emphasises the assessment process on the grounds that, without a behaviour baseline, casework can not be judged (Barber, 1991). This involves a detailed examination of specific behaviours to establish how they have been acquired and maintained as habitual ways or paths that people 'walk', day in, day out, step by step, so we think that the best way this map can be described is an Ordnance Survey map – one which 'blows up' small areas of territory to expose every detail.

As with psychodynamic social work, the application of learning principles to social work was initially lifted straight out of clinical psychology and then adapted to a wide range of social work situations. We will identify two main strands of learning theory in this chapter: traditional behaviourism, consisting of three types of learning based on the work of Pavlov (1960), Skinner (1958) and Bandura (1969, 1977), and cognitive behaviour modification, consisting of four types based on Werner (1970), Beck (1967), Ellis (1962) and Seligman (1992) respectively. The cognitive part of the map looks at how habitual ways of thinking can be considered as habitual behaviour, with an emphasis on how unhelpful thinking can be replaced by learning and practising more helpful thinking, and on how these ideas develop useful assessments that can accommodate both quantitative and qualitative aspects of change. First, we examine traditional behaviourism as this remains central to much behavioural social work.

We begin looking at traditional behaviourism by considering *respondent* (classical) conditioning, which is mainly based on the work of Ivan Pavlov, a Russian physiologist working in 1911. Any basic text in psychology will tell the story of how Pavlov conditioned dogs to salivate at the sound of a bell by associating the sound of the bell with the arrival of food. This was described in the language of experimental psychology: the bell being said to be a stimulus (S) and salivation a response (R). This is known as classical conditioning, with a stimulus always preceding a response:

$$S \rightarrow R$$

Responses are not only learned, but can also be unlearned or become extinguished; for example, if food did not follow the stimulus of a bell, Pavlov's dogs ceased to salivate after a while. Probably the most common application in clinical psychology of respondent learning is in dealing with phobias. Here the assessment involves the development of a hierarchy of responses to the feared object before the sufferer is gradually helped to relax and then presented with the item at the bottom of the hierarchy. More greatly feared items are not presented until each step has been successfully achieved. This process is called systematic desensitisation. In other words, the person's reflex responses to the fear such as increased heart rate are gradually removed.

The $S \rightarrow R$ sequence of learning, however, explains only a narrow range of learning opportunities that involve reflex actions, while *operant* conditioning explains a more extensive form of learning. It has a very wide application in addressing a range of human behaviours in which reflex actions are not necessarily present. This part of the theory also derives from animal experiments. For example, Skinner (1953) demonstrated how pigeons could learn to peck at a set of levers to obtain corn. The reward of food followed their effort, reinforcing the behaviour. In operant conditioning, it is the person's actions that operate on the environment; any one act is still labelled a response (R) and the consequence a stimulus (S), even though in operant conditioning responses precede stimuli. The stimulus then elicits a stronger response (R2).

$$R \rightarrow S \rightarrow R2$$

This clumsy use of jargon terms may seem confusing, but as Hudson and Macdonald (1986, p. 28) say:

> do not be exercised over it, simply think of them as different animals, having a familiar meaning in the respondent paradigm (stimulus eliciting response) and an unfamiliar one in the operant paradigm (the association of a behaviour with a consequence).

Operant conditioning is often referred to as the ABC approach. A stands for Antecedents, that cue in the start of the behaviour; B stands for the Behaviour itself; and C stands for the Consequence, which reinforces. Stuart (1974) gives considerable attention to antecedents as a key focus for intervention. He distinguishes between four types of antecedent:

1   *Material and competence antecedents.* These are the tools and skills without which the behaviour cannot occur. For example, a student needs a quiet place, books and other materials, plus essential ability, to be able to make progress with an assignment.
2   *Instructional antecedents.* These are rules, requests and expectations, not always explicit, set by others. For example, parents often unfairly criticise children for not doing what they were not asked to do, saying they should have known it was expected.
3   *Potentiating antecedents.* These consist of a set-up in which the rewarding impact of the consequence is increased. This can happen in three ways:
    ● By restricting the consequence so that it follows only when the desired behaviour has happened. For example, no television viewing until after an assignment has been completed.
    ● By providing a sample of the consequence for a person who has never experienced it, for example only after the excitement of canoeing has been experienced and enjoyed can it be used efficiently as a reward for completed work.
    ● By offering a person a choice of consequence from a menu of options, for example going out for a burger, playing pool or going bowling. This has been shown to heighten the reward effect.
4   *Signal cues.* These may be associated positively or negatively with the resulting reward. Thus there may be positive discriminative stimuli associated with a pleasant outcome. For example, where a person has many pleasant memories of a partner, the presence of the partner is a cue for social approach. Alternatively it may be a negative stimulus delta. For example, where there is a history of

unsatisfactory marital interaction, the presence of the partner is a neutral or aversive cue that does not signal approach behaviour.

In assessing problematic behaviour, therefore, it is essential to begin by examining its antecedents and considering how their effect could be either increased or reduced. The behaviour itself (B) must also be mapped out in detail. Sheldon (1982) says that a behavioural assessment takes place independently of the definitions and labels that others place on problems. For example, a behavioural assessment would not state that a person is deluded, but rather it would state precisely what behaviours were involved.

The consequences of behaviour (C) in operant conditioning strengthen or weaken subsequent behaviour. Rewarding consequences, or reinforcers, make it more likely that a behaviour will occur. Positive reinforcers strengthen (reward) behaviour by gaining/giving a wanted/positive consequence, for example money, whereas negative reinforcers strengthen (reward) behaviour by removing an unwanted/ negative consequence, for example, pain. The unwanted consequence may be present, for example a twisted arm, in which case the required behaviour enables the subject to escape the pain; or it may be threatened, for example 'You will be grounded unless you behave well from now until 3.00 pm', in which case the subject avoids the unpleasant consequence by behaving well for that period.

Confusion, however, is common here. Because avoiding threatened sanctions is a negative reinforcer, we are apt to think punishment is the same as negative reinforcement. While punishment is usually unwanted or aversive, it does not necessarily remove or reduce behaviour; often it encourages endurance or the avoidance of being observed in the behaviour. This adds to the confusion in that punishment can be either positive (giving unwanted pain) or negative (taking away a want, for example money). Figure 8.1 may help to clarify matters.

There are no absolute examples of positive and negative reinforcers because what is perceived by one person as negative or bad may be considered by another as desirable, and vice versa. Something unpleasant or painful would probably be considered negative by most people, but others may enjoy it or see it as a macho proof of strength, for example. Thus the terms positive and negative (like good and bad) must always be seen *as perceived by the service user*.

A vital part of a behavioural assessment, therefore, is establishing what is or is not rewarding for the particular service user: 'It is a good general rule that the "customer knows best"' (Sheldon, 1982, p. 113).

When making behavioural assessments, social workers should expect to find both positive and negative reinforcements operating with unwanted behaviour being reinforced. You may be part of this learning process. For example, the social worker who rushes round to the foster home each time a child exhibits unwanted behaviour and never visits at times when the behaviour is acceptable may be unconsciously reinforcing unwanted behaviour.

REWARD (that is wanted/liked) STRENGTHENS the behaviour that precedes it This REINFORCEMENT can be:		An AVERSIVE consequence (that is not liked) WEAKENS the behaviour that precedes it This PUNISHMENT can be:	
POSITIVE or NEGATIVE		POSITIVE or NEGATIVE	
Gaining a positive, e.g. sweets	Avoiding or ending a negative, e.g. not getting caught, or pain stops	Getting a negative, e.g. pain or a shout	Losing a positive, e.g. money fines
Behaviour is also weakened by the absence of reinforcers			

Figure 8.1 Reinforcement and punishment

Reinforcement is more effective the nearer in time it is to the behaviour and when it is consistent, although there are different schedules of reinforcement, mostly continuous or intermittent ones. Intermittent reinforcements have a more lasting effect on behaviour, although one of us sometimes thinks that the schedule of reinforcement in catching salmon is all too intermittent. Schedules of intermittent reinforcement may be 'fixed ratio', like pay for piece work, or 'fixed interval', like a weekly wage. There are also variable ratios in which the number of performances of the behaviour is varied before the reward is given, and variable intervals where the time between rewards is varied. These variable schedules provide the most lasting effects on behaviour, so consideration of these variables will provide useful indicators for the most effective intervention in changing behaviour.

The third type of traditional behaviourism is based on Bandura's (1977) social learning theory, or vicarious learning. Very briefly, the theory says that we learn by observing and imitating others. These models give advance information about the likely consequences of behaviour, and social learning theorists claim that this is a more efficient way of learning than is classical or operant conditioning. Here, learning is further facilitated if the observer sees the model's behaviour being rewarded, if the model is reasonably like the observer, which aids identification, if the model is popular or of high status, for example a professional sports person or a television personality (the 'wannabee' syndrome), and if the observer can practice the behaviour immediately and gain reinforcement. The theory acknowledges that there can be expectation of rewards, thus taking into account the fact that people are not simply victims of their environments but can deliberately act to influence them. This adaptation of traditional behaviourism addresses some of the early criticisms of learning theory that appeared to view the nature of people as essentially passive, a 'determinism' not unlike that of Freudian theorising. This means that an assessment needs to examine how and what models influence behaviour. For example, a social worker hoping that a delinquent client will benefit from a therapeutic relationship may need to consider that a peer group may have much more influence on the client as it will probably contain people who are similar to the client, of high status and rewarded for their behaviour, making them more effective models than the social worker.

In using the traditional part of this Ordnance Survey map, assessment begins after a 'get to know you' phase, with a detailed description of the target behaviour(s) or required behaviour(s) in precise terms. This requires the direct observation of current behaviour, either by the social worker, the client or a third party, who counts the frequency of certain behaviours in certain circumstances, listing antecedents, behaviours and consequences. A log may be useful here, for example that suggested by Schwartz and Goldiamond (1975) (Figure 8.2).

Time	Activity	Where	Who was there	What you wanted	What happened
7.00					
8.00					
9.00					
10.00					
11.00					
and so on until bedtime					

Figure 8.2 Record of behaviour

The behaviour modification approach promotes several techniques that are useful for reducing unwanted behaviour and strengthening wanted behaviour; social workers may wish to check through a list of these ideas and consider which might be the most effective for the removal of a particular problem.

In general, as Fisher and Goceros (1975) say, operant techniques are appropriate for operant behaviour problems and respondent techniques for respondent problems. For example, with an individual problem such as a specific phobia, systematic desensitisation, which has been found to be highly successful where the client is well motivated and involved in the problem selection, would generally be favoured. Classical conditioning, however, has little practical application in social work as few problems involve solely reflex actions. On the other hand, social learning approaches, for example social skills training, will be more appropriate where problems are located within interpersonal interactions. However, it is operant conditioning techniques that have the widest application.

Finally, Schwartz and Goldiamond (1975) also present a 'constructional' approach to behavioural social work. This consists of viewing problematic behaviours as patterns that successfully produce desirable and even logical consequences but at a distressful cost. Persistence with behaviour despite distressing consequences suggests that such behaviour might be the result of choice alternatives, given the history and circumstances of the person involved. The task is therefore to help construct new ways of producing these positive consequences that might be accompanied by less distress. Where there are very limited choices:

> Assessment procedures are also used to examine the links between behaviour and contingencies in the client's immediate environment. The apparently unreasonable or underdeveloped behaviour of the client may result from an unreasonable or weak set of contingencies, as with the problem of institutionalisation in hospital and residential care. (Sheldon, 1982, p. 99)

A traditional behavioural assessment would attempt to establish a baseline of behaviour using points in the following sequence:

- Decide on the goals with the client in strict behavioural terms, that is those which are not only clear to the client but also capable of measurement.
- Where, when and how often is the new behaviour required?
- How would the client measure success?
- What will other people notice about the behaviour when this happens? This could be at home, at work or at leisure. You also need to work out how often and how much the behaviour needs to be demonstrated.
- How will this differ from what is happening *now*?
- What areas of life will be changed for the better?

- Why change now?
- Has there been any condition under which the problem was not a problem?

Next set a *baseline* for the current behaviours (wanted and/or unwanted), showing how often they occur, hourly or daily, over a period of a week or two. Then decide whether the problem is one of an excess of unwanted behaviour or the lack of wanted behaviour, using the following questions:

- What behaviours are in excess and what behaviours deficient?
- What behaviours need to be increased or decreased?
- What behaviours are occurring in the wrong place and at the wrong time?
- If it is a matter of removing unwanted behaviour, how is it being maintained or reinforced?
- Is the consequence one of positive reinforcement or negative reinforcement?
- Can these reinforcers be removed?
- What alternative behaviour could be put in its place? This should be carefully considered because behavioural change techniques have been shown to have more power in strengthening than weakening responses, so 'no deceleration technique should ever be used unless alternative behaviours are positively reinforced' (Stuart, 1974, p. 411).
- What are the antecedents or cues
    - material/competency?
    - instructional antecedents?
    - potentiating antecedents?
- If the behaviour is acquired by modelling, can contact with the model be discontinued?

If it is a matter of needing to develop wanted behaviour, ascertain:

- what new behaviour could be desirable;
- what antecedents are missing and need to be put in place;
- what is considered by the client to be rewarding;
- what reinforcers are available or could be gained;
- because reinforcers need to be administered immediately and consistently, who would be available to do this; and
- whether the new behaviour could be acquired by modelling; and if so, is an appropriate model available?

If it is a matter of strengthening current behaviour, check out:

- What are the antecedents?
- What are the consequences?
- How can more rewarding consequences be achieved and by whom?
- What schedule or reinforcement would be most efficient?

The answers to these questions should be used to build up a baseline. Your data display would look something like this:

CASE EXAMPLE
A student has a problem with doing college assignments on time.

Goal: Wants to get next essay finished on time.

- This requires a considerable amount of reading and note-taking.
- If he read a chapter an evening and made notes on it, he could be better prepared.
- This could be done in the bedroom, away from distractions.
- A daily log of chapters read could be kept.
- This will be better than wasting time watching television.
- Change is needed now because of college deadlines.
- Unless dealt with, the problem will continue until the course is passed.

The student's difficulty could be seen as an excess of unwanted behaviour (watching TV) or as a deficit of wanted behaviour (study). Because it is easier to strengthen weak behaviour, he decides to look for ways to strengthen studying and he decides the bedroom is the best location.

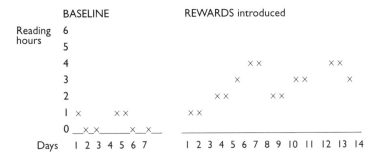

Figure 8.3 Behavioural baseline

The consequences (in the longer term) of more effective studying is passing the course and avoiding the embarrassment of failing. Since negative reinforcement is more powerful, the student asks his partner to remind him of this consequence. There is also something (a certain crunchy chocolate confection) that he finds very rewarding, so his partner acquires some of this and shares it when a chapter has been read. (The rewards of watching TV cannot easily be removed, this is a further reason for concentrating on rewarding the study behaviour.) However, modelling can be assisted by the partner also reading instead of watching TV at study time. The emphasis, in the short term, is on the pleasant consequences of having the chocolate following a period of study. In the long term, the student knows that this work will avoid dreaded failure as well.

Cognitive behavioural theory

The cognitive dimension to behavioural approaches suggests that behaviour is mediated through thought processes just as much as through a series of responses to stimuli. This is particularly relevant to social work, which seeks to individualise client behaviour but does not always find this easy; insight does not necessarily change behaviour, nor does traditional behaviour modification always prove effective. Indeed, although the latter seems scientific, logical and accessible, each human situation contains so many variables that even Skinner commented on this in his novel (*Walden Two*), saying that predicting behaviour is rather like making a weather forecast. And we all know how accurate weather forecasting is.

Research into the outcomes of behavioural social work (Sheldon, 1995) suggests that a combination of traditional behavioural approaches and cognitive approaches produces better results, and the cognitive dimension is being increasingly applied to a wider range of problems. As the term implies, the cognitive dimension considers 'how behaviour is guided by the perceptions and analysis of what we see' and how 'irrational thoughts or disturbances in perception lead us to process our view of the world incorrectly' (Sheldon, 1995, pp. 184–5). The cognitive dimension would provide a better explanation of the salmon-fishing behaviour referred to earlier as it would take into account an entire set of thoughts about fishing rather than just the inter-mittent reinforcement resulting from a fish taking the fly.

Within this cognitive model, there are numerous variations, but we will confine ourselves in this brief outline to the ideas of Werner (1970), Beck and Tomkin (1989), Ellis (1962) and Seligman (1992). The work of Beck and Ellis has been further developed by Burns (1992) and Dryden and Yankma (1993).

The acknowledgement on the part of behavioural theorists that there is a cognitive element brings the theory both nearer and yet further away from psychodynamic approaches. Adherents of the psychoanalytic approaches have long wrestled with cognitive issues, originating explicitly with Adler, who parted company with Freud in about 1911. Rather than seeing the mind as three sections at war with each other, Adler maintained the mind was a unified whole and that conflicts were not within its structure but between it and the world, these being associated with distorted and antisocial thinking. He maintained that it is this 'private logic' of faulty thought processes that is the main determinant of behaviour. Following his death in 1937, there was a decline of interest in Adler's ideas, but, following republication of his ideas in the 1950s, he aroused the interest of the behavioural theorists, most notably Ellis (1962). A cognitive approach had been implicit in the ego psychology of the 1940s, but Ellis and Beck (1967) redefined emotions as clearly cognitive in essence, Ellis (1962) describing them as a strongly evaluative kind of thinking resulting from what he termed self-talk, internalised sentences and self-verbalisation.

Werner (1970) emphasises a behavioural rather than a psycho-deterministic approach: 'emotion is a feeling a person experiences after estimating what an event *means* to him' (p. 254), inferring that people must be confronted with the disparities between their perception and reality and offered alternatives to inaccurate perception, the discrepancies between stated goals and actual behaviour being addressed. Contrary to the psychoanalytic notion of insight being gradually gained, the focus in Werner's approach is on examining goals, perceptions and lifestyles. He sees behaviour as shaped neither by unconscious inner drives nor by externally conditioned habits but by a third force, cognition, the self-determination of the individual who *uses* both internal forces and the external environment. He accepts that internal urges and strongly conditioned responses can start behaviour moving in a particular direction but that 'action is not completed unless conscious thought processes support it' (Werner, 1970, p. 252).

This cognitive theory attempts to explain irrational behaviour by taking the notion of what psychoanalysts would call defence mechanisms but applying a behavioural analysis to this phenomenon. Werner sees choosing goals, evaluating events and self, and solving problems as the three conscious cognitive processes intimately associated with personality development. Personality development, in behavioural terms, is not seen as static or linear, as in psychoanalytic explanations. Certainly, there is no emphasis on a guiding force, such as sexuality, although motivation is important. For Werner (1970), change in the three elements listed above results in changes in personality. For example, a person whose personality is characterised by withdrawn behaviour is not necessarily seen as fixated at one stage of development. Instead, this is probably due to frequent failure to attain desired goals, and a 'personality change' can be effected if that person experiences success in goal achievement. This leads him to ask the following questions in making an assessment:

Goals
● What are the current expectations of life?
● Are the goals constructive?
● Are they realistic?
● What information, for example, about options and alternatives, might be needed?
● What early recollections are there of aims/expectations?
● Who were the opponents of these aims?
● Do the goals represent an attempt to compensate for feelings of deficit?

Perceptions of reality
● Are there any distortions?
● Are there any limitations?
● What feelings do clients have about interpersonal relations, formal or informal?
● Are any of these distortions or feelings due to family atmosphere?
● Could the family atmosphere be classified as rejective, authoritarian, martyrdom, inconsistent, suppressive, hopeless, indulgent, pitying, high standards, materialistic, competitive, disparaging or inharmonious?
● What private logic is operating?
● What cognitive deficiency is evident?
● Are there any early recollections of trauma, struggles, disabilities or oppressions?
● What are the implications of one's gender, race or religion?
● What uncertainty or confusion exists?
● What perceptions might be influenced by significant others? Note how Werner seeks to connect early experiences and rearing with current thought processes, thus blending two approaches.

Lifestyle, in so far as it shows the pattern by which a person goes through life:
● What pattern of past behaviour is significant?
● What pattern of current behaviour is evident?

- Is the lifestyle pampered, withdrawn, self-sacrificing, controlling, inadequate, joyful, obsequious, altruistic?

In the case of the student mentioned earlier, these questions discover that, while his goals are constructive and realistic, there is a possible opponent in that the children do not understand or agree with them; the family atmosphere is 'indulgent' but also reasonably competitive. A private logic of 'Do I really have to be so hard on myself?' operates, and there are early recollections of being sent to the bedroom as a punishment, so there is quite a mix of emotions and perceptions, the clarification of which is helpful both as an understanding of the difficulty and as providing signposts towards a solution.

Werner's set of questions develop an understanding of how current thinking helps or hinders the attainment of goals. Ellis (1962), on the other hand, was primarily interested in anxiety and depression states and how these were caused or maintained by thoughts, remaining closer to traditional behavioural approaches. He developed an ABC alternative to that of operant conditioning. For Ellis, A is the Activating event, such as loss of employment; B is the Beliefs one has about that event, such as 'My whole life is ruined'; and, C is the emotional Consequence, mostly for Ellis, 'I'm depressed'. He suggests that cognitive processes, rather than simple reinforcements, influence behaviour, with people usually blaming the Activating event for the Consequential emotion. Ellis seeks to break this A–C connection and show the service user that the emotion follows from the Beliefs (B) about the event rather than from the event itself (A). This explains why different people react differently to the same event. Ellis would say that A–C thinking is a distortion and needs to be replaced by B–C thinking.

Ellis (1962) also outlined a whole set of cognitive distortions, the most common being that people oppress themselves by believing they *must* do, or have, or achieve certain things. He coined the words 'musterbation' to challenge this process in the application of cognitive therapy and 'awfulising', the process whereby merely unpleasant or uncomfortable experiences are described as worse than 100 per cent bad. For example, when the bus is late, some people will refer to this as disgusting. Burns (1992) added to this list of damaging cognitive distortions:

- *All or nothing thinking*: what is short of perfect is a total failure.
- *Over-generalisation* : a single failure is a never-ending pattern of failure.
- *Mental filter*: selecting and dwelling only on the negatives.

- *Disqualifying positives*: rejecting them as not counting.
- *Jumping to conclusions*: making negative judgments on little evidence and also mindreading that ascribes negative rather than positive intent.
- *Magnification/minimisation*: exaggerating one's faults or another's strengths, or shrinking one's own strengths (also known as reversed binocular vision).
- *Emotional reasoning*: 'I feel it, so it must be true'.
- *'Should' statements*: by which one whips and punishes oneself before one can be expected to do something. Additionally, 'should' statements directed at others lead to anger and frustration.
- *Labelling/mislabelling*: 'I am a loser', 'He is a dirty rat'.
- *Personalisation*: seeing oneself as the cause of negative events.

In cognitive therapy, Ellis (1962) strongly debates with, confronts and challenges people to correct these distortions and replace them with more rational reasoning. Such rational reasoning is supported by (behavioural) rewards in the first instance until the client achieves the self-rewarding effect of attaining an agreed goal. Beck and Tomkin (1989) have a more gentle style that leads people to reconsider their beliefs and is, perhaps, more rigorous in the assessment stage of therapy. They developed a system of identifying negative automatic thoughts, for example, 'I can't make real friends', 'I'm stupid', 'I always say the wrong thing', 'Everyone knows how disorganised I am', 'I'm no good'. Burns suggests the keeping of a daily log to identify the details of both the behaviour and the accompanying cognitive processes which might look something like Figure 8.4.

	Situation	Emotion	Automatic thought	Rational response	Outcome
Date					
Time					

Figure 8.4 Response record

An automatic thought will usually be a form of self-criticism, whereas a rational response will be a self-defence or a rebuttal of an automatic thought. For example, parents experiencing problems with their children may catch themselves thinking 'Where did I go wrong', while a more rational response might be 'I am not a bad parent; I do try; I cannot control all that goes on in my children's lives'. Keeping an assessment record such as that shown above becomes the therapy in that the client comes to appreciate the improved emotional and relational outcomes of more rational responses. Burns (1992) provides a selection of checklists and self-evaluation instruments that a client completes. These facilitate data collection and diagnostic analysis because they include many of the assessment questions a social worker needs to consider.

Cognitive approaches have their own specialised therapeutic offshoots, such as the Institute for Rational–Emotive Therapy, which suggests that clients list irrational beliefs, then dispute them, before putting 'effective rational beliefs' in their place. An example of an irrational belief is: 'I can't stand it when he… ' or 'I can't stand it when I do not have the drug', an effective rational alternative being 'It's unpleasant and uncomfortable, but I can stand it'. Equally, the irrational belief 'I cannot be happy unless I have someone to love me' could be replaced by a rational response such as 'As an independent person I can love myself, so I can always be loved, and this will make me more attractive to others'. Yapko (1988) suggests some further examples of distorted thinking that may lead to depression: 'It's me'; 'It will always be this way and it affects everything I do'; 'It can only be this way'; 'Life always has been bad, therefore it will always be bad'; 'The whole thing is ruined'.

This approach leads to the following questions during the assessment phase:

- What cognitive distortions can be heard in the client's story?
- What automatic thoughts enter the mind when things are not right?
- How is the person putting him/herself down?
- How can these irrational beliefs be disputed?
- How can rational beliefs be developed?

Cognitive theorists also became interested in the concept of learned helplessness (Seligman *et al.*, 1992). This is a state that results from repeated exposure to unpleasant events that are beyond the control of the individual so that whatever a person does has no predictable effect one way or another. An example of this is a woman who sometimes gets battered when she does something and sometimes gets battered when she does not do the same thing. This information about the lack of connection between effort and outcome grows into an expectation or belief that responding to one's situation is futile, that all future efforts will fail in the same way and that it will always be so. For example, a social worker arrived at a home to find the wife being beaten violently by her husband. She hurried the woman and her four children into her car but was amazed at the woman's behaviour. This woman had become so accustomed to the futility of any action on her part during violent episodes that she sat perfectly still in the car, apparently calm, while her husband beat the car with a spade. This learned helplessness continues even after some good outcomes; good days are attributed to luck or to the efforts of others and only serve to prove one's own helplessness. There are some similarities with the hostage syndrome, in which victims of kidnapping become attached to their captors and blame themselves for the trouble, although the main features of learned helplessness are lack of energy, negative mood, self-condemnation and withdrawal.

As these features are similar to those of depression, Beck and Tomkin (1989) draw on Seligman's (1992) notion of learned helplessness in his cognitive approach, suggesting that people in this state have an unrealistically negative view of themselves that will yield to cognitive therapy techniques. Similarly, Sheldon (1995) maintains that depressive and anxious people attribute success to good luck or the task being easy, while attributing failure to lack of effort or poor ability, adding that irresponsible people do the opposite. However, Brown (1986) argues that the depression of learned helplessness may well be realistic – life may actually be that grim. Social work that uses this concept accepts the notion of cognitive structuring in so far as the internal attributions need to be addressed in order to empower service users to attribute blame to appropriate external causes, but its exponents would not always describe themselves as behavioural in orientation (see, for example, Barber, 1991).

Advantages of a behavioural approach to assessments

Behavioural approaches have considerable appeal for social workers because they offer a systematic, scientific approach that makes it possible to structure the work: 'The objective is spelt out clearly, the method pre-defined, and the end product always measurable' (Davies, 1981, p. 54). The initial stages of assessment are given prominence in this approach, and the production of behaviour baselines aids data display. Additionally, a strict behavioural approach has the advantage of going some way towards meeting the values of social work in that client participation is encouraged, labelling discouraged and accountability made evident. Sheldon (1982) argues that a behavioural assessment has the advantage over other approaches of not 'squeezing out' the client's story or shaping the evidence to fit a favourite theory, so this careful attention to detail is particularly useful in 'blowing up' aspects of client situations so that all variables can be explored. When the ideas about learned helplessness are taken on board, this has the potential to bridge the gap between psychological and sociological explanations of behaviour and maintain the focus on social as well as individual factors.

Disadvantages of a behavioural approach to assessments

Despite the claims of behavioural social workers that the approach is value-free and client friendly, it remains in practice largely psychologically reductionist. Usually, it is only the immediate environment of the client that is examined; even with behavioural groupwork, it tends to yield little more in the way of solutions than the establishment of token economy regimes. Whatever the value of these, they do not take into account the realities of, for example, children's experiences in residential care where homes are understaffed, underfunded and, in some cases, abusive.

Also, the approach is not as value-free as it claims. For example, Ellis's (1962) rational therapy is really all about appropriate white, masculine assertiveness. The instruments used by behavioural theorists are basically masculine; for example, Sain's (1996) study of the psychological sequelae of domestic violence for women found that the questionnaires designed to assess individuals' responses to lack of control in their lives included such items as 'Whether or not I get into a car accident depends mostly on how good a driver I am' and 'Whether or not I get to be a leader depends whether I am lucky enough to be in the right place at the right time'. It would be difficult to challenge many women's 'irrational' beliefs as they may well be embedded in the 'rational' context of patriarchal relations.

The scientific nature of traditional behavioural assessment rests on modernist assumptions about certainty, and, in practice, assessments need to include the cognitive aspects. Even then, there often appears to be a tendency to go for a rushed solution after a limited assessment; see, for example, the modified and limited use of social skills training in groupwork. One is left with the same basic criticism as we made of psychodynamic approaches: it is usually easier to bend the theory so that the assessment suggests an intervention that changes how an individual accommodates their lot rather than actually look at whether that 'lot' should be changed. This is, of course, the perennial problem of social work, as it always seems easier to change an individual than challenge the *status quo*.

In conclusion, the traditional behavioural approach can be used on its own, as can the cognitive dimension, but added together they provide a more powerful analysis of a wide range of troubled situations, examining what precedes and follows behaviour environmentally, and also what thoughts and resultant feelings precede, accompany and follow from the behaviour, giving clear indications of which interventions are most likely to be helpful.

Summary

- Behavioural approaches offer a detailed and thorough method for the analysis of problems, suggesting useful techniques to aid assessment.
- These approaches are most effective in developing strategies to strengthen behaviour.
- Despite the advantage of rigour in the assessment of behavioural problems, this approach is little used by social workers.
- Cognitive behavioural approaches that emphasise the role of thought processes in behaviour offer a more acceptable approach to assessment and intervention for many social workers as they help them to understand the emotional component of behaviour difficulties.
- The emphasis on learned helplessness gives behavioural approaches the potential to deal with anti-oppressive practice issues, but the scope is limited as much of the theory is based on white, male, Western norms of behaviour.

9

The Handy Tourist Map:
Task-centred Approaches

The map presented in this chapter has much in common with the cognitive element in the previous map, but it moves further towards social constructionism and also towards acknowledging and dealing with external social factors in human difficulties.

Task-centred theory

This chapter addresses the increasingly popular task-centred approach to social work assessment and intervention. This theoretical map differs from those in preceding chapters in that, while it is implicitly behaviourist and cognitivist, it did not originate in clinical psychology but is based on research into social work practice, written specifically for social workers. We refer to it as a handy tourist map because it involves no elaborate or complex theory, its principles could fit on a folded card and social workers use many of its elements, perhaps without naming them, as a guide to where they need to get to in much of their work.

The task-centred approach arose from disenchantment in the 1960s with the existing open-ended and long-term ways of working. William J. Reid's dissertation at Chicago University in 1963 was the first statement of the ideas, which were then developed over a 20-year period by Reid and Shyne (1969), Reid and Epstein (1972), Reid (1978) and Epstein (1988). The main British publication is that of Doel and Marsh (1992).

There are certain assumptions underlying this approach, many of them drawn from the (cognitive) philosophical writings of Goldman (1970) and from the crisis intervention ideas of Parad (1965). Briefly these are:

- The usual and best way to get what you want is to take action.

- Action is guided by beliefs about the world and self, and these are the basis for plans of action.
- Many psychosocial problems reflect only a temporary breakdown in coping.
- Time limits help to motivate service users, before the edge of discomfort becomes blunted with time.
- One positive problem-solving experience improves one's ability to cope with the next difficulty.
- 'Normal life consists of one damn thing after another' (Dorothy Sawyer's character Lord Peter Whimsey). Difficulties are mostly normal; they become problems only when they become 'the same damn thing over and over' (O'Hanlon, 1995) as a person becomes stuck.
- We are what we do, and feelings flow from behaviour.
- Feelings can be viewed as beliefs about wants.

From wants to goals

Problems are defined by Reid (1978) as unmet or unsatisfied wants as perceived by the service user. These perceptions may often be unclear, but, more importantly, an unmet want is often attributed to the potential service user by someone else. For example, person A may say 'My partner B has a drink problem – he needs to control his drinking'. This is the attribution of a problem by person A (the 'referrer') to person B. A is seeking help for B, so A's want/problem is really 'I have a problem with my drinking partner'. That is the only 'acknowledged' problem so far. B has not acknowledged any want; he is not an 'applicant', and it is mainly service users who are applicants in some way that concern us in the detailed use of this map.

Of course, in statutory agencies especially, many of the people we work with are 'referrals' rather than 'applicants'. They are the unwilling people whom courts, child protection panels, schools, parents and families refer to us. These people may say they have no unmet want with which they wish us to help. In these situations, task-centred work does not move forward unless, and until, some want is acknowledged, even if it is only 'I want you off my back'. Unwilling 'referrals' can be engaged by exploring how it is that others see them as having problems or as being problems, how the situation is affecting them, whether there is something they would like to see changed, and whether there is something they could do that would free them from interference in their lives. When they acknowledge some such want they become 'applicants'. In this approach, therefore, the first step in assessment is to establish whether this person has any want, that is 'Is there anything you want to change?', 'Do you want my help in achieving it?'. Some people see themselves as confirmed failures in life and may not believe that any help will make a difference. They may need to consider the questions 'If effective help was available, what would you like it to tackle?' and 'Are any of the attributed problems real problems for you in any way?'

This approach takes nothing for granted and asks the most basic and obvious questions, respecting potential service users' states, seeking to start where they are and looking at life through their perception of it. Epstein (1988) describes this phase as the 'Start up', in which the worker establishes whether there are acknowledged wants in the mind of those referred for help.

The next step focuses on *wants*, assessing whether they are specific and achievable and, if so, in how much time, particularly how short a time. This consideration of time-limited work is seen as crucial for motivation and clearly fits well with the current requirement that assessments should include the costing of interventions.

Many potential service users will have more than one want; these are prioritised at the assessment stage and usually no more than three are targeted. Once agreed, these (three) problems become the basis of the goals of the work. Where, when and with whom these problems arise is explored, as are the consequences of behaviours, the meaning the problem has for the person and for significant others, and also the social context.

Three considerations arise at this point:

- What needs to be done or changed?
- What constraints make this difficult?
- What tasks will be required of the service user and/or the worker, mainly the service user, in order to begin to improve matters?

We also recommend the Want Sheet (Figure 9.1) designed by Masson and O'Byrne (1984), which is particularly useful where two or more people are involved, as in family conflicts.

Instruments such as these help people to clarify wants or, often more importantly, to express wants. The vagueness arising from an inability to explain, clarify and express wants is often a further problem compounding the original problems.

NAME	What I want from them	My chances of getting it	What they want from me	Their chances of getting it from me
Dad				
Mum				
Kate				
Paul				

Figure 9.1 Want Sheet

Clarification at the assessment stage is in itself also a major part of helping. Since the aim is to help or 'coach' service users in taking action to deal with the problem themselves, the service user, rather than the social worker, being the main agent of change in this approach, clarity and agreement are vital at this point. Each member of a family or group can be asked to complete a Want Sheet and then share it with each other, giving them an opportunity to challenge misconceptions about each other's expectations within the group. Such exchanges can give valuable information about the potential of the group for sorting out its problems through its own action. The approach therefore is essentially an empowering one with the social worker serving/servicing the user(s).

The meeting of a want is equivalent to reaching a goal. Every social work text will stress the need for clearly defined realistic goals that are salient to the service user; however, there may be a tendency among some social workers to busy themselves with tasks and miss out on the work of identifying goals, which in turn makes evaluation difficult. The task-centred approach sees the clarification of wants as a crucial step in the assessment and helping processes.

Problem classification

The next step in problem analysis is that of classification. This is particularly useful if, as is often the case, there is more than one problem. Reid (1978) classifies problems into eight types:

1   *Interpersonal conflict*: interactions with others are presenting difficulties; 'We don't get along'. The problem is in a relationship be it marital, parental, school or work conflict.
2   *Dissatisfaction with social relationships*: 'I am not assertive; I get picked on'. The problem here is more general, within the individual rather than between them and others.

3 *Problems with formal organisations*, such as housing, schools, hospitals and state benefits systems.
4 *Difficulty in role performance*, such as parent, spouse, worker or student.
5 *Problems with decisions.*
6 *Reactive emotional distress*, such as depression or anxiety resulting from the situation.
7 *Inadequate resources*, such as of money, food, work or housing.
8 *Others*, not included in the above, such as behavioural problems associated with addictive or compulsive patterns, substance abuse, crime and gambling.

In the assessment stage of task-centred work, it is also important to seek out how various problems are *interconnected*. This can arise in two ways. First, actual problems in different categories can be interconnected, such as drinking, unemployment and lack of money. Having identified these connections, the social worker can consider which would be the most useful to tackle first as, in dealing with that problem, others may take care of themselves. The second way in which interconnectedness can arise is in the problems of different people, for example two parents where the problem of one is maintaining the problem of the other in each of their cases. We find that service users find it helpful to be given a scale, setting out the eight types in a way such that they can write in the problems and score them at the beginning of work and again at the end (Figure 9.2).

Next, there is an analysis of the *cause(s)* of the problem. This is where there is a major shift of thinking from earlier approaches to social work. In this approach, there is no question of seeking out the original cause of a problem. Even where a prior event, for example a loss, is recognised as starting the problem, it is what the service user is making of that loss here and now that matters. The event cannot be changed, but the person can be helped to grieve, to accept the reality and to plan a new life without the lost person or status. Of problems, it is said that they simply happen. Rather than searching for complex 'original' causes, social workers look for those factors that are contributing to *maintaining* the problem in existence. It is those 'causes' of the problem continuing to be that really matter. The removal of these obstacles will allow the change to happen. The focus, therefore, is mainly on the here and now, with perhaps some attention to the recent past, because irrespective of the original cause that started the problem off, the cause that counts is the cause that is 'blocking' the resolution of the problem in the present, namely those factors that are 'causing' the problem to persist. These are current things that the service user and worker can do something about – we can do nothing about changing history. It is important in this approach not to interpret service users' behaviour and explanations in terms of irrational behaviour, resistance or defence mechanisms. Doel and Marsh (1992) refer to this as 'shooting the reflective parrot' that sits on the shoulders of many social workers trained in essentially psychosocial approaches.

	NIL	LOW	SOME	A LOT	SERIOUS
Interpersonal					
Social relations					
Formal organisations					
Roles					
Decisions					
Emotional distress					
Resources					
Other					
Other					

Figure 9.2 Problem scale

In a task-centred assessment, 'cause' equals *obstacle* preventing the problem from being moved. There are four main obstacles:

1 *The social system.* This could be the family, extended family, community, formal or informal networks, or society at large (as in

the case of many oppressions). Here the task-centred approach is clearly saying that the cause of problems can be outside the individual. Where that is the case, to see it anywhere else would be unjustly to pathologise the service user. However, causes are frequently complex and can include both internal and external elements.

2 *Beliefs or constructs* about the world, life, self and the problem. Beliefs can be factual or evaluative, and their accuracy or consistency can be challenged.

3 *Emotions*, which are translated into beliefs about wants. For example 'What I want is lost or unobtainable' = depression; 'What I want is wrong' = guilt. Moving feelings to an explicit cognitive level makes them easier to deal with, since the underlying beliefs can be disputed. For example, a person feeling guilty about being sexually abused can be helped to see that it was not they who initiated the behaviour.

4 *Attempted solutions*, or actions being taken, that are making matters worse. There are three main types of attempted solution that can become obstacles:
   - Seeking utopian goals, or aiming too high, such as wanting children to be 'angels'.
   - Trying too hard to do what can only be spontaneous, for example trying to get to sleep or trying to get a stepchild to love you.
   - Seeking to change attitudes when the service user could settle for behaviour, or wanting someone to want something they do not want. Examples of these attempted solutions include challenging children for stomping up stairs to bed because they do not think they should have to go so early, or complaining that a child is not enthusiastic about going to school. In both cases, not settling for the behaviour concerning going to bed and to school will turn a minor difficulty into a problem. If the 'attitude' were simply ignored, there would be a better chance that it would go away.

This assessment process in a task-centred approach checks out which of the main obstacles might be operating in any given situation – the social system, beliefs, emotions or attempted solutions, namely utopianism, trying too hard or changing attitudes. By this point, some analysis and ideas about what might be helpful in working towards the goal will be developing, and a working agreement begins to be formulated as the assessment proceeds to the next stage.

Task selection

The next step is task selection, working out with the potential service user which tasks could be attempted to bring about change. A wide range of tasks is usually developed, and these are discussed, the social worker and potential service user collaboratively assessing which would be the most useful, which are within the potential service user's repertoire and, if they are not immediately capable of being done, how much help, coaching and rehearsal the potential service user would need in order to be able to do them. If outside resources are needed, the assessment needs to consider what are they and who should get them.

In this step of the assessment process, decisions are made jointly with the potential service user, discussing the task options available and considering:

- the potential benefits of each;
- the work involved in carrying them out;
- any obstacle that may make a task difficult;
- what practice, rehearsal or guidance may be needed;
- the overall plan for carrying out the task; and
- how and when progress will be reviewed.

It is only at this stage, having made the above preliminary assessment, that tasks can be selected or set. The following are some of the options available in selecting tasks:

1 *Exploratory tasks*. These further examine the problem or challenge factual beliefs. A parent may say, 'My son is always disobedient', so the task could be to count up the occasions when he obeys or disobeys over the next week and set out to catch him being obedient as much as possible, or at least once.
2 *Interventive tasks*. These are used to make a change or move towards solving the difficulty or meeting the want, such as parents going out together more. Attempting such intervention by way of experiment provides valuable evidence for the assessment.
3 Tasks can be *simple* (one action) or *complex* (several actions or parts). However, simple tasks are preferred in this approach.
4 *Single* (done by one individual) *or reciprocal tasks* (someone does something and another person reciprocates).
5 *Physical or mental tasks*. It is recommended that mental tasks be made as physical as possible, for example by making lists of one's ideas or observations.

6 *Incremental tasks*, beginning with small steps and then increasing in difficulty as the client gains in confidence and skill.
7 *Pretend tasks*, such as pretending that something has changed, for example a depression having lifted, noting the difference or seeing if someone else notices anything different.
8 *Reversal tasks.* These entail doing the opposite of what the service user has being doing to tackle the problem. These are especially recommended where the attempted solution is the main cause of the problem being stuck.
9 *Paradoxical tasks.* These may be considered where straight-forward tasks have failed and where they can be preceded by a positive reframe of the problem. These ask the service user to not change or to make the problem worse, and, unlike any of the above tasks which are negotiated with the service user and which hope for compliance, these are not negotiated or discussed. The hope is for refusal, the intention here being that the service user will recoil from the injunction and thereby change.

Task review

When reviewed, all interventive tasks provide useful information not only about the problem, but also about the most helpful way of addressing it, about the motivation and capacity of the service user and about the likely time and effort that will be required. The final step, therefore, is task review. If the tasks are carried out and some progress is found, the assessment is well on its way to completion; we already know what needs to be done – it is only a matter of estimating how long it will take to complete. If, however, the tasks are not done, or they have made no difference, we know that further analyses and changes are required. If the tasks are completed but ineffective, this is valuable information that will increase the likelihood that more effective tasks can be and will be designed. So the step of task selection is retaken. If, however, the agreed tasks have not been carried out, a further set of issues need to be considered:

1 Has the service user a clear understanding of the task and its relevance?
2 Has the service user any adverse beliefs, such as thinking that the task has little value or that doing it will be frightening? Has s/he the necessary self-confidence to perform the tasks?
3 Does the service user have the necessary skill to perform the task completely and consistently? If not, how can this be acquired?
4 Does the service user have the necessary concrete resources to

carry out the task? These may be money, accommodation or the support of friends.
5   Are there reinforcements necessary to encourage the service user in the persistent carrying out of the tasks? If so, from whom could they come?
6   Are the social worker's attitudes affecting the service user's performance? Does the service user's forgetfulness or anxiety annoy the social worker, or does his/her behaviours or attitudes make the social worker feel contemptuous in any way?

The task review will not only seek to discover any reasons for tasks not being carried out, but will also include supportive discussion, especially of any beliefs and anxieties that may be impeding progress. This is followed by the planning of more appropriate tasks or rehearsal for their performance.

In summary, the following assessment questions arise from this map.

Type of user
- Is this case a matter of a referral or an application?
- Is the service user's want attributed or acknowledged?
- What do others want?
- If change is wanted by others, is that a problem for the service user?
- What does the service user want to do about it?
- Does the service user want help to do that?

Type of goal
- If the service user is an 'applicant' – 'What do you want?'
- Is the want specific?
- Is the want achievable?
- What constraints make change difficult?
- What needs to change?
- How long will it take to reach the goal?
- Where, when, how often and with whom does the problem arise?
- What meaning does the problem have for the service user and others?

Analysis of 'cause'
- How is the problem maintained: by beliefs, emotions, the social system or attempted solutions?
- What are service user's beliefs about the situation and about the want?
- If the 'cause' is an attempted solution, is it seeking utopian goals, trying too hard or seeking attitudinal change?

- How can the problem(s) be classified?
- Is there any interconnectedness between problems?

Task selection
- What tasks will be required to make the necessary change?
- Will the service user be able to carry them out?
- What help or rehearsal will be needed to prepare for task implementation?
- What other resources will be needed?

On first reading, these questions may seem to be too obvious and simplistic, but that is really their strength. It is all too easy to make assumptions and end up putting words into the mouths of service users; it is good practice to take nothing for granted and to ask all the 'fundamental' questions possible. Even where the nature of the problem is clear and specific, we still need to learn from service users how best to help them proceed in small steps towards their goals. Encouragement over small achievements and seeing them as a cause for optimism are vital elements in the 'coaching' process.

A case example

A social services department received a complaint from neighbours that they could hear shouting, and what seemed like a child being hit coming from the K family's house.

The visiting social worker explained who she was and the purpose of the visit, making use of good engagement skills to gain access to the home despite some early hostility and fearfulness on the part of the Ks. The couple had been together for 3 years and there were two children, Sarah aged 12 and Jason aged 3. Sarah was Mrs K's child from an earlier relationship, and Mrs K had lived alone with Sarah for several years. She had a low-paid, part-time job and struggled to pay her way, accumulating £4500 in debts. Mr K had not been aware of the debts until about 18 months previously when a court letter arrived. He had felt very angry and had started to drink more than usual, often on his own. He also had back trouble and had been unemployed for the past 6 months, which was getting him down. Mrs K also said she felt a bit depressed and that everything seemed to be falling apart. They agreed that there had been loud arguments; he was angry over the debts and she would respond that his drinking and attitude was making things worse. Over the past 18 months, they seemed to talk only when they rowed; he had hit her once (a 'slap on the face') and he had lost his patience with Sarah. They both said he had not hit Sarah but he had frightened her and made her cry. At one point, he had briefly left the family, returning for Jason's sake.

Given these data, the worker was able to establish that Mrs K wanted to be less depressed and more able to deal with the debts (her two main acknowledged wants), and she felt that Mr K should help her more in the home instead of just shouting about things. Mr K wanted his wife to be honest over the debts and to be more firm in dealing with Sarah (two 'attributed' problems), but he did acknowledge that he needed to watch his temper in order to avoid hitting anyone in the family. Both Mr and Mrs K, however, expressed feelings of hopelessness about the future in that debt, unemployment and health problems were seriously frustrating and heightening the risk of abuse and family break-up. This led to a vague acknowledgement that they needed some help or guidance of some sort. At this stage of the assessment, they could be said to have a mixture of attributed and acknowledged problems, some vague goals and many constraints.

The social worker next showed them a 'problem scale' and, talking them through it, asked them to enter their problems and use ticks to show how serious they considered the issues to be. With some encouragement and advice, they produced the sheet shown in Figure 9.3.

This exercise helps to set out the situation in a non-blaming way so that, for example, Mr K was able to accept that drinking was at least a minor problem. The completion of the scale led to some discussion on the interconnectedness of the problems. Did the fighting make the depression worse? Did this affect their ability to tackle the debts better? Did the drinking make the rows and the debts worse, or were they causing it? Where would the most effective starting point be? At this point, they were not ready yet to face up to the problems of their relationship, their inability to talk things out or their lack of social life. They were, however, more clear that something needed to be done, and they were willing to have the worker see them again to plan some action together. Before leaving, the worker left two copies of the Want Sheet with them and suggested the task of completing their sheets separately and privately, then sharing them for discussion one evening when the children were in bed. A second visit was arranged for a week later.

As she departed, the worker began to consider what obstacles might be blocking this couple from satisfactory functioning:

1   *Beliefs*. As she had listened to their accounts, she had a sense that they believed they were each being blamed by the other, that they were caught for ever in growing debt and that they had lost any

real hope of financial coping or of happiness. Mr K seemed to think that his back was permanently damaged, but he had not continued with medical check-ups.

	NIL	LOW	SOME	A LOT	SERIOUS
Interpersonal Aggressive arguments				✔	
Social relations Few friends					✔
Formal organisations Courts		✔			
Roles Budgeting				✔	
Decisions	✔				
Emotional distress Feeling depressed			✔		
Resources Debts, no job			✔		
Other Drinking		✔			
Other Backache				✔	

Figure 9.3 Mr and Mrs K's completed problem sheet

2 *Emotions*. The belief in the loss of prospects could explain the depression. Mrs K was also isolated in that there was little communication with Mr K, so she might have been feeling unloved and alone.
3 *The social system*. Reduced welfare benefits and a shortage of employment were affecting the family, as was the lack of nursery school places in the area.
4 *Attempted solutions*. How had they gone about the debt issue? Was Mr K's drinking an attempted solution? There was no evidence of

utopian thinking in the session. It would be useful to check what efforts, if any, Mr K had made to respond to his wife's depression. Attempts like 'cheer up' tend to make the other person feel worse!

In the next session, the social worker planned to use these questions to obtain a more in-depth assessment of their situation and review the task with them. By the end of the second meeting, the couple were clearly saying they wanted help in improving their relationships in terms of talking with each other and their children. Using incremental steps, Mr K decided he would visit his doctor about his back and both parents would attend for debt counselling. Additionally, they agreed to spend 15 minutes talking, at least two nights a week, without the television on and when the children were in bed. This constitutes three simple tasks that would be monitored over four more sessions with the social worker, who by now was well placed to write a report on this family and the likely prospects of their being able to care safely for their children. The review element of the task-centred approach would provide further assessment should the tasks not be done or should they fail to bring about the service users' desired changes.

Advantages of a task-centred approach to assessment

Reid (1978) suggests that this approach is suitable for any specific, acknowledged psychosocial problem that is capable, with some help, of resolution by the service user's own action. It can serve 'as a basic approach for the majority of clients served by social workers' (p. 98). Used in full, as the sole method, its range is narrower than if it is used along with other approaches. For example, as well as engaging in tasks, victims of trauma and people in grief may need to talk at length to an understanding listener who can facilitate their self-expression. Given some creativity in developing appropriate tasks, this approach is suitable, therefore, for most potential service users who are capable of rational discussion, perhaps with the exception of those with existential problems, seeking for meaning and identity. These need time for a lengthy, 'searching and free-ranging self examination' (ibid. p. 99).

Various texts criticising the relevance of Eurocentric approaches to social work with black service users and their families (see, for example, Logan *et al.*, 1990; Devore and Schlesinger, 1991) find task-centred approaches less problematic than those in the maps described earlier. Logan *et al.* (1990) maintain that this is because the task-centred approach acknowledges the person–environment interaction and the place or impact of the social system on the personal. It also respects the beliefs, values and perceptions of the service users and listens to their definitions of their problems and their concerns. In this approach, 'the problem' is always 'the problem as defined by the service user'.

This approach also encourages service users to select the problem they want to work on and engages them in task selection and review. Logan *et al.* (1990) found that minority ethnic groups preferred this level of personal responsibility, as well as the action orientation of the task-centred approach. They add, however, that white workers need to concentrate on keeping a 'strength focus', assuming the existence of community and cultural strengths and seeking to locate them. The task review is clearly vital for checking cultural appropriateness and whether different world views are being overlooked. Issues such as language differences also need to be addressed. Staying with specifics reassures members of some minority ethnic groups who may feel threatened when a lack of specificity by social workers suggests that they are attempting to take over the person's whole life. Last, it clearly helps to develop service users' confidence in social workers if the latter show themselves willing to carry out their share of tasks, especially if they show themselves to be assertive brokers of services, actively helping to remove environmental barriers, locating information and conferring with other agencies and with those the service user considers relevant, such as community leaders. And, just as they review the efforts of the service user, they ought to review their performance of tasks, what they have and have not done, and the reasons why. This accountability is assisted by the clear data display developed in the assessment process. In this way, the approach can be seen to be truly collaborative and empowering.

It will be clear that, because this approach prefers to assess during intervention rather than before it, time and care must be spent in carrying out a useful assessment. However, because tasks will have been tried out, much more realistic practical information will be available. In a period of 3 weeks or so, a considerable number of trials/experimental tasks can be completed, provided these are started at the end of the first meeting without waiting to plan the perfect action. In this way, service users have an opportunity to demonstrate their capacities as well as their needs and, together with the worker, gain a useful understanding of what is maintaining the problematic situation and what might be a helpful way of dealing with it. It is also our experience that this collaborative style, with its focus on actions rather than feelings, sets the scene for the mutual bridging of difference gaps in an unthreatening way. The tasks are set to attack the problem and they, and not the person as such, are the focus.

Disadvantages of a task-centred approach to assessments

In our view, there are few disadvantages of this approach if it is used rigorously. For example, although it has the capacity for empowerment, this perhaps needs to be more explicit. In the case example above, the child is not directly empowered or involved; children should be heard and their views taken into account. Some social workers, believing the approach to be value-free and intrinsically non-oppressive, take this as read and make no further efforts to address issues of empowerment and anti-oppressive practice. The coaching role of the worker could be open to abuse, perhaps encouraging an overworked social worker to be overly directive. Like all other approaches, it needs to be accompanied by the values set out in Chapter 5. Additionally, the emphasis on simple tasks may give rise to concrete solutions that can obscure the advocacy role mentioned earlier.

Although, in theory, the approach should be ideal for group and community work, there are few examples of this happening. It may be that, like other approaches, it lends itself most easily to individual and family problems.

Summary

- The task-centred approach includes some behavioural ideas but it is mainly a cognitive approach.
- In the main, it views difficulties as temporary breakdowns in coping.
- It defines problems as unmet wants.
- It sees the 'causes' of problems as those obstacles that prevent resolution, that is in the four obstacles that maintain problems, namely beliefs, emotions, attempted solutions and the social system.
- Once obstacles are removed, people can work towards their wants mainly by their own efforts.
- It offers a unique problem classification and problem clarification process.
- Goals are reached by taking action, by performing tasks.
- Coaching in task selection and task preparation is central to the helping process.
- Time limits and task reviews aid motivation and promote optimism and empowerment.
- A sound assessment is best made after task analysis and task experimentation. The more time there is for this, the better.

10

The Navigator's Map: Solution-focused Approaches

This chapter presents the fourth and last of the detailed maps in the framework. It is the most constructionist part of the book, putting into practice social constructionism in an explicit way.

Solution-focused theory

A solution-focused approach has features in common with a task-centred approach: it is largely a cognitive approach and frequently leads to tasks to be carried out by the service user. However, the focus is quite different. While task-centred approaches focus on understanding *problems* and seeking ways of removing or at least alleviating them, solution-focused work focuses on understanding *solutions*, maintaining that it is not necessary to understand a problem in order to understand its solution. This approach begins at the end (the solution) and works back from there, rather like a navigator plotting a sea journey, pinpointing the destination first and then drawing a line back to the present position.

This approach originates in work developed at two centres: the Milwaukee Centre for Brief Therapy, with Steve de Shazer and his colleagues, and the Australia New Zealand partnership of Michael White and David Epston. We will look at de Shazer's approach first.

de Shazer acknowledges that social workers have several roles to play, mainly those of social controller, mobiliser of external resources and therapist. He stresses that, although social workers will be in one role or another at different times during their an involvement with a service user, social workers rarely clarify this either to themselves or to the service user. He suggests that, in order to remind themselves and service users, social workers should ideally have three chairs and move from one to the other as the work changes. The work carried out in the first two chairs is fairly clear, if difficult to carry out effectively. Much of the more difficult aspects of assessments is for the third chair, dealing with personal change and how it can be achieved. This map outlines work in that chair as it figures most prominently in the literature.

In a succession of publications over the past 10 years, de Shazer (1985, 1988, 1991, 1994) set out the solution-focused approach, which can be described as postmodern and constructionist. His philosophy is largely based on the psychotherapeutic ideas of Milton Erickson (1959) and on the theories of language and meaning of Derrida (1973) and Wittgenstein (1980). This solution-focused approach seeks to find the seeds of solution in a person's current repertoire, seeking those occasions, however small or rare, when the problem is less acute in order to identify when and how that person is doing or thinking something different that alleviates the problem. This involves listening carefully to, and then utilising, what the person brings to the encounter, focusing on problem-free moments, constructing an envisaged future when the problem is no longer there, and getting a very detailed description from the person of what will be different then and whether any of that is already beginning to happen. In partnership, both the person and the worker build a picture of a possible future without the problem. From this assessment process, messages and tasks emerge for the service user to consider between sessions.

This approach thus has a view of assessment different from most others. Rather than assuming that information about a problem will help to find its solution, the assumption is that we can understand a solution without necessarily knowing a great deal about the problem. Searching for an understanding of a problem usually leads to a laundry list of deficits or negatives, whereas this approach says that what is needed is a list of positive strengths and *exceptions* to the problem. Lists of deficits often risk overwhelming both the service user and the social worker, engendering hopelessness and a tendency on the part of the social worker to use such expressions as 'unmotivated', 'resistant' or 'not ready to change'. The solution-focused approach, on the other hand, 'can be summed up as helping an unrecognised difference become a difference that makes a difference' (de Shazer, 1988).

As Durrant (1993) puts it, psychological assessment tends to assume that qualities are measurable entities, that there are 'normative' criteria for determining healthy functioning and that we need to identify deficit and fault before planning intervention. He contrasts this with the solution-focused approach, which assumes that the meaning of behaviour and emotion is relative and constructed, that psychological and emotional characteristics are partly a product of the observer's assessment and interpretation, that intervention need not be directly related to the problem, and that social workers should build on strengths rather than attempt to repair deficits. This approach therefore develops an apparently 'atheoretical, non-normative, client determined view' (Berg and Miller, 1992, p. 5) of difficulties in which change is regarded as constant and inevitable. As a result, it makes sense to find what bits of positive change are happening and to use them to develop a solution. If social workers do not look carefully for what the service user is doing when the problem is not happening, or is not perceived to be a problem, these exceptions will go unnoticed. The most striking example of this is the 'pre-session change' question. Because de Shazer's team believe that change is constant, that 'nothing always happens' (de Shazer, 1988), new service users are asked what has changed since the appointment was arranged. The team found that a considerable proportion of people reported some change. By then asking 'How did you do that?', they quickly got a solution-focused assessment under way.

Of course, referrers, for example school teachers of disruptive pupils, will have many complaints about a potential service user, and these concerns should be listened to and taken seriously if one is to engage the teacher in a way that will be helpful. We can, however, change the information we collect by asking teachers to help in the development of a solution by listing, in detail, those times when the pupil is or was *doing better* in class. Examples of times might include 'When she sits with a certain person' or 'When she is reminded to write down her homework'. How social workers and service users 'see' situations is crucial in a solution-focused approach. Once we 'see' a pupil as 'troublesome', we see only trouble, so we need to consider in what ways s/he is not troublesome, and we also need to consider what difference it will make when the pupil sees him/herself differently and is not seen to be troublesome. This involves an explicit awareness that we and referrers can suffer from 'delusions of certainty' and 'a hardening of the assumptions' (O'Hanlon, 1989, personal communication) in the sense that people tend to see what they believe or expect.

Kral (1989) produced an assessment device, the 'solution identification scale' (S-Id), to aid this process. Referrers are asked to score 39 different positives as not at all, just a little, pretty much and very much, examples of positives being such details as 'sleeps OK', 'is happy', 'is considerate', 'tells the truth' and 'shows honesty'. While this helps to focus attention on strengths, and allows weaknesses to be acknowledged, it also ensures that positives are not ignored, thus providing a better chance that the location of steps towards solutions can be found. It has the added advantage that it can be completed by potential service users as well as referrers, giving tangible evidence of a partnership approach.

Kral also suggests four basic questions at the initial assessment stage:

1 To estimate self-concept, he asks 'Think about the best person you could be and give that person 100 points. Now tell me how many points you would give yourself these days'. Most people without serious problems give themselves between 70 and 85. If a service user says, for example, 60, this would influence the second question.
2 'On a scale of 1 to 10, how much are you satisfied with your score of 60?' If highly satisfied, the person is not considered likely to be a good 'customer' (a term that will be explained shortly).
3 'When you move from 60 to 70, what will be different that will tell you that things have changed?' or 'Have you been at 70 before and if so what was happening then?' or 'What is the highest you have ever been and what was going on then?' Although these variations of the same question ask nothing about the problem, they open the door to finding exceptions, in which will lie the seeds of solutions. They also clarify for the service user what change is within his/her control.
4 'What are the chances, on a scale of 1 to 10, that you could do that again?' This question hints that the person should make such a change, thus helping to estimate commitment and pave the way for a task assignment.

Clearly, these questions have nothing to do with why the problem is happening. They are about goals, where people are positioned in their situations and what the service user is doing that is different when there is less of a problem or no problem. They are about 'putting difference to work' (de Shazer, 1991): the questions explore what is different when the problem is not happening.

de Shazer and his colleagues also developed two particularly useful questions: the 'miracle' question and 'scaled' questions. The miracle question asks the service user to describe life in which a miracle has happened and goals were reached overnight while the service user was asleep. It continues, 'Because you were asleep you do not know yet that it has happened; so what is the first thing you would notice that would tell you?' The morning after the miracle is constructed more easily because the subject can 'describe what they want without having to concern themselves with the problem and with traditional assumptions that the solution has to be connected with understanding or eliminating the problem' (de Shazer, 1994, p. 273).

Scaled questions are probably particular to this approach (an example being the 1 to 10 question quoted above from Kral). These questions can be directed at service users' estimations of the gravity of their difficulty, at their level of confidence about reaching their goal or at their willingness to work hard to make progress. The question is normally put like this: 'Suppose we had a scale of 0 to 10, with 0 being the "pits" and 10 being "there is no problem", where would you put yourself on that scale?' This scale is set up 'in such a way that all numbers are on the solution side' (de Shazer, 1994, p. 104), but it is impossible to be sure about what any number really means, even for the service user. They and we know that 5 is better than 4 and less good than 6, so answers provide a way of grading progress – or its lack – for both social worker and service user. But, more importantly, scaled questions and their answers help to make concrete what is not concrete, making it easy to describe what is hard to describe.

Numbers get their meaning from the scale to which they belong; they are content free in so far as only the subject has any idea what they mean. But when we ask 'How will life be different when you move from 5 to 6?' and 'What will important people in your life notice that is different?', these future-orientated questions help the service user to begin constructing progressive change.

In discussing a problem such as depression, scaled questions help us to get away from the idea that one is either depressed or not, as if depression had an 'on–off' switch. Suppose a worker asked, 'So if 0 is how depressed you were when you asked for help and 10 is when you will be unaware of any depressing feelings, where are you now?', any reply above 0 would indicate that the depression was less bothersome now and that things are already moving towards the goal (de Shazer, 1994).

We now offer two flow diagrams (Figures 10.1 and 10.2) to set out the solution-focused approach, the first in the initial meeting with a service user and the second in subsequent meetings. In this process, the boxed questions are central not only to assessment, but also to intervention. Like a task-centred approach, there is not really an assessment that precedes intervention as the two processes intertwine.

To explain the terms used, a 'customer' is a person who acknowledges the need to make some personal change and who wants to be helped. A 'complainant' is a person who wants the social worker to change someone else but does not wish him/herself to change. A 'visitor' is a person who is neither a customer nor a complainant but is visited by, or visits, the social worker because there is no choice, for

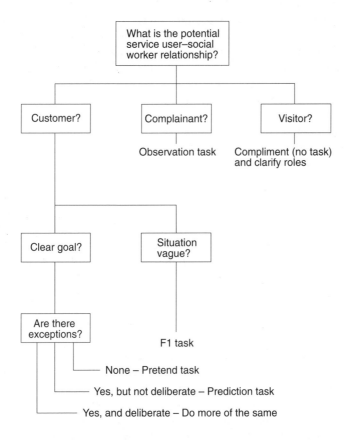

Figure 10.1 Solution-focused work – session 1

example where contact is mandated by statute, a parent or another person in authority. In the case of visitors, it is essential to clarify, as one does with 'referrals' in a task-centred approach, that while the social worker may have a controlling role, s/he is also willing to be helpful should the potential service user agree. This help could relate to getting rid of the statutory order, usually by developing those behaviours for which the order was intended. In the case of complainants, who have been observing the problem that led to the referral, they are encouraged to do more observation, but this time of the positives or the exceptions to the problem, and then to report back. This is because they are more likely to comply with what they are good at and also because engaging them provides the opportunity that they may become customers, should that be helpful to the solution or helpers.

With 'customers' for whom a situation is vague, a 'formula' (or standard) first session (F1) task is given, asking service users to list all those things that are happening in their life that they want to continue to happen. By listing what does *not* need to change, this exercise helps the clarification of appropriate goals.

When a service user is unable to recall an exception, a pretend task is suggested, for example pretending to be not depressed one half of the week and noticing what is different or what other people see is different. This helps to develop and identify possible exceptions that make a difference to the problem.

Where exceptions are spontaneous or the result of other people's efforts, that is not deliberate on the service user's part or seen as outside their control, service users can be asked to predict when spontaneous exceptions are going to happen. For example, a service user who compulsively steals could be asked to predict when the urge to steal will or will not come. It has been found that service users can improve their ability to predict this correctly with practice, and, of course, when they can get a high proportion of predictions correct, the question is 'Are the exceptions really spontaneous?'

An alternative flow diagram has been developed (Wilgosh *et al.*, 1993) for second and subsequent sessions (Figure 10.2).

This diagram shows how progress, or the lack of it, is assessed in this approach and how changes, or the lack of them, are responded to. Where something is better, this is explored in detail, using the EARS process:

- eliciting from the service user what exactly the changes are;
- amplifying these changes by asking the service user what difference the changes made, who noticed the changes, what they saw that was different, and so on;
- reinforcing the change by complimenting the service user; and
- starting again, discussing any further changes that are reported by the service user and how s/he can 'do more of the same'.

White and Epston (1990) have a different approach to solution-focused work, which draws more heavily on a 'narrative' metaphor. Although they agree that solutions are constructed in narrative with the service user, and the more a future without the problem is described and envisioned the more real it becomes, they prefer to deconstruct

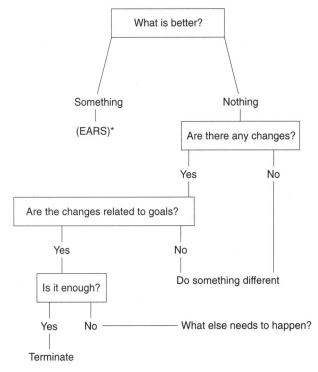

(* Elicit, Amplify, Reinforce and Start again)

Figure 10.2 Solution-focused work – session 2

the problem before moving on to constructing the solutions. Because the deconstruction provides a deadly exposé of the problem, endless possibilities are made available for the service user to be able to reclaim his/her life. By 'deconstruct the problem', these authors mean reflecting with service users on how they came to be 'recruited into a problem saturated story'. This includes discussing that story in a way that separates the problem from the person and develops a sense of alienation between the person and the problem. This externalising conversation is helped by giving the problem a name and by asking questions that help to establish the influence of the problem on the person and their influence on it. The service user, having been invited to explain the effects of the problem, for example 'It gets between me and my parents', is then asked if that is something they want or not (an evaluation of the problem). If they say they do not want it, they are asked to justify that evaluation by explaining, for example, why not. In this way, they make a decision to start reclaiming their life from the problem, which clearly makes for a very promising assessment. The process then leads on to finding 'unique outcomes' (exceptions) when they resisted the problem. Examples of such questions would include:

- How did the problem seduce you into thinking that way or into going along with it?
- What influences led to your enslavement by the problem?
- What prevented you from resisting it? What were the restraints?
- Does it really suit you to be dominated by it?
- What effect or influence does the problem have on your life, on that of those close to you, on your relationships, on your self-image?
- What effect or influence do you have on the life of the problem?
- Given a choice between life with the problem and life free of the problem, which do you chose?
- Why do you not want to keep the problem in your life?
- When there are unique outcomes, what are the implications for the sort of person you are when you refuse to cooperate with the problem's invitations?
- What does it say about your ability to undermine the problem?

Note that the last two questions are reflecting on the qualities of the person rather than on their actions. By adding this 'landscape of consciousness/identity', the new story, with its 'language of action' (exceptions), is enriched. The language is the language of resistance and liberation, and it is used to understand how the service user submitted to the problem's ways and how these ways are not liberating or ideally suited for the service user. This involves looking back at the past to some extent, before going on to becoming future and solution focused, but it is not a blaming look at the past or a search for deficits. It is empowering in that it develops a sense of the service user as being intrinsically OK, as not *being* the problem but as being oppressed by it and sometimes colluding with it. Thus the explanation that is developed is not one that seeks the cause of the problem in the person but one that seeks to understand how this (basically OK) person became ensnared by the problem's invitation. Frequently, part of that ensnarement is caused by societal attitudes, such as attitudes suggesting that the consumption of alcohol is socially necessary or that women should be the main carers in families. More accurately, people are *restrained* in these ways from resisting the problem or from taking responsibility in various ways. A narrative style, storying the separate lives of the person and the problem, encourages a sense of authorship of one's life, a sense that service user and worker can co-author a future story, breaking away from the performance of the unhelpful past story and thus experiencing the capacity to create change. New narratives yield a new vocabulary and construct a new meaning, new possibilities and new self-agency. White (1991) has found that more service users than expected are able to re-author their lives, and we cannot assess their capabilities to do so until we afford them the opportunities created by narrative promptings. However, the issue of responsibility is not avoided; the question 'What influence do you have on the life of the problem?' seeks out how the service user might be, deliberately or unwittingly, helping the problem to dominate and remain in their life.

Concerning exceptions to the problem (unique outcomes), White and Epston write, 'The narratives in which [people] are storying their experiences, and/or in which they are having their experiences storied by others, do not sufficiently represent their lived experiences... there will be vital and significant aspects of lived experience that contradict these dominant narratives' (White and Epston, 1990, p. 40). Only a fraction of experience can be storied – much of it falls outside the dominant story. It is in that fall-out that we can search for unique outcomes and new options. Then, as these are storied, talked about with an audience, the possibility of 'personal agency' grows as a life without submission to the problem becomes a reality. Therefore the service user is invited to choose between the unique outcomes, along with what they 'say' about the service user, and enslavement by the problem. When a choice of life without the problem has been made, the final step is to bring this new 'story' to life by narrating it to an audience, such as friends who would believe it easily in the first place, and then to others. So the concluding questions in this approach would include 'To whom could you tell the story of your decision to fight the problem?', 'Because it is easier to tell the story to people who are willing to believe it, who would be the best person to start with?' and 'How could the audience be increased?' The final step is one of finding an audience and telling the new story, thus constructing the solution. Telling leads to performing.

White (1991) states very clearly that, while the narrative offered may be seen as part of radical constructionism, he does not accept that anything goes if we simply give it a new name. Because narrative is 'constitutive' of people's lives, shaping and structuring them, we must be accountable to those we seek to assess or help. Not all stories are equally good in their effects. For a very helpful account of this approach, we recommend Gilligan and Price (1993). This book presents the Steve de Shazer and the Michael White approaches as different, and opposing in some ways, giving a particularly clear analysis of White's approach. Meanwhile, O'Hanlon (see, for example, O'Hanlon and Beadle, 1994) has been combining the American and the Australian approaches in a creative fashion that stresses the importance of language. In his view, language can easily make difficulties sound, and be, fixed. His aim is to reconnect people's sense of 'possibility' and hope when things seem unchangeable. He is concerned about the danger of 'iatrogenic inquiry' whereby problems are caused or worsened by an assessment or an attempted intervention. He stresses the importance of avoiding negative assessment procedures 'that discourage, invalidate, show disrespect or close down possibilities for change' (O'Hanlon and Beadle, 1994, p. 10), and he maintains that since service users are the experts on their lives, social workers need to check their work with them as they might with an expert. Included in this approach is Milton Erickson's principle of 'utilisation', considering carefully how a social worker can identify and use fully the strengths, exceptions or 'unique outcomes' or solution seeds that the service user brings. Like White, O'Hanlon holds service users accountable for behaviour that impacts on others, but this is about *accepting responsibility*, rather than blaming, looking for bad intention or suggesting that service users are bad people. People are presumed to be resourceful enough to deal with changing, the social work task being to connect them with their often unrecognised resources and join with them in locating these and any other resources they may need, be these external, personal, interpersonal or spiritual – in a word, possibilities.

The location of responsibility for behaviour that impacts adversely on others may seem to neglect victim perspectives and involve rather convoluted semantics, but we suggest that solution-focused approaches do, in fact, take into account all the elements of risk assessment. This can be explained in terms of a particular psychological theory, prospect theory, because the whole approach is framed in terms of gains rather than losses. Prospect theory will be addressed more fully in the next chapter.

Case examples

The social worker is part of a team attached to a GP practice/health centre. The service user is L, aged 65 and living alone. She coped satisfactorily until her husband died from an alcohol-related disease. L denies that, while her husband was alive, her consumption of alcohol was heavy, but since he died she has been drinking heavily, neglecting to eat sufficiently or to care for herself. In addition, there have been a few incidents of minor self-harm. The agency had referred L to social services for home care support and meals-on-wheels services. Even though these were in place, L was not making progress, and over a period of several months she was repeatedly admitted to hospital, stabilised, returned home and admitted again after a few weeks. She was consuming large amounts of whisky. By now several professionals were involved and, after working with her on three admissions, the hospital consultant told the new social worker that it looked as if 'we are going to lose her'.

The social worker began by visiting L at home, daily at first, encouraging her to tell the story of her life, her husband and her loss. This took several hours of listening and supporting L in her grief, validating her story. Meanwhile, the social worker was listing L's needs and strengths so that she could shift the work from grief counselling to solution-focused work. She explored what was different in L's life when she was not drinking. L talked of how she was more busy and talking to her neighbours at these times. Following a scaled question about how well she was coping with her loss, she said she was at 3. There was a discussion about what would she be doing when she was at 4, which included visiting the day centre that people had been talking about where she would meet some old friends. She still cried over her husband at times, and the social worker decided to wait until L was ready for more future-orientated discussions. When asked a scaled question about her motivation to change, she put herself at 5, and when asked what she would need to do to move up one step at a time, she was clearly able to describe this.

It was only at this point that the social worker, new to this approach, risked the miracle question. L responded well to it, talking of how she would be smiling like she used to, getting up at a reasonable time, looking forward to keeping her house nice and having a laugh with her next-door neighbour. She was complimented on her strengths and asked what else she would be doing, so that a detailed picture emerged of life after the solution, along with what support she would like. At the next meeting, the worker felt that L had reached the point of belief in her ability to control her drinking and to improve her quality of life. This was a very different assessment from that made by the hospital consultant. Over the next few weeks, it became clear that it was correct, as L went from strength to strength. Note that there was no attempt to explain or understand why L had developed such a problem.

David Epston (White and Epston, 1990) approaches solution-focused work in a way very similar to that of Michael White, but he makes greater use of writing letters (sometimes quite long ones) to service users. Many other workers, in the family therapy field in particular (see, for example, O'Byrne, 1990), have used letters as a powerful means of reframing situations and eliciting responses from people which might otherwise be difficult to get. Epston maintains that, due to people needing to reflect in their own time on carefully worded letters about themselves and the impact of the written word, assessments made following such letters are more full of positives and possibilities, and the time taken to craft the letter is saved many times over. This is illustrated in the following case example.

Paul was a bright man of 24. He had been to university and obtained a Certificate in Electrical Engineering. For the past year, he had worked as a technician and lived in a rented flat. He had a leg injury as a child that had left him with a permanent slight limp, but this did not affect his work. However, his family became increasingly worried about his ability to care for himself or manage his finances. Despite a steady income, he had wasted his money in an impulsive fashion, mainly on small treats for himself, chocolate bars, cream cakes, and so on. Money ran through his fingers constantly in numerous ways, and he felt he 'had nothing to show for his work' except mounting debts, loans and overdrafts. In addition, he agreed fully with his parents that he was usually unwashed and untidy. He dare not invite anyone to his flat and he had no friends. Efforts by his family to help him were to no avail, but he was willing to seek help and did so. He was also concerned that, as he put it, he had no self-esteem left and he was often lying to people to cover up – a 'problem-saturated story'!

The first session with Paul was along the Michael White (1988) lines, seeking to separate the person from the problem, to externalise and name the problem, to explore its influence on him and his influence on it, and to alienate him from it. Paul's response to the session was minimal, and one could easily assess that the situation was not promising. Even though he was obviously an intelligent and articulate man, his response to the work was rather flat and unenthusiastic. The social worker decided to write a follow-up letter, saying she would have to think over how the session had gone before making any suggestions for action. This is her letter:

Dear Paul,

I have been thinking about our meeting and I would like to sum up my ideas and offer some further thoughts for you to consider.

Firstly, YOU are OK but you have some enemies. YOU are not the problem. The problems are the problem, that is those enemies who are conning you, oppressing you, subjugating you into their ways. Once you defeat them by dealing with their persuasions and by breaking free from them, your progress to success will be assured.

So who are they? Well, we saw two main characters:

1 Self-Carelessness (SC), who brings his cousin, Low Self-Esteem.

2 Unplanned Spending (US), who brings his cousins Indulgence and Debt.

Scruffy SC has managed to get you to neglect personal hygiene, your clothes and your flat, while greedy US has 'conned' you into wasting your resources and stuffing yourself with what you don't always need.

If we look at the past for a moment we might be able to see how these two crept into your life. Your life-history probably created *restraints* that made it hard for you to tackle them with your full forces, for example feeling hurt over your disability and abuse at school games might tempt you into escaping from struggle by putting things off or even lying to yourself about things. (I see your disability not as the problem, or even the cause of the problem, but merely as a restraint in dealing with SC and US, who are the problem, so your gym work will help to cut you loose from that restraint).

OK, so events led to your being restrained in your attack on SC and US so that they got a foothold and once they got you into certain habits they were able to persuade you that those ways of coping were all right; after all you got a job etc.

You are probably still rather restrained in attacking SC and US, so can I add another piece of philosophy about life that might help? It is from Scott Peck's *The Road Less Travelled*.

Life is not meant to be easy. Doing even reasonably well in life *is* a hard road to climb. The climb involves some (not all!) pain and self denial, in a word, self discipline regarding doing without nonessentials. The joys of life come only *after* we have pressed on with it. But our two enemies tell us seductively that life should be easy and they tempt us to avoid frustration and discomfort by saying that we deserve a treat *now* or an escape via some indulgence. The devilment of this however is that in fact, after we have had a little enjoyable downhill trip, we are left with a steeper climb if we are to get back on track. Staying on track, on the other hand, requires delaying gratification until we can afford it, whereas their 'con' is that acting on impulse (play now – pay later) will serve us better.

I think there are two other lies they tell us (two 'cons' to ensnare us), Non-responsibility and Non-truthfulness.

We know however that Responsibility means taking it on our own shoulders to tackle the enemies, avoiding excuses like 'I can't' or 'I had to'. Life is about 'I ought to – it's my responsibility – no one else can do it for me'.

As regards Non-truthfulness (or lack of frankness), I think this is an old trick used by all subjugators – if they can get us to lie to ourselves then they have 'cracked it' – they don't need to lie to us anymore – we do it for them. None of us likes being challenged about what we are doing, so the temptation of not being frank (taking short cuts with truth) is an obvious first choice of the oppressor.

So much for Scott Peck and my interpretation of him. To sum up the enemies' tactics, they use the 'cons' of 'life should be easy, so take a downhill trip', 'You're not fully responsible for straightening your climb in life' and 'Its OK to dodge challenges about your behaviour by not being totally honest, even with yourself'. So putting off self-care chores and self-management tasks, not checking the spending budget, not saying no to yourself, not facing things honestly, are all part of the scheme to enslave you.

But now is a good time to take stock of what *effect* these two enemies are having on your life, on your relationships and on those close to you. Perhaps you could begin to list those effects for yourself. The second list to make is of those ways in which you have affected the lives of your two enemies, i.e. ways in which you have entertained then, strengthened them even, in your life.

By now you will be ready to plan some ways by which to stand up to the wiles of SC and US, ways to spot them coming, answers to make to their lies.

Finally, you could start to think whom could you tell about your new plans for a new life story besides me.

I realise this is a long and full letter which will take a few readings over the next few days and some time to think about it.

I look forward to hearing about how often you have been able to smell SC and US creeping into your head, and what 'cons' you have spotted, when we meet again. I suspect you know these two guys so well that you could start straight away rehearsing your answers for them when they next whisper in your ear!

Good luck.

In our view, while this letter has many helpful features and builds on the language developed in the meeting with Paul, it is too much of a homily. We would prefer less exhortation and more detail from the meeting. Tasks, too, are pushed too much at Paul. Nevertheless, at the next meeting Paul was much more engaged with the ideas, and he had started to make progress in dealing with the problems. Because of this, a more positive and optimistic assessment was possible at the end of the second contact.

These examples provide substance to Allen's (1996) suggestion that the ideas of de Shazer and White (1988) can be combined in various ways. The most obvious of these is beginning with White's look at the past, learning about how life for the service user was oppressed or subjugated by the problem and how the life of the problem may be explained by a set of constraints preventing a problem-free life, and then using de Shazer's miracle question and scaled questions to construct life without the problem by building on the exceptions to it.

Both the examples given involve work with individuals. However, this approach is widely used with groups as diverse as support groups for people with schizophrenia, community groups among aboriginal people tackling problems of diabetes that are partly the result of poverty, and groups of AIDS workers in villages in Malawi. Externalising conversations have been shown to lead to an exposé of the problem that empowers the taking of community and political action (see various reports in *The Dulwich Centre Newsletter*, Adelaide). For White, 'the personal becomes social and the social includes the personal' (personal communication, 1996).

In summary, using a solution-focused map would lead a social workers initially to ask:

- What is the service user: a visitor, a complainant or a customer?
- Is the situation clear, and is there a goal?
- Are there any exceptions to the problem, and are they deliberate or not?

Then, later:

- Are things getting better or not?
- Are changes goal related?
- Are they enough?
- What else needs to happen?

If using the Michael White variation, a social worker would ask:

- How did you get recruited into joining up with this problem?
- Have there been times when you did not have it in your life, or when you stood up against it?
- Which suits you better: life with the problem or life without it?
- As you reject the problem and start life without it, you will need an audience for your new story, so who would be a good audience to start with, who will be likely to believe you?
- Problems are like habits that can be named and fought against. Sometimes they win and sometimes we win. When we win we need to explore 'How did we do that?'

Advantages of a solution-focused approach to assessments

Solution-focused approaches have a very wide application, but their main advantage is in the emphasis on listening to the service user's story and focusing on exceptions, which is both anti-oppressive and empowering, seeking solutions within the user's life rather than in the worker's head. Additionally, the way in which service users' situations are framed to emphasise gains reduces risk in practice and increases creativity.

Disadvantages of a solution-focused approach to assessments

We find it difficult to think of any major disadvantages, but this may be because we have a strong personal preference for this approach to social work. However, because it involves a complete change of emphasis from the ones traditionally used by social workers, there is a danger that the technique might be applied as a sort of quick fix or, for some readers perhaps, as a 'pet' theory used inappropriately or uncritically. It is essential for social workers hoping to employ these approaches to get into the habit of reframing situations and listening carefully to service users. Although the approach creates a good flow to the work, it still requires careful analysis. Using it well is not as easy as it sounds. As we have said of other maps, this one too needs to be used in conjunction with the weather map. The notion of understanding a solution without understanding the problem could be misread for finding a solution before knowing anything about a problem. If this latter reading were taken out of context, it could result in muddled work in which people are not sure what they are doing or why they are doing it. Properly understood, however, solution-focused theory is not saying this. The problem is not ignored but it is not necessarily deconstructed in the traditional way.

Summary

- There are three types of service user: visitors, complainants and customers. It is vital to assess which type each service user belongs to and to treat them accordingly.
- The person is not the problem; the problem is the problem. Thompson (1995) says that the problem is not in the person rather the person is in the problem. Either way, this approach avoids pathologising service users.
- de Shazer holds that problems simply happen and that it is not necessary to understand the problem in order to develop the solution; solutions can be constructed without deconstructing problems.
- White holds that the deconstruction of problems by a liberating narrative is helpful and promotes the separation of the person from the problem.

- We maintain that workers can draw from both White and de Shazer, using a deconstructing narrative followed by miracle and scaled questions.
- The seeds of, or clues to, solutions are in the exceptions to the problem. There are always exceptions; if the person cannot believe this, s/he can be helped to see exceptions by pretend tasks and 'problem-free' talk.
- There is a strong future focus. Talking about 'life after the problem' constructs a future without the problem.
- The approach offers three 'rules of thumb': if it ain't broke don't fix it, if something works do more of it, and if something doesn't work do something different.
- Searching for difference is valuable: what is the person doing that is different when the problem is less of a problem?
- Epston shows that written language helps people to reflect on how to break free from difficulties.

11

Making and Finalising the Judgment

Having looked in some detail at the theoretical maps that can be used to guide social workers towards helpful analyses, we turn in this chapter to the issues around finalising an assessment in a report.

Problems of trying to keep an open mind

We suspect that social workers would find it preferable to use the exchange model of interviewing recommended by Smale and Tuson (1993) as the main route to assessment if potential service users all entered into the assessment process voluntarily. As is evident by the wide range of terms in the literature describing recipients of different social work interventions, the assessing social worker rarely meets with an individual on a truly voluntary, partnership basis. Some social work methods of intervention make clear distinctions about the differing levels of partnership that may be possible. For example, solution-focused work suggests three different levels of participation and partnership. In a discussion on ethical issues, Wise (1995), however, makes the distinction based on power differentials. While she finds it appropriate to use the term 'service user' for the recipients of social work interventions voluntarily entered into, she retains the term 'client' for those who have social work imposed upon them because the social worker has a mandated responsibility to protect vulnerable members of society. In either situation, social work intervention involves unequal power relations because the social worker can do something to people against their will which they cannot do to social workers, or because social workers have something people want and can decide whether or not to give it to them. Inevitably, this means that decisions are made involving some sort of judgment.

Social workers are regularly exhorted to retain an open mind about their judgments. Indeed, judgmentalism has become a dirty word in social practice to such an extent that we sometimes find practitioners tolerating harmful circumstances for some family members in their efforts to avoid appearing judgmental of other family members – usually older ones. For example, rather than be seen to impose 'middle-class' standards of housekeeping on working-class families, some social workers we have met seem to feel they must sit in considerable discomfort in filthy homes. We worry that such workers do little about the children of such homes who attend school smelling of urine-soaked beds. There is a very important distinction, however, between 'making a judgment' and 'being judgmental'. Social workers must face the challenge and responsibility of the former in order to be helpful; they must avoid the prejudice, closed-mindedness and blaming implicit in the latter. The avoidance of making a moral judgment remains in itself a moral judgment; as Davis and Ellis (1995) say, social workers are, at the very least, responsible for accommodating the complexity and individuality of people's living situations within the confines of bureaucratic decision-making.

Social workers have to assess needs, evaluate risks and allocate resources in a way that is as equitable as possible for a wide range of people in various situations. Inevitably, the rights and entitlements of some people will be restricted. We suggest that coping with this difficult balancing act cannot be facilitated by attempting to avoid making judgments, assuming that holding the 'right' values will make it any easier, or attempting to promote partnership where it patently does not exist. Keeping an open mind is particularly problematic because *all* people are liable to be biased in *all* their assessments of each other. Good will and well-meant activity are no guarantee of impartiality. Social psychology suggests that we are all 'cognitive misers' in that we do not use fresh eyes each time we assess another person because we simply lack the time that this would involve. So we use quick and 'dirty' cognitive processes to move information speedily through our system of organised social knowledge (Forsyth, 1986). And we make mistakes. This chapter outlines some of the more common decision-making distortions.

Individual decision distortions

Selective attention

Although we all probably pride ourselves on our objectivity, research shows that we commonly weight some evidence from our assessments more heavily than others. Traits that have extreme value carry more weight than traits with moderate value. For example, child protection case conference minutes often contain positive statements about a father's intelligence and ability to impose order on a disorganised household (traits with extreme value), while failing to comment on traits that may have a negative impact on the children, leading to judgments such as 'He is the better parent of the two' (Kelly and Milner, 1996a). Also, the value we ascribe to various traits is influenced by factors such as race. For example, Denney (1992) argues that black physicality has more extreme value than white physicality in probation reports on male offenders. Similarly, social workers are more likely to give more weight to mothering behaviours than fathering behaviours as the former are more detailed and prescribed (Milner, 1996), particularly when the information is negative, because we have a tendency to give more weight to negative and less to positive information. This tendency becomes more pronounced the longer a person is 'socialised' into social work (Case and Lingerfelt, 1974).

There are also two other effects of selective attention: vivid, distinctive or unexpected data are perceptually more salient, and primacy effects overwhelm recency effects, giving truth to the old adage about the need to make a good first impression. The subjects of social work assessments are most likely to encourage these effects, the reason for their referral being usually one which is distinctive. As they will initially be seen when they are at their 'worst' (an overload of negative information), they will then present the assessor with an initial impression that is difficult to dislodge. Social workers have traditionally attempted to overcome this bias by developing a sort of optimism (for an overview, see, for example, Corby, 1993), although this tendency can be counteracted more easily in certain interventions. For example, the 'assessment through intervention' style of the tourist map and the navigator's map help to address the issue since the social worker waits to see what change is possible.

Stereotyping

Data collection must not be simplified by stereotyping that permits the classification of people into ready-made compartments so that responses are prepared for particular persons. Unfortunately, there can be some truth in stereotypes – indeed, people give strong signals by the way in which they present themselves, indicating the categories to which they consider themselves to belong. Social workers in anoraks with bulging diaries under their arms should not be surprised if people make assumptions about them based on stereotyping effects.

The danger is that information on which categorisation is made may be faulty because of the selective attention errors mentioned above, or because differences from a stereotype that indicate a person's uniqueness may be ignored. For example, a social worker with a stereotype of Asian families to do with the importance of family networks assessed an Asian woman as depressed due to social isolation because she had no links with her extended family. This completely ignored the fact that she had made a conscious decision to move away from her family, whom she saw as the cause of her problems in the first place.

Primacy effects work on stereotyping in a peculiar manner. If the first impression is a good impression – which will be weighted heavily for both salience and primacy effects – a halo effect then sometimes operates in which a person's very positive characteristics colour one's perception of their various other characteristics. This is quite different from picking out positives as well as negatives in assessment work and can have grave consequences. For example, positive stereotyping about the strengths of black mothers meant that Tyra Henry's grandmother was assumed to be sufficiently competent to safeguard Tyra's welfare despite severe financial, emotional and material privation (London Borough of Lambeth, 1985).

Another inherent danger in stereotyping is that it tends to produce negative as well as positive self-fulfilling prophecies about people. Putting people into erroneous categories tends to perpetuate myths about them, as has been amply demonstrated by research into social class, race and gender effects on educational achievement. Wider stereotyping effects are also clearly demonstrated in research into gender and ethnic differences in pain tolerance and response.

Woodrow *et al.* (1975) conducted a huge study of 40 000 subjects from different countries, subjecting them to a heel test. They found that men tolerated pain better than women; whites tolerated more pain than oriental people, with black people occupying an intermediate position;

and that tolerance to deep pain decreases with age. These results seem impressive at first glance – it is a large study and seems to have involved an equal and valid indicator of pain. This study confirmed stereotypes of women, black people and old people being less resilient than white, young men. However, these stereotypes did not match the day-to-day experiences of a group of nurses who reassessed the research on pain using real-life situations (Davitz and Davitz, 1980). They undertook a 3-year cross-cultural study among nurses in 13 countries. There were some serious flaws with the research methodology; for example there was a tendency to stereotype 'oriental' as one group – which they are patently not – and, interestingly, the Nepalese group rejected psychological motivations of behaviour. They argued that these were a facet of Western thinking which was not found in Nepalese thinking.

Despite these limitations, the study came up with quite different findings from the Woodrow study, highlighting stereotyping effects rather than revealing absolute truths. For example, they found that nurses in China reported low levels of psychological distress because they believed in 'inner peace', while Chinese nurses in America were stunned by what they saw as the unreasonable turmoil evidenced by American patients. Similarly, English nurses in America found it difficult to comprehend a culture in which dramatic expressions of pain were not considered abnormal or demanding. This led them to be in conflict with their patients, who perceived them as uncomfortable and reserved – efficient but 'hard boiled' – while the nurses perceived the patients as demanding and over-emotional.

Social workers who pride themselves on their lack of prejudice and susceptibility to stereotyping effects may dismiss this research as having little bearing on their realities; after all, they have probably engaged in extensive anti-oppressive training. However, the results of research into social work attitudes shows that social workers are, like everyone else, susceptible to stereotyping effects, with concomitant self-fulfilling prophecies. Davis and Ellis (1995) found that when social workers were responsible for allocating scarce resources, they labelled people who appeared knowledgeable about their entitlements as 'demanding' and those who tried to exercise choice or challenge workers' judgments as 'fussy' or 'manipulative'.

Two studies using vignettes in which the only significant difference between different children was race also reveal unconscious stereotyping effects. Osuwu-Bempah (1994) found that social workers were more likely to ascribe identity problems to 'black' pupils and prescribe the need for a strong male model than they did to the 'white' pupils. Similarly, Blyth and Milner (1996) undertook an assessment exercise with practising social workers. They were given the following scenario in small groups and asked to make tentative hypotheses about the nature of the problem before the first visit. They all received the same information although the child's name varied:

N school have referred Darren/Delroy/Shaheen to the service following an assault on a teacher. Darren/Delroy/Shaheen is the eldest boy/girl in a family of five children. She/he is known to the service who investigated his/her poor attendance record at junior school. This was explained by his/her mother as a result of a severe chest infection and the case was closed.

Since starting secondary school, his/her attendance has been patchy, she/he is disruptive and not achieving his/her full potential. His/her friends include one boy/girl who is the most difficult pupil in the class.

An assault was triggered by the class teacher's response to a note delivered by Darren/Delroy/Shaheen, requesting permission for him/her to be off school for a four week family holiday. The teacher said that it would be most unlikely that permission would be granted and Darren/Delroy/Shaheen then 'went wild'.

The group assessing Darren viewed the problem of one of a single mother struggling to bring up a family on a low income. They thought that Darren's behaviour might be due to hyperactivity because of junk food and were worried that he would lose the opportunity of a 'holiday of a lifetime' – probably to visit relatives in Canada. The group assessing Delroy viewed the problem as one of an out-of-control boy, lacking a father figure. They referred to his history of 'violence', although there was none in the scenario. They also suggested that he had written the note himself.

The group assessing Shaheen viewed the problem as one of an overburdened girl in a large two-parent family. They also thought that the family might have unrealistic academic expectations for her. Health was seen as a factor by this group who assumed some deficiency of diet. With regard to the holiday, the group were sure that Shaheen was bound for an arranged marriage in Pakistan and were anxious to avoid this.

Thus each group managed to display stereotyped views around class, race and gender without any supporting evidence. Indeed, so strong were their stereotypes that they found it difficult to believe that they each had the same scenario and they continued arguing about this for some time in the feedback session. They were quite convinced that they were assessing different children, even though they had *constructed* these differences.

This seemed to us to be a dramatic and perhaps unusually marked display of stereotyping so we replicated the experiment with a group of social work students, timing the experiment to follow immediately after a lecture on stereotyping effects. Here, the difference in names led to

the students considering that the child might be subject to racist interpretations of their behaviour by professionals other than themselves.

Attributional bias

All of us wish to make sense of social interactions so that we can
control and predict events (Heider, 1958). That is, if we can decide why
someone has done something, it will help in deciding our own behaviour towards them, as well as being able to predict what they will do.
We are biased towards looking for causes and making inferences (attributions) that are subject to a range of irrational biases (see, for
example, Nisbett and Ross, 1980). The attribution process is switched
on whenever people attract our attention through the selective attention
effects mentioned above, and when events and actions do not meet our
expectations and need an explanation that fits with our ideas about the
nature of people.

By and large, we attribute our successes to our own efforts and our
failures to events outside ourselves. However, we judge other people
oppositely. This is called an attributional bias. The first part of this,
attributing positive outcomes to stable, personal factors and negative
outcomes to unstable, external factors, is called a self-serving bias
(see, for example, Miller and Ross, 1975). This is actually a healthy
thing because it not only helps us to make sense of unexpected events,
but also protects our self-esteem and public image. For example, if one
gets a cold, one is likely to think that this is the result of being
surrounded by cold germs at work, whereas if one is the only person at
work who escapes getting the cold, one is likely to attribute this to
something one has done – such as taking vitamin C or not smoking.
Perhaps, a little nearer home, the social worker who is named in a child
death inquiry will see this as resulting from a lack of resources or bad
luck, while all other workers will be quite sure that their assessments
would have been better.

The tendency to attribute causes oppositely when observing other
people is called 'fundamental attribution error'. This arises from over-
attribution and defensive attribution, both of which serve to insulate
observers from anxiety. If other people are considered *personally*
responsible for their misfortunes, the same fate cannot befall the
observer. This means that we are all predisposed to victim blaming –
even where the 'victim' is clearly constrained and controlled by situational factors. Thus it can be seen that we have an inbuilt tendency to
prefer social work interventions that locate the problem within the

subject. It is not just that it is easier to 'work' on the subject rather than social circumstances, but it makes us each feel more individually secure. For example, it is more comfortable to locate the reasons for a rape attack in the victim's personal behaviour than to accept that the circumstances make us all vulnerable to such an attack.

While ordinary people make attributions in the way mentioned above, depressed people seem to be quite different. Seligman (1992) developed and refined the notion of learned helplessness to explain the state that occurs when events are uncontrollable. Then emotional, cognitive and motivational debilitation sets in, manifested in symptoms of depression – lack of energy, negative moods, helplessness, self-condemnation and withdrawal. What is interesting about learned helplessness is that the perception of uncontrollability is more important than the uncontrollability itself. This means that even when action could be taken, a person who has learned helplessness is unlikely to try anything and any successes will be considered to be the product of chance rather than effort. Barber (1991) describes this as a psychology of powerlessness, which explains the passivity of many recipients of social work services – single mothers on income support, disabled persons dependent on others, victims of child abuse and domestic violence.

Learned helplessness and depression have similar features, and a depressed person who is characterised by such an attributional style may well have acquired this quite early in life. Beck (1967) considers that depressive attributional style distorts the truth: a bias against the self, an unrealistically negative view of the self. Brown (1986) suggests that life may actually be 'that grim' and that the depression may be realistic – he reviews the research evidence demonstrating that depressive people do indeed take the darkest possible view but says that it would be worth examining the possibility that there is an insidious attributional style, conceivably grounded in reality, that is the antecedent for depression.

Learned helplessness highlights the need for social workers to combine psychological and sociological factors – not only to attend to external resources, but also to mobilise internal resources, considering the dispositional factors within each person. Additionally, it may be more immediately helpful and empowering for the service user in the short term if accessible dispositional factors are changed while situational factors are addressed as part of a long-term strategy. It is important to bear in mind that attributions are not just the product of an individual's mind, but are also influenced by culture. When internal attributions are addressed, the service user may then be empowered to make more appropriate external attributions. In assessing learned helplessness, Barber (1991) suggests using the following questions:

47

- How long have things been bad?
- What efforts have you made to change things?
- How much success have you had?
- How much good times have you had compared with bad times?
- What do you put your good times down to?
- What do you put your bad times down to?
- If attributed to internal causes, do you put it down to effort or ability? (Effort is easily improved.)
- If attributed to external causes, do you put it down to luck or task difficulty? (Real luck is totally outside our control, but some luck can be self-made.)

Sensory distortions

Not only do we make judgments about people as a result of the mental processes outlined above, but we also make inferences about people's whole characters simply from the way they look, smell and speak. Our 'cognitive miserliness' may help us to take short cuts in assessment, but it is rarely accurate. The most obvious sensory distortion in personal perception is the effect of physical appearance on judgments. Good-looking people are usually ascribed positive personality traits – a factor that belies the saying that beauty is only skin deep. Physical appearance is, of course, the most 'salient' and 'recent' impression we receive. All social workers know of some young, handsome charmer who escaped a realistic assessment of his/her behaviour, but far more serious for social work subjects is the bias against those with unfortunate physical appearances. For example, the rapid increase in the number of exclusions from school shows some evidence that it not necessarily the most badly behaved children who are most frequently excluded – it is the under- or oversized, peculiar looking ones who have little appeal for the hard-worked teacher (Hayden, 1996). And in a society whose people spend a fortune eliminating body odours, smell is important in assessments – the child or old person who smells of stale urine is not likely to be assessed positively for strength of character.

There are obvious gender and ethnic biases that operate with regard to speech. Many apparently natural aspects of men's and women's voices cannot be explained simply in terms of anatomical differences between the sexes but are acquired as speakers learn the cultural norms of feminine and masculine behaviour (Graddol and Swann, 1989). Language reflects gender divisions, a masculine tone being regarded as the voice of authority. Service users are unlikely to be able to afford the voice coaching that Margaret Thatcher used to lower the tone of her voice. Indeed, their voices are likely to lack 'authority' as a result of the stress of their circumstances making them more shrill than usual.

What is depressing for the conscientious and enthusiastic social work assessor about these unconscious distortions is that they are *universal* features of human behaviour. Social work values teaching can have little impact on such robust behaviours. And what sense can we make of psychoanalytic explanations of defence mechanisms when it is obvious that the entire population engages in a sort of mass projection via attribution bias? How can the assessing social worker ever claim to be non-judgmental, warm and empathic in all human situations? To do so would be to go against the grain of ordinary human behaviour – and would lead to a lowering of the social workers' own self-esteem. Before attempting to answer this horrible question, we have to confess that the reality of making an objective assessment is even more elusive when one examines the effectiveness of interagency meetings in improving the standard of social work assessments. The results of group decision-making paint an even bleaker picture.

Interagency distortions and risk assessment

Much of the drive towards interagency meetings as a check against individual errors in assessment work comes from the child protection field, although the notion of the case conference has now become popular in other areas of social work, such as the assessment of risk in probation practice, the identification of children with special educational needs and the management of community care for elderly and disabled people. The case conference is generally thought to be particularly effective in assessing risk (see, for example, Home Office, 1991). We query the wisdom of viewing the case conference as an effective check against individually biased assessment. We do not believe that two heads are necessarily better than one, and we support our argument with generic psychological explanations of group and individual decision-making processes.

Groupthink

One popular explanation of reasons for defective decision-making in groups is the concept of groupthink. This describes decision-making in groups under stress where a group engages in particular types of behaviour. When Janis and Mann (1977) studied several disastrous policy decisions, they found that these behaviours include shared rationalisations to support the first apparently adequate course of action suggested by an influential group member, a lack of disagreement between group members and a consequent high level of confidence in the group decision. This concept of groupthink has already been aired in the child protection literature, and suggestions for improving case conference performance with reference to making corrections to the symptoms of groupthink have been promoted in training packs (Lewis *et al.*, 1991). However, there are two fundamental problems with the application of correctives. First, the concept of groupthink itself suggests that once a group is subject to its symptoms, it will be too deeply entrenched in its behaviour to change. Second, it may be the case that an individual can exert far more influence on the decisional direction of the group due to framing effects.

Prospect theory

Kahnemann and Tversky (1979) offered an explanation of how individuals make decisions that tend towards the direction of risk or caution depending upon whether or not the initial choice is framed in terms of options that involve gains or losses. If the possible options are framed in terms of gains, individuals will be risk averse, that is they will opt for a certain, although perhaps smaller, gain as opposed to another larger gain that is uncertain or risky. In other words, they will be less likely to gamble or risk losing the certain gain. However, if the options are framed in terms of losses, individuals will be more risk-seeking and will tend to avoid a certain, although smaller, loss in favour of another, larger loss that is uncertain. They will be more likely to risk the gamble, exposing themselves to a potentially greater risk. Positive framing leads to caution, and negative framing to risk-taking. The various options open to social workers are often all unattractive, desired outcomes usually having a low probability and less desirable outcomes having a high one. All the options can usually be framed either positively or negatively, and this will affect riskiness in decision-making.

The principle was demonstrated recently with a group of 120 delegates attending an international conference on child protection. They were asked to choose between two unattractive options in the following scenario (Kelly and Milner, 1996a):

A known paedophile is about to be discharged from prison after serving the full term of a three-year sentence. He intends to resume a relationship with a previous partner who has six children aged two to sixteen years. She knows that he will not be allowed to live with her and the children but you suspect that he will visit at night. You have devised two child care plans which will secure the safety of the children but both have consequences for the children's relationship with their mother.

Half the group were asked to make a choice between two losses:

- If you choose plan A, four of the children will lose contact with their mother.
- If you choose plan B, there is a third likelihood that none of them will lose contact with their mother and a two thirds likelihood that all of them will lose contact with their mother.

The other half were asked to make a choice between two gains:

- If you choose plan C, two of the children will remain in contact with their mother.
- If you choose plan D, there is a two thirds likelihood that none of the children will maintain contact with their mother and a one third likelihood that all of them will maintain contact.

The odds are identical in both halves of the exercise since plan A and plan C are the same, although framed differently, as are plans B and D. Still, of those making the choice in terms of losses, 100 per cent opted for plan B, avoiding a certain loss but risking a greater one that was uncertain. Of those making the choice in terms of gains, 55 per cent opted for plan C and only 45 per cent opted for plan D (the risky gamble). Those making the decision in terms of trying to avoid a certain loss therefore exposed themselves to the possibility of a greater loss for all the children and were risk-seeking, whereas the other half were more risk-averse, that is cautious.

Many of the dilemmas in social work involve choices between two unattractive options. For example, a social worker is regularly faced with leaving a child in an abusive family or admitting the child to care, with leaving a potentially dangerous offender in the community or recommending he be sent to prison. Similarly, the choice for many frail elderly people is between an unsafe home environment and an old person's home. While respite care and adequate domiciliary services remain underdeveloped, the first option in these examples is highly desirable for the social worker, but, in opting to avoid a certain loss, other possible (uncertain) losses are ignored and risky behaviour sets in (see, for example, Kelly and Milner, 1996b). It is common to hear social workers say that risk-taking is a vital component of good practice, but we maintain that the converse can be true. Cautious behaviour, that is seeking to achieve certain gains, is more likely to lead not only to re-evaluation and contingency plan-making, but also to creative and effective social work.

Unfortunately, social work legislation often encourages risk-seeking behaviour. For example, the Children Act 1989 has no definition of what constitutes the welfare of a child in terms of gains, the criterion for an order being the possible losses to welfare in comparison with a similar child. Social workers are therefore usually faced with choices between losses. To avoid the shift towards risk-taking, they need to reframe options in terms of certain and uncertain gains.

Before leaving prospect theory, social workers, when involved in the management of risky situations, need also to listen carefully to the frames that service users are using. If they are in the domain of gains as they frame their options, they may be less prone to high risk-taking (for example, offending), whereas if they are in the domain of losses, more vigilance is suggested as they may be more prone to gamble on a high risk. So both they and the social worker need to be helped to move into the domain of gains. Solution-focused approaches facilitate this more than do other types of intervention.

Group polarisation

Whyte (1989, 1993) suggests that rather than alter the original framing of the problem, a group would be subject to the effects of group polarisation, and this would *accelerate* the tendency to risk or caution of the original framing, group polarisation effects demonstrating that people in a group take a more extreme position than they would as individuals (Moscovici and Zavalloni, 1969). This, suggests Whyte, means that rather than act as a countercheck to any unwarranted optimism, if the decision is framed in terms of losses, the group will commit resources to a course of action initially agreed on by the group, even when it is failing. Group members will bolster this decision by self-justification, such as 'The plan needs more time to work' or 'We need more resources'. The group then has the potential to become so risky that there is always the possibility for a decision fiasco. This group behaviour is not only found in social work assessments of risk. As Leiss and Chociolko (1994, p. 31) comment on industrial risk assessment:

> the significance of an event's probability tends to decrease as conceivable consequences increase, until what is possible becomes more feared than what is probable.

An analysis of child protection case conference decisions (Kelly and Milner, 1996b) showed that most child protection assessments are framed in the domain of losses; that the *key decision-maker* is the individual social worker who deals with the initial referral and prepares the report for the case conference; that the case conference does not act as a check against this initial assessment (it does, as Whyte predicted, escalate rather than reduce risky decision-making); and that, although individual social workers perceive other case conference members to be more powerful than themselves, these members actually have little influence on the decision.

In probation practice, the new emphasis on public safety in the risk assessment of potentially dangerous offenders (Home Office, 1991) has had the effect of altering the decision frame for some probation officers. Where they frame the risk assessment in terms of public safety, not only are their decisions more cautious, but they are also able to use the interagency group more effectively for the development of a monitorable management plan. The probation officers who frame the risk assessment in terms of avoiding the loss of freedom for the potential offender (alternatives to custody) tend to make risky decisions with imprecise management plans (Hayles *et al.*, 1996) and define success in terms of establishing a relationship with offenders or diverting them from custodial sentences rather than in terms of re-offending rates (Denney, 1992).

This does not imply notions of unwarranted optimism or careless assessment work on the part of social workers. The social psychological theory explaining these effects is universal and there is no evidence that other case conference forums are any more effective in realistically assessing risk (Whyte, 1989, 1993). What it does imply is that an individual social worker would make less risky decisions than a group when a losses frame is applied and that an interagency group can operate more effectively when a gains frame is applied.

Recording distortions

For most social workers, recording is a chore that detracts from the real business of social work – the interpersonal nature of the social work relationship. Once having learnt the agency format of records and reports, 'learning the forms and words of a specific discourse' (Rojek and Collins, 1988, p. 613), social workers spend much more time developing their intervention skills. This, we suggest, is seriously to undervalue the importance of the case file. Once something is written down, it gains authority. White and Epston (1990) suggest that the invention of the case file enabled individuals to be captured and *fixed* in writing:

> In our world, language plays a very central part in those activities that define and *construct* persons, and if written language makes a more than significant contribution to this, then a consideration of modern documents and their role in the redescription of persons is called for. (White and Epston, 1990, p. 188, emphasis added)

This is particularly important in social work practice since recording has become diagnostic rather than simply factual. As Kagle (1991) comments, the case file is both selective and analytic, but analyses are often retrospective reconstructions of the worker's thinking processes rather than a prospective aid to assessment. As we noted earlier, analyses of case files and case conference minutes reveal evidence of selective use of facts, inaccurate information and 'shaping'. The written word has such power that social workers could usefully re-examine their attitudes towards recording. The process of individualising service users in reports and records should not be allowed to slip into pathologising.

Pathologising the individual arises mainly from an emphasis on the subject of the case file, obscuring the fact that the social work relationship involves two people – the *subject* and the *author* of the document. White and Epston (1990, p. 188) argue that the author has 'a library of terms of description that have been invented by and considered the property of this particular domain of expert knowledge'. This expert knowledge, combined with the invisibility of the author, creates the impression of the possession of an objective and detached view that does not actually exist. For example, adherents of psychodynamic social work practice carefully chart the resistances and manipulations of clients while viewing their own resistances and manipulations as 'therapy'. They are able to bolster a view of the therapy as essentially beneficial and the therapist as rational and scientific through the construction of the subject within their specialised discourse in a way which hides the moral assumptions implicit in it (for a fuller discussion, see, Ingleby, 1985).

It is unfair, though, to blame particular areas of social work expertise for all the distortions that occur in social work records. Much of the shaping of data has its roots in the sexist and racist nature of language itself. Language reflects racial and gender divisions, and there is an interplay between language and social structure, with language helping to reproduce social values. For example, feminine is a 'marked' category in language where there are pairs of words, such as actor and actress. The term 'actor' functions as a neutral term but 'actress' is formally marked as feminine. Close examination of descriptions in case records will usually indicate 'marking' for subjects who are neither male nor white. For example, Denney (1992) shows how the word 'space' has different meanings for the black and white subjects of probation reports. For black subjects, space is used to describe physical space, whereas for white subjects it indicates ontological space in which the subject can explore feelings and have space to think. There is also linguistic derogation of women with other pairs of words that do not match, for example, fathering and mothering.

There are also linguistic gaps, such as a dearth of expressions that refer to a women's sexual activity in a positive way. For example, women cannot be 'virile', although there are many pejorative words such as 'promiscuous'. The lack of words for the activities of women and black people not only reflect recording practices, but also add up to what feminist and black researchers refer to as 'silences' in social research in which whole areas of women's and black people's experiences are ignored (Maynard and Purvis, 1995). These gaps in research affect recording in that essential detail is often missing from records. For example, it is not uncommon to read in case files to do with child development issues that a child has 'blossomed', but there seems to be no equivalent that supplies detail about what would be the evidence for 'wilting'. Additionally, the social work discourse is mainly within a micro domain, therefore racism, for example, is a macro concept that is not readily accessible within this:

> It was noteworthy that individual assessments for all clients appeared to be based upon highly individualised descriptions of personality... the probation officer appeared to be creating a certain form of reality which was meant to represent the nature of the offender and the offender's problem. (Denney, 1992, p. 96)

With the introduction of service user access to files, there is also a reluctance to record assumptions, although they remain in the social worker's head. This manifests itself in the form of Chinese whispers in the interagency group or the use of euphemisms in reports, particularly court reports. Euphemisms may seem kinder to the service user but have the disadvantage that they cannot be challenged. They are often nothing more than coded insults; for example, 'He tries his best' actually means 'He has failed'; 'manipulative' means 'She/he will not do what I suggest'. Additionally, euphemisms can have coded meaning for the reader; for example, 'The house is typical of this estate' means 'This is a filthy house, like most others in the area'.

Reports are particularly prone to distortion as they often have the purpose of persuading the reader to accept a recommendation as well as informing and explaining. This means that reports usually contain either a 'pitch' or a 'denunciation' (Emerson, 1969) that involves the writer in 'recycling the evidence' (Aronsson, 1991). A 'pitch' will attempt to individualise or victimise the subject and will use words such as 'unfortunately' and 'however', which then cast doubt on statements of fact. A 'denunciation' will use similar words but give them a negative connotation. There is no reason why reports should recycle the evidence; a more factual account would leave the reader to make up his/her own mind, and any statements of opinion could be labelled just that. For further discussion of linguistically sensitive language, see Pugh (1996).

Conclusion

Thus social psychology tells us that we are pretty ineffective at making accurate assessments in *any* social situation. And the human tendency to make attributions, develop stereotypes and increase risk-taking in groups is such robust behaviour that exhortations to keep an 'open mind' are quite worthless. We simply don't keep our minds open at all, although we do sometimes pretend that our judgments are non-judgmental. Not only would it be against our self -interests to do so in terms of our own mental health, but it would also be incredibly time-consuming – and no-one would listen to us when we had done so anyway. Are we a truly horrible lot; is the ideal of the non-judgmental social worker quite impossible? Is there anything we can do?

Modestly, we would suggest that there is a way forward. First, this would involve removing the interagency group from social work assessments. By all means, consult with all the people in your action/

target system, but by no means give them the mandate to make judgments. Accept the individual responsibility for your own judgments. This is not to say that the interagency group has nothing to offer the individual social worker in terms of resources and management of the individual decision. Neither is it to say that you need not listen carefully to service users but, at the end of the day, you must state *your* judgment and note differences of opinion.

Second, be aware of the importance of your first assessment because this will underpin all your subsequent decisions and may hinder the process of evaluation. The only way in which you can reasonably engage in evaluation of your assessments, we suggest, is by ensuring that you have multiple frames at the outset. Consider the maps outlined earlier even where they do not fit comfortably with your theories about people. For example, it will be obvious to the reader that we do not particularly like psychoanalytic explanations of human behaviour as it works against our own self-efficacy efforts, but we include it as a possible truth that we must consider even if we are both more likely to begin with a cognitive explanation of events. These frames need to be written down in terms of possible hypotheses to provide the means by which you actually evaluate your outcomes or else you will engage in the self-justification efforts described earlier.

Third, test each frame by checking your hypotheses against the outcomes by asking the subject of your assessment. Continuous bridging of the gap between assessor and subject will assist this process.

Fourth, check your case files for language usage that pathologises rather than individualises the subject.

Finally, set out your report in a logical order using some adapted version of the headings listed in Chapter 3. These are based loosely on the work of Meyer (1993) and, as the reader will have realised by now, they reflect the layout of this book and mirror the six stages of the process of making assessments.

1 *Define the 'case'*: its boundaries and systemic context.
2 *List the data*: what facts, happenings, oppressions and supports are present.
3 *Weigh the data.* How is the person(s) functioning in the circumstances? How is the balance of strengths and limitations, reactions and resources, affecting the situation? These should be based on your use of social science 'knowledge' (see Chapters 2 and 3).
4 *Analysis, inference and explanation.* Interpret the interaction between the variables. Make causal connections. Check

hypotheses. This should be based on the use of the general
theoretical maps (Chapters 4 and 5) and the more detailed method
maps (Chapters 6 to 10). A final check should be made against
distortions at this point.

5 *Situation definition/summary*. What are the needs, what needs to
be and can be done, internal/external change first or both, what
workers can the service offer, what are the priorities, what risks
are involved?

6 *Recommendations*. What would be the best focus of
attention/intervention? What could be attempted? What is the
preferred method? What is an alternative method? Is the time
frame brief time-limited, episodic or open ended? Who is the best
person to take action? What is the expected outcome? What are
the criteria for evaluating the outcome? What about cost?

Summary

- Assessments necessarily involve making a judgment that is the
  responsibility of the individual social worker.
- Objectivity in assessment work is subject to a range of distortions:
  selective attention, stereotyping, attributional and sensory biases.
- Interagency groups are even more prone to biases than individual
  decision-makers and do not act as a safeguard against risky
  decision-making.
- Case recording and report writing practices rarely acknowledge
  the power of the writer to construct the subjects of social work
  interventions.
- Language reflects the racial and gender divisions of society, so the
  language used in reports often reproduces dominant social values.
- Social workers need to build a series of checks into their
  individual assessments and take responsibility for them.

12

Conclusion

We hope that the comprehensive framework that we have presented will, first, help social workers to be theory conscious at least in their reflections and that, with a clearer idea of how various theories reflect different explanations of human behaviour, they will be encouraged to draw more deliberately on the theoretical maps as they journey towards helpful analyses of situations.

Social workers will continue to approach assessments from their favoured theoretical standpoint, and each theoretical approach has its own usefulness and limitations. The psychodynamic approach, we suggest, offers a considerable analysis of a person's *individual* problems but is severely limited in *social* work practice because it largely ignores important 'weather conditions' such as oppressions to do with sexuality, gender, race and class. Adherents of behavioural approaches claim to be more value-free and rigorous in their assessment of behavioural problems, but the reality is often that this approach is used selectively in assessment work with a tendency to go for a 'quick fix'. Strict behavioural assessments need careful attention to behavioural baselines if the assessment is to yield testable outcomes.

Task-centred approaches to assessment are essentially value-free and non-oppressive as they emphasise service user involvement in the analysis, but there is a danger here that this may be taken as read and that social workers may be lulled into a false sense of security about their abilities to empower service users through this approach. The solution-focused approach to assessment differs from all the others in that it rejects the therapeutic preoccupation with problems. As such, it has enormous potential for anti-oppressive assessment practice, but it still requires the social worker to undertake a careful analysis to avoid a tendency to psychological reductionism.

There is, of course, no reason why all the maps we outline should not be used in making an assessment, as long as the process is carefully and systematically carried out and the competing and contradictory nature of the various approaches is understood.

Second, we hope that practitioners' confidence about the identification, placing and use of theory will enable them to relax with it, in the sense of being comfortable with uncertainty, in such a way that they will seriously listen for service users' views and take time to construct mutual dialogue and engagement despite differences of race and gender. Indeed, the greater the differences, the more time and care is required for this.

What must be emphasised is that assessment is complex, time-consuming and fluid. So our third hope is that practitioners who are better rooted in theory will endeavour to be more research-minded and keep track of the outcomes of their assessments, with a view to being able to identify what they do that is different, either in the process or in the theoretical map chosen, when the outcome is satisfactory. But, of course, good outcomes will never remove all problems from people's lives – our definition of good progress is moving from the stuckness of the same damn thing over and over to the normality of one damn thing after another.

The main hallmark of effective professional practice, however, is when theoretical knowledge acts as a basis of professional expertise (Sibeon, 1991), but, as theory informs practice, so practice develops theory. We hope, therefore, that practitioners will become less ambivalent about theory, that they will seek to own it rather than abandon it to academics. Commitment to social work values, to caring, to high standards and to effectiveness will involve much thinking as well as doing, and much reflection before and after the doing. Theoretically informed practice in assessment work is more likely to provide a clearer basis for interventions and their evaluation. Perhaps one of the obstacles to the integration of theory and practice is the mystique that sometimes surrounds theoretical discussion. We hope that, by focusing on making assessments useful, we have been able to cut away some of the mystique and bring theory down to earth, making it more useable in the real world.

For those who are interested in our fundamental orientation, readers will have noticed that our approaches are anti-positivist and that we consider human action to be conditioned, but not entirely determined by, external factors. People are not passive objects but are 'conscious social actors who play an active part in plotting the course of their lives' (Thompson, 1995, p. 43). But, while we reject positivism, we do not reject all social science – we accept the hermeneutical approach that focuses on the interrelationship between the objective world and social actors, and we accept the critical approach that seeks to integrate this with wider social and political factors. Thus we are very interested in postmodernist issues and in the current growth of literature relating them to social work (see, for example, Parton and Marshall, in press) and we are particularly attracted to social constructionism and narrative approaches. We agree with Thompson (1995, p. 46) that we need 'to understand not only individual subjectivities but also shared subjectivities in terms of membership of social groups'. Our philosophy is also influenced by existentialism, which is a philosophy of lived experience, of freedom and of responsibility; it does not seek to be prescriptive or to tie people down to specific practices (Thompson, 1992).

Theory on its own is not able to provide ready-made solutions for practice, but it can guide and inform it. Messy uncertainty remains part of reality, and the best we can do is 'continue to struggle through our confusion, to insist on being human', as R.D. Laing used to say. In social work, we are dealing with unique difficulties each day, and we therefore need to carry on what Sibeon (1992, p. 163) calls a 'reflective conversation with the situation'. What we make of situations includes our own contribution to them, and service users can be helped to see this too. This approach embraces uncertainty, encouraging its creative use. It also means there are no guaranteed outcomes, hence the need for evaluating assessments when their outcomes are known. This is a far cry from the mechanistic application of theory or expecting theory to fit perfectly with reality.

Also, in order to embrace anti-discriminatory practice, it is necessary to become aware of how the structure of psychocultural assumptions and biases constrains our view of others and take action to counteract them when they lead to inequality. In other words, we need to avoid assuming that our theories, social roles and expectations are not problematic for others. Such practice is about seeking to make the best use of the theory that is available, learning how to make it more useful or helpful and learning from our mistakes. To do this, we need to work in partnership with service users for they are well, if not best, placed to reflect on the usefulness of the partnership.

Finally, assessment necessarily involves making a judgment for which social workers need to take responsibility. There are many biases that can shape assessments to desired decisions, and these biases are universal. We do not think that social workers are a special breed whose training makes them any less likely than other mortals to be free from distorting service users' realities. Additionally, we question the ability of multiagency groups to act as a check against inadequate initial assessments and faulty decision-making. What we do consider to be important in assessment activity is the need to emphasise the critical role of the individual social worker's professional judgment. Thus, individual accountability for these judgments, through a series of checks such as routine consumer and interagency feedback, is essential. We realise that making assessments in the way we have detailed will demand much effort at an early stage of the social work process, but we envisage that it will result in improved confidence in professional abilities and help to put the *social* back in social work. At all times, however, seek and keep balance. Like Fisch *et al.* (1983), we see theory as important and indeed necessary for practice, yet theory can be over-elaborated or taken too seriously – deified – until it hampers direct observation and the clear interpretation of situations.

References

Abbott, P. and Wallace, C. *An Introduction to Sociology Feminist Perspectives*. London: Routledge, 1990.

Aggleton, P. and Chambers, H. *Nursing Models and Nursing Process*. London: Macmillan, 1986.

Ahmad, B. *Black Perspectives in Social Work*. London: Venture Press, 1990.

Ainsworth, M.D.S., Blehar, M.C., Waters, E. *et al. Patterns of Attachment*. Hove: Lawrence Erlbaum Associates, 1978.

Alexander, F. and Ross, H. *The Impact of Freudian Psychiatry*. Chicago: Phoenix, 1961.

Allen, E.F. 'Psychoanalytic theory', in Turner, F.J. (ed.) *Social Work Treatment*. New York: Free Press, 1974.

Allen, L. 'Combining solution-focused ideas with White/Epston-style therapeutic letters', *Context*, **26**, 1996, 34–5.

Arber, S. and Ginn, J. *Gender and Later Life*. London: Sage, 1991.

Aronsson, K. 'Social interaction and the recycling of evidence', in Coupland, M., Giles, H. and Weimann, J.M. (eds) *Miscommunication and Problematic Talk*. London: Sage, 1991.

Audit Commission *The Community Revolution: Personal Social Services and Community Care*. London: HMSO, 1992.

Austin, L.N. 'Trends in differential treatment in social casework', *Social Casework*, June, 1948.

Baldwin, S. *The Myth of Community Care: An Alternative Neighbourhood Model of Care*. London: Chapman & Hall, 1993.

Bandura, A. *Principles of Behaviour Modification*. New York: Holt, Rinehart & Winston, 1969.

Bandura, A. *Social Learning Theory*. Englewood Cliffs, NJ: Prentice Hall, 1977.

Barber, J.G. *Beyond Casework*. London: Macmillan/BASW, 1991.

Barker, P. *Basic Family Therapy*. London: Granada, 1981.

Barker, V. *Promoting Partnerships Through Consultation*. Lyme Regis: Russell House, 1994.

Barr, V. 'Change in women', in Ernst, S. and Maguire, M. (eds) *Living with the Sphinx*. London: Women's Press, 1987.

Bateson, G. *Steps to an Ecology of Mind*. New York: Ballantine Books, 1977.

Bayley, R. 'Making a success of marriage', *Family Policy Studies Centre Bulletin*, November, 1995.

Beck, A.T. *Depression: Clinical, Experimental and Theoretical Aspects*. London: Hoeber, 1967.

Beck, A.T. and Tomkin, A. *Cognitive Therapy and Emotional Disorders*. London: Penguin, 1989.

Bee, H. and Mitchell, S. *The Developing Person*. London: Harper & Row, 1985.
Beecher, S. in Marchant, H. and Waring, B. *Gender Reclaimed*. Sydney: Hale & Iremonger, 1986.
Belsky, J. and Nezworski, *Clinical Implications of Attachment*. Hillsdale, NJ: Erlbaum, 1988.
Berg, I.K. and Miller, S.D. *Working with the Problem Drinker*. New York: Norton, 1992.
Berne, E. *Games People Play*. New York: Grove Books, 1964.
Berne, E. *A Layman's Guide to Psychiatry and Psychoanalysis*. London: Penguin, 1978.
Bibring, G.L. *et al*. 'A study of pregnancy', *Journal of Social Casework*, c.1960.
Blair, M. 'Interviews with black families', in Cohen, R. and Hughes, M. with Ashwort, L. and Blair, M. *Schools Out: The Family Perspective on School Exclusions*. London: Family Service Units and Barnardos, 1996.
Blaug, R. 'Distortion of the face to face: communicative reason and social work practice', *British Journal of Social Work*, **25**(4), 1995, 423–39.
Blyth, E. and Milner, J. 'The process of interagency work', in Violence Against Children Study Group, *Taking Child Abuse Seriously*. London: Unwin Hyman, 1990.
Blyth, E. and Milner, J. 'Black boys excluded from school: race and masculinity issues', in Blyth, E. and Milner, J. (eds) *School Exclusions: Interprofessional Issues for Policy and Practice*. London: Routledge, 1996.
Blyth, E. and Milner, J. 'Young black people excluded from school'. Paper presented at Current Developments in Child Care: Linking Practice with Research. Leeds: Leeds University, 1995.
Blyth, E., Saleem, T. and Scott, M. *Kirklees Young Carers Project*. Huddersfield: Kirklees Metropolitan Council and The University of Huddersfield, 1995.
Bocock, R. *Sigmund Freud*. London: Tavistock, Ellis Horwood, 1983.
Bowlby, J. *Child Care and the Growth of Love*. London: Penguin, 1964.
Bowlby, J. *Attachment and Loss*. London: Hogarth Press, 1982.
Bowlby, J. and Parkes, C.M. 'Separation and loss within the family', in Anthony, E.J. and Koupernik, C. (eds) 'Growing points of attachment theory and research' *Monographs of the Society for Research in Child Development*, **50**(1–1), 1970, 3–35.
Boykim, W. and Toms, F.D. 'Black child socialisation: a conceptual framework', in McAdoo, H.P. and McAdoo, J.L. (eds) *Black Children: Social, Educational and Parental Environments*. London: Sage, 1985.
Braye, S. and Preston-Shoot, M. *Practising Social Work Law*. London: Macmillan, 1992.
Braye, S. and Preston-Shoot, M. *Empowering Practice in Social Care*. Buckingham: Open University Press, 1995.
Brayne, H. and Martin, G. *Law for Social Workers*. London: Blackstone, 1993.
Bretherton, I. 'The origins of attachment theory: John Bowlby and Mary Ainsworth', *Developmental Psychology*, **28**(5), 1992, 759–75.
Brown, R. *Social Psychology: The Second Edition*. London: Free Press, 1986.
Bruner, E. 'Ethnography as narrative', in Turner, V. and Bruner, E. (eds) *The Anthropology of Experience*. Chicago: University of Illinois Press, 1986.
Bruner, J. *Acts of Meaning*. Cambridge, MA: Harvard University Press, 1990.
Burman, E. *Challenging Women*. Buckingham: Open University Press, 1996.

Burnard, P.A. 'Method of analysing interview transcripts in qualitative research', *Nurse Education Today*, **11**, 1991, 461–6.

Burns, D.D. *Feeling Good*. New York: Avon, 1992.

Burr, V. *An Introduction to Social Constructionism*. London: Routledge, 1995.

Byng Hall, J. 'The family script: a useful bridge between theory and practice', *Journal of Family Therapy*, **7**, 1985, 301–5.

Caplan, G. *An Approach to Community Mental Health*. London: Tavistock, 1961.

Carter, E.A. and McGoldrick, M. *The Family Life Cycle and Family Therapy; A Framework for Family Therapy*. New York: Gardner Press, 1980.

Case, L.P. and Lingerfelt, V.B. '"Name calling": the labelling process in social work interviews', *Social Services Review*, **48**(1), 1974, 75–86.

Cavanagh, K. and Gee, V. (eds) *Working with Men. Feminism and Social Work*. London: Routledge, 1996.

Challis, D. and Davies, B. *Care Management in Community Care*. PSSRU: University of Kent at Canterbury, 1986.

Challis, D., Chessum, R., Chesterman, J. *et al. Case Management in Social and Health Care*. Canterbury: PSSRU, University of Kent, 1990.

Challis, D., Darton, R., Johnson, L. *et al. Care Management and Health Care of Older People*. Canterbury: PSSRU, University of Kent, 1995.

Channer, Y. *I am a Promise. The School Achievement of Black African Caribbeans*. London: Trentham Books, 1995.

Cicirelli, V.G. 'Feelings of attachment to siblings and well being in later life', *Psychology and Ageing*, **4**, 1989, 211–16.

Cicirelli, V.G. 'Attachment theory in old age: protection of the attachment figure', in Pillemer, K. and McCartnery, K. (eds) *Parent–Child Relations Across the Life Course*. Hillsdale, NJ: Erlbaum, 1991.

Clark, H., Dyer, S. and Hansaran, L. *Going Home: Older People Leaving Hospital*. London: Polity Press in conjunction with the Joseph Rowntree Foundation and *Community Care Magazine*, 1996.

Clifford, D. 'Towards an anti-oppressive social work assessment method', *Practice*, **VI**(3), 1994, 226–38.

Cockburn, C. *In the Way of Women. Men's Resistance to Sex Equality in Organisations*. Basingstoke: Macmillan, 1991.

Corby, B. *Child Abuse: Towards a Knowledge Base*. Milton Keynes: Open University Press, 1993.

Cordery, J. and Whitehead, A. 'Boys don't cry: empathy, collusion and crime', in Senior, P. and Woodhill, B. (eds) *Gender, Crime and Probation Practice*. Sheffield: Pavic, 1992.

Coulshed, V. *Social Work Practice: An Introduction*. London: Macmillan, 1988.

Crittenden, P.M. 'Distorted patterns of relationship in maltreating families: the role of internal representation models', *Journal of Reproductive and Infant Psychology*, **6**(3), 1988, 183–200.

Curnock, K. and Hardiker, P. *Towards Practice Theory: Skill and Methods in Social Assessments*. London: Routledge, Kegan & Paul, 1979.

Dale, P., Morrison, T. and Waters, J. *Dangerous Families: Assessment and Treatment of Child Abuse*. London: Tavistock, 1986.

Dale, P., Davies, M., Morrison, T. *et al.* 'A family therapy approach to child abuse: countering resistance', *Journal of Family Therapy*, **5**, 1983, 117–45.

Dalrymple, J. and Burke, B. *Anti-oppressive Practice. Social Care and the Law*. Buckingham: Open University Press, 1995.

Davies, M. *The Essential Social Worker: A Guide to Positive Practice*. London: Heinemann, 1981.

Davis, A. and Ellis, K. 'Enforced altruism or community care', in Hugman, R. and Smith, D. (eds) *Ethical Issues in Social Work*. London: Routledge, 1995.

Davitz, L.L. and Davitz, R.J. 'Nurses' responses to patients suffering', in Copp, L. (ed.) *Perspectives on Pain*. London: Churchill Livingstone, 1980.

Dearden, C. and Baker, S. *Young Carers: The Facts*. Sutton: Community Care, 1995.

Denman, G. and Thorpe, D. 'Particpation and patterns of intervention in child protection in Gwent'. *A Research Report for the Area Child Protection Committee, Gwent*. Lancaster: University of Lancaster, 1993.

Denney, D. *Racism and Anti-Racism in Probation*. London: Routledge, 1992.

Department for Education. *Code of Practice on the Identification and Assessment of Special Educational Needs*. London: Department for Education, 1994.

Department of Health. *Protecting Children: A Guide for Social Workers Undertaking a Comprehensive Assessment*. London: HMSO, 1988.

Department of Health. *Community Care in the Next Decade and Beyond: Policy Guidance*. London: HMSO, 1990a.

Department of Health. *Child Abuse: A Study of Enquiry Reports 1980–1989*. London: HMSO, 1990b.

Department of Health. *Adoption: the Future*. London: HMSO, 1993.

Department of Health. 'Study of working together', *Area Child Protection Committee Series Report No.1*. London: HMSO, 1994.

Department of Health. *Carers (Recognition and Services) Act*. London: HMSO, 1995a.

Department of Health. *Looking After Children*. London: HMSO, 1995b.

Department of Health/Scottish Office. *Care Management and Assessment. Practitioners' Guide*. London: HMSO, 1991.

Derrida, J. *Writing and Difference*. Chicago: Chicago University Press, 1973.

de Shazer, S. *Keys to Solution in Brief Therapy*. New York: Norton, 1985.

de Shazer, S. *Clues: Investigating Solutions in Brief Therapy*. New York: Norton, 1988.

de Shazer, S. *Putting Difference to Work*. New York: Norton, 1991.

de Shazer, S. Verbal communication, at Glasgow conference, Solutions in Brief Therapy, 1993.

de Shazer, S. *Words Were Originally Magic*. New York: Norton, 1994.

Devore, W. and Schlesinger, E.G. *Ethnic-sensitive Social Work*. New York: Macmillan, 1991.

Dobash, R.E. and Dobash, R. *Women, Violence and Social Change*. London: Routledge, 1992.

Doel, M. and Marsh, P. *Task Centred Social Work*. London: Ashgate, 1992.

Dryden, W. and Yankma, J. *Counselling Individuals – A Rational Emotive Handbook*. London: Whorr, 1993.

Durrant, M. *Creative Strategies for School Problems*. Epping, NSW Australia: Eastwood Centre, 1993.

Edley, N. and Wetherall, M. 'Masculinity, power and identity', in Mac an Ghaill, M. (ed.) *Understanding Masculinities*. Buckingham: Open University Press, 1996.

Edwards, R. *Women Students: Separating or Connecting Family and Education?* London: Taylor & Francis, 1993.

Ellis, A. *Reason and Emotion in Psychotherapy*. New York: Lyle Stuart, 1962.

Emerson, D. *Judging Delinquents*. Chicago: Aldine, 1969.

Epstein, L. *Helping People; The Task Centred Approach*. Columbus, OH: Merrill, 1988.

Epstein, N.B., Bishop, D.S. and Levin, S. 'The McMaster model of family functioning', *Journal of Marriage and Family Counselling*, **IV**, 1978, 19–31.

Erikson, E.H. *Children and Society*. Harmondsworth: Penguin, 1948.

Erikson, E.H. *Childhood and Society*. London: Granada, 1977.

Erickson, M.H. *Hypnotherapy: An Exploratory Casebook*. New York: Irvington, 1959.

Evans, J. *Feminist Theory Today*. London: Sage, 1995.

Everitt, A. *et al. Applied Research for Better Practice*. London: Macmillan, 1992.

Family Policy Study Centre. *Families in the European Union*. London: Family Policy Study Centre, 1994.

Fawcett, B., Featherstone, B., Hearn, J. and Toft, C. (eds) *Violence and Gender Relations Theories and Interventions*. London: Sage, 1996.

Feeney, J. and Noller, P. *Adult Attachment*. London: Sage, 1996.

Field, P.A. and Morse, J.M. *Nursing Research: The Application of Qualitative Approaches*. London: Croom Helm, 1985.

Fisch, R., Weakland, J.H. and Segal, L. *The Tactics of Change*. New York: Jossey Bass, 1983.

Fisher, J. and Goceros, H. *Planned Behaviour Change*. New York: Free Press, 1975.

Forster, N. 'An analysis of company documentation', in Cassell, C. and Symon, G. (eds) *Qualitative Methods in Organisational Research*. London: Sage, 1994.

Forsyth, D.R. *Social Psychology*. Monterey, CA: Brooks Cole, 1986.

Fox-Harding, L. *Perspectives in Child Care Policy*. Harlow: Longman, 1991.

Fraiberg, S. (ed.) *Clinical Studies in Infant Mental Health*. London: Tavistock, 1980.

Freire, P. *Pedagogy of the Oppressed*. Harmondsworth: Penguin, 1972.

Freud, A. *Ego and the Mechanisms of Defence*. New York: International Universities Press, 1936.

Freud, A. *Ego and the Mechanisms of Defence*, 2nd edn. London: Hogarth Press, 1968.

Freud, S. 'Constructions of analysis, vol. 23', in Strachey, J. (ed.) *The Standard Edition of the Complete Psychological Works of Sigmund Freud*. London: Hogarth Press, 1937.

Furman, B. and Ahola, T. *Solution Talk*. New York: Norton, 1992.

Gambrill, E. *Casework: A Competency Based Approach*. London: Prentice Hall, 1982.

Gilligan, C. *In a Different Voice*. Cambridge, MA: Harvard University Press, 1982.

Gilligan, S. and Price, R. *Therapeutic Conversations*. New York: Norton, 1993.

Glaser, B. and Strauss, A.L. *The Discovery of Grounded Theory: Strategies for Qualitative Research*. Chicago: Aldine, 1969.

Goldman, A.I. *A Theory of Human Action*. Englewood Cliffs, NJ: Prentice Hall, 1970.

Gorell Barnes, G. *Working with Families*. London: Macmillan, 1984.

Graddol, D. and Swann, J. *Gender Voices*. New York: Norton, 1989.

Grossman, K.E. and Grossman, K. 'The wider concept of attachment in cross-cultural research', *Human Development*, **13**, 1990, 31–47.

Grossman, K., Grossman, K.E. and Spangler, G. *et al.* 'Maternal sensitivity and newborns' orientation responses as related to quality of attachment in Northern Germany', in Bretherton, I. and Waters, E. (eds) Growing points in attachment theory and research, *Monographs of the Society for Research in Child Development*, **50**, 1985.

Haley, J. *Problem Solving Therapy*. New York: Jossey Bass, 1976.

Hall, C.S. *A Primer of Freudian Psychology*. London: New English Library, 1954.

Hall, E. 'The gender of the therapist; its relevance to practice and training', in Horobin, G. (ed.) *Sex, Gender and Care Work: Research Highlights in Social Work*. London: Jessica Kingsley, 1987.

Hamilton, G. 'The underlying philosophy of social casework', *Family Journal of Social Casework*, July, 1941.

Hammersley, M. *What's Wrong with Ethnography*. London: Routledge, 1992.

Hanmer, J. and Statham, D. *Women and Social Work*. London: Macmillan, 1988.

Haralambos, M. and Holborn, M. *Sociology: Themes and Perspectives*. London: Unwin Hyman, 1990.

Harris, T. A. *I'm OK – You're OK*. London: Pan, 1970.

Harris, T. 'Getting off the conveyor belt from childhood adversity: what we can learn from naturalistic studies'. Paper presented at Surviving Childhood Adversity, 2–5 July. Dublin: University College Dublin, 1991.

Harrison, H. 'Child assessment and family support.' Paper given at conference Assessing the Needs of Individual Children, 31 October. London: National Children's Bureau, 1995.

Hayden, C. 'Explaining exclusion from primary school: an analysis of the reasons behind the rise in the recorded primary school exclusions in the early 1990s'. PhD Thesis. Portsmouth: University of Portsmouth, 1996.

Hayes, N. *A First Course in Psychology*. London: Edward Arnold, 1984.

Hayes, N. *Foundations of Psychology*. London: Routledge, 1994.

Hayles, M., Kelly, N. and Milner, J. *Public Protection: Assessment Skills and Decision-making in the Process of Risk Management*. West Yorkshire: West Yorkshire Probation Service, 1996.

Hearn, J. 'Men's violence to known women; men's accounts and men's policy developments', in Fawcett, B., Featherstone, B., Hearn, J. *et al.* (eds) *Violence and Gender Relations*. London: Sage, 1996.

Heider, F. *The Psychology of Interpersonal Relationships*. New York: John Wiley & Sons, 1958.

Hollis, F. *Social Casework: A Psychosocial Therapy*. New York: Random House, 1964.

Home Office/Department of Health/Department of Education and Science/ Welsh Office. *Working Together under the Children Act 1989: A Guide to the Arrangements for Inter-agency Cooperation for the Protection of Children from Abuse.* London: HMSO, 1991.

Home Office/Department of Health/Welsh Office. *National Standards for the Supervision of Offenders in the Community.* London: Home Office Probation Services Division, 1995.

hooks, bell *Talking Back: Thinking Feminist Thinking Black.* London: heba, 1989.

hooks, bell *Yearning.* London: Turnaround, 1991.

hooks, bell *Sisters of the Yam: Black Women and Self-Recovery.* London: Turnaround, 1993.

Howe, D. *On Being a Client.* London: Sage, 1993.

Howe, D. *Attachment Theory for Social Work Practice.* London: Macmillan, 1995.

Huberman, A.M. and Miles, M.B. 'Data management and analysis methods', in Denzin, N.K. and Lincoln, Y.S. (eds) *Handbook of Qualitative Research.* London: Sage, 1994.

Hudson, B.L. and Macdonald, G.M. *Behavioural Social Work: An Introduction.* London: Macmillan, 1986.

Hughes, B. 'A model for the comprehensive assessment of older people and their carers', *British Journal of Social Work*, **23**(4), 1993, 345–63.

Hughes, B. and Mtezuka, M. 'Social work and older women: where have older women gone?', in Langan, M. and Day, L. (eds) *Women, Oppression and Social Work: Issues in Anti-Discriminatory Practice.* London: Tavistock/Routledge, 1992.

Hugman, R. and Smith, D. *Ethical Issues in Social Work.* London: Sage, 1995.

Hussain, N. 'An investigation of the placement arrangements made for children and young people "looked after" in relation to cultural and religious origins'. Dissertation. Department of Behavioural Sciences, University of Huddersfield, 1996.

Ingleby, D. 'Professionals as socialisers: the "psy complex"', in Spitzer, S. and Scull, A.T. (eds) *Research in Law, Deviance, and Social Control.* New York: Jai Press, 1985.

Janis, I.L. and Mann, L. *Decision Making.* New York: Free Press, 1977.

Jones, E. 'The early development of female sexuality', *International Journal of Psychoanalysis*, **8**, 1932, 459–63.

Jones, W. 'Research expertise on the World Bank', in Walford, G. (ed.) *Researching the Powerful in Education.* London: University College London Press, 1994.

Jordan, B. *Social Work in an Unjust Society.* Hemel Hempstead: Harvester Wheatsheaf, 1990.

Jordan, J. *Moving Towards Home. Political Essays.* London: Virago, 1989.

Justice, B. and Justice, R. *The Abusing Family.* New York: Human Sciences Press, 1976.

Kagle, J.D. *Social Work Records.* Belmont, CA: Wadsworth, 1991.

Kahneman, D. and Tversky, A. 'On the psychology of prediction', *Psychological Review*, **80**, 1973, 237–51.

Kahneman, D. and Tversky, A. 'Prospect theory: an analysis of decisions under risk', *Econometrician*, **47**, 1979, 263–91.

Kahneman, D. and Tversky, A. 'The psychology of preferences', *Scientific American*, 1982, 136–42.

Kelly, L. 'The interconnectedness of domestic violence and child abuse: challenges for research, policy and practice', in Mullender, A. and Morley, K. (eds) *Children Living with Domestic Violence. Putting Men's Abuse of Children on the Child Care Agenda*. London: Whiting & Birch, 1994.

Kelly, N. and Milner, J. 'Decision-making in child protection practice: the effectiveness of the case conference in the UK'. Paper presented at ISPCAN Eleventh International Congress on Child Abuse and Neglect. University College, Dublin 18–21 August, 1996a.

Kelly, N. and Milner, J. 'Child protection decision-making', *Child Abuse Review*, **5**(2), 1996b, 91–102.

King, N. 'The qualitative research interview', in Cassell, C. and Symons, G. (eds) *Qualitative Methods in Organisational Research: A Practice Guide*. London: Sage, 1994.

Kline, P. *Fact and Fantasy in Freudian Theory*. London: Methuen, 1972.

Kohlberg, L. 'The child as a moral philosopher', *Psychology Today*, **II**, 1968, 25–30.

Kral, R. *Strategies that Work: Techniques for Solution in the Schools*. Milwaukee, WI: Brief Family Therapy Centre, 1989.

Lawrence, M. 'Women's psychology and feminist social work', in Langan, M. and Day, L. (eds) *Women, Oppression and Social Work. Issues for Anti-Discriminatory Practice*. London: Routledge, 1992.

Leiss, W. and Chociolko, C. *Risk and Responsibility*. Quebec: McGill-Queen's University Press, 1994.

Lewis, A., Shemmings, D. and Thoburn, J. *Participation in Practice – Involving Families in Child Protection: A Training Pack*. Norwich: Social Work Development Unit, University of East Anglia, 1991.

Lloyd, S. and Degenhardt, D. 'Challenges in working with male social work students', in Cavanagh, K and Gee, V. (eds) *Working with Men, Feminism and Social Work*. London: Routledge, 1996.

Logan, S.L. *et al. Social Work Practice with Black Families*. New York: Longman, 1990.

London Borough of Lambeth. *Whose Child? The Report of the Panel of Enquiry into the Death of Tyra Henry*. London: HMSO, 1985.

McNay, M. 'Social work and power relations', in Langan, M. and Day, L. (eds) *Women, Oppression and Social Work Issues in Anti-Discriminatory Practice*. London: Routledge, 1992.

Mac an Ghaill, M. (ed.) *Understanding Masculinities*. Buckingham: Open University Press, 1996.

Mackinnon, C. *Feminism Unmodified: Discourses on Life and Law*. Cambridge, MA: Harvard University Press, 1987.

Macleod, M. and Saroga, E. 'Challenging the orthodoxy: towards a feminist theory and practice', *Feminist Review*, **XXVIII**, 1988, 16–56.

Marchant, H. and Waring, B. *Gender Reclaimed*. Sydney: Hale & Iremonger, 1986.

Marshall, J. 'Pansies, perverts and macho men: changing conceptions of male homosexuality', in Plummer, K. (ed.) *The Making of the Modern Homosexual*. London: Hutchinson, 1981.

Marshall, W. 'Professionals, children and power', in Blyth, E. and Milner, J. (eds) *School Exclusions: Interagency Issues for Policy and Practice*. London: Routledge, 1996.

Marvin, R.S. and Stewart, R.B.A. 'A family system framework for the study of attachment', in Greenberg, M., Cichetti, D. and Cummings, M. (eds) *Attachment Beyond the Pre-School Years*. Chicago: University of Chicago Press, 1990.

Maslow, A.H. *Motivation and Personality*. New York: Harper, 1954.

Masson, H. and O'Byrne, P. *Applying Family Therapy*. London: Pergamon, 1984.

Masson, H. and O'Byrne, P. 'The family systems approach: a help or a hindrance', in *Violence Against Children Study Group. Taking Child Abuse Seriously*. London: Unwin Hyman, 1990.

Maturana, H. and Varela, F. *The Tree of Knowledge: Biological Roots of Human Understanding*. Boston: New Science Library, 1987.

Mayer, J.E. and Timms, N. *The Client Speaks: Working Class Impressions of Casework*. London: Routledge, Kegan & Paul, 1970.

Maynard, M. and Purvis, J. *Researching Women's Lives from a Feminist Perspective*. London: Taylor & Francis, 1995.

Mead, G.H. *Mind, Self and Society*. Chicago: Chicago University Press, 1934.

Meredith, B. *The Community Care Handbook: The New System Explained*. London: Age Concern, 1993.

Meyer, C. *Assessment in Social Work*. New York: Columbia University Press, 1993.

Miller, D.T. and Ross, M. 'Self-serving biases in the attribution of causality: fact or fiction?', *Psychological Bulletin*, **82**, 1975, 213–18.

Miller, J. Baker (ed.) *Psychoanalysis and Women*. Harmondsworth: Penguin, 1973.

Miller, P. and Rose, N. (eds) *The Power of Psychiatry*. Cambridge: Polity Press, 1986.

Mills, C. Wright 'The professional ideology of social pathologists', *American Journal of Sociology*, **49**, 1943, 165–80.

Mills, C. Wright *The Sociological Imagination*. London: Oxford University Press, 1970.

Milner, J. 'A myth dispelled', *Community Care*, **397**, 1982, 4 February, 23–8.

Milner, J. 'A disappearing act: the differing career paths of fathers and mothers in child protection investigations', *Critical Social Policy*, **38**(13), 1993, 48–68.

Milner, J. 'Men's resistance to social work', in B. Fawcett *et al.* (eds) *Violence and Gender Relations: Theories and Interventions*. London: Sage, 1996.

Minuchin, S. *Families and Family Therapy*. Cambridge, MA: Harvard University Presss, 1974.

Morgan, G. *Images of Organisations*. London: Sage, 1986.

Moscovici, S. and Zavalloni, M. 'The group as polariser of attitudes', *Journal of Personality and Social Psychology*, **12**, 1969, 125–35.

Murphy, K. 'Men and offending groups', in Newburn, T. and Mair, G. (eds) *Working with Men*. Lyme Regis: Russell House, 1996.

Myake, K., Chen, S. and Campos, J. 'Infants' temperament, mothers' mode of interaction and attachment in Japan: an interim report', in Bretherton, I. and

Waters, E. (eds) Growing points of attachment theory and research, *Monographs of the Society for Research in Child Development*, **50**, 1985, 276–97.

Neill, J. *Assessing Elderly People for Residential Care: A Practical Guide*. London: National Institute for Social Work, 1989.

Newburn, T. and Mair, G. (eds) *Working with Men*. Lyme Regis: Russell House, 1996.

Nice, V. 'Them and us. Women as carers; clients and social workers', *Practice*, **2**:(1), 1988, 58–73.

Nisbett, R.E. and Jones, L. *Human Inference: Strategies and Shortcomings of Social Judgement*. Englewood Cliffs, NJ: Prentice Hall, 1980.

O'Byrne, P. 'The Chinese duet – the Tao of resistance', *Journal of Family Therapy*, **12**, 1990, 31–4.

O'Hagan, K. and Dillenburger, K. *The Abuse of Women Within Child Care Work*. Buckingham: Open University Press, 1995.

O'Hanlon, B. Conference on solution focused work. London, 1995.

O'Hanlon, B. and Beadle, S. *A Field Guide to Possibility Land*. Omaha: Possibility Press, 1994.

Olsen, M. *Social Work and Mental Health*. London: Tavistock, 1984.

Osuwu-Bempah, J. 'Race, identity and social work', *British Journal of Social Work*, **24**(2), 1994, 123–36.

Packman, J., with Randall, J. and Jacques, N. *Who Needs Care? Social Work Decisions About Children*. Oxford: Basil Blackwell, 1986.

Parad, H.J. *Crisis Intervention: Selected Readings*. New York: FSA of America, 1965.

Parkes, C. Murray *Bereavement: Studies of Grief in Adult Life*. New York: International Universities Press, 1972.

Parkes, C. Murray *Bereavement*. London: Tavistock, 1986.

Parton, N. (ed.) *Social Theory, Social Change and Social Work*. London: Routledge, 1996.

Parton, N. and Marshall, W. 'Postmodernism and discourse approaches and social work', in Adams, R., Dominelli, L. and Payne, M. (eds) *Social Work*. London: Macmillan, in press.

Pavlov, I.P. *Conditional Reflexes: An Investigation of the Psychological Activity of the Cerebral Cortex* (translation). New York: Hover Publications, 1960.

Payne, M. *Modern Social Work Theory*. London: Macmillan, 1991.

Pearson, G., Treseder, J. and Yelloly, M. *Social Work and the Legacy of Freud*. London: Macmillan, 1988.

Penfield, W. 'Memory mechanisms', *AMA Archives of Neurology and Psychiatry*, 1952, **67**, 178–98.

Piaget, J. *The Origin of Intelligence in the Child*. Harmondsworth: Penguin, 1977.

Pincus, A. and Minahan, A. *Social Work Practice: Model and Method*. Itasca, IL: Peacock, 1973.

Pinsof, W.M. 'An overview of integrated problem solving therapy', *Journal of Family Therapy*, **16**(1), 1994, 103–20.

Pocock, D. 'Searching for a better story', *Journal of Family Therapy*, **XVII**, 1995, 149–74.

Polanski, N. *Damaged Parents: An Anatomy of Neglect*. Chicago: Chicago University Press, 1981

Pozatek, E. 'The problem of certainty', *Social Work*, **XXXIX**, 1994, 396–404.

Pringle, K. *Men, Masculinities and Social Welfare*. London: UCL Press, 1995.

Pugh, R. *Effective Language in Health and Social Work*. London: Chapman & Hall, 1996.

Punch, M. 'Politics and ethics in qualitative research', in Denzin, N.K. and Lincoln, Y.S. (eds) *Handbook of Qualitative Research*. London: Sage, 1994.

Radke-Yarrow, M., Cummings, E.M., Kuxcinsky, L. *et al.* 'Patterns of attachment in two- and three-year-olds in normal families and families with parental depression', *Child Development*, **56**, 1985, 884–93.

Ramon, S. 'The category of psychopathy: the professional and social context in Britain', in Miller, P. and Rose, N. (eds) *The Power of Psychiatry*. Cambridge: Polity Press, 1986.

Reder, P., Duncan, S. and Gray, M. *Beyond Blame: Child Abuse Tragedies Revisited*. London: Routledge, 1993.

Reid, W.J. 'An experimental study of the methods used in casework treatment'. Doctrinal dissertation. New York: Columbia University Press, 1963.

Reid, W.J. *The Task-Centred System*. New York: Columbia University Press, 1978.

Reid, W.J. and Epstein, L. *Task-Centred Casework*. New York: Columbia University Press, 1972.

Reid, W.J. and Shyne, A. *Brief and Extended Casework*. New York: Columbia University Press, 1969.

Renzetti, C.M. and Lee, R. *Researching Sensitive Topics*. London: Sage, 1993.

Rich, A. *Of Woman Born: Motherhood as Institution and Experience*. London: Virago, 1977.

Richards, J. *The Sceptical Feminist*. London: Routledge, 1980.

Richards, M. 'Developing the content of practice teaching', *Social Work Education*, **6**(2), 1987.

Richmond, M. *What Is Social Care Work?* New York: Russell Sage, 1917.

Robson, C. *Real World Research*. Oxford: Basil Blackwell, 1993.

Rojek, C. and Collins, S.A. 'Contract or con trick revisited. Comments on the reply by Corden and Preston-Shoot', *British Journal of Social Work*, **18**, 1988, 611–22.

Rorbaugh, J.B. *Woman: Psychology's Puzzle*. London: Abacus, 1981.

Rose, N. *The Psychological Complex: Psychology, Politics and Society in England 1869–1939*. London: Routledge & Kegan Paul, 1985.

Roys, C. 'Two reports on feminism and family therapy – a conversation with Marianne Walters'. *Association of Family Therapy Newsletter*, **7**(3), 1987, 12.

Rutter, M. *Maternal Deprivation Reassessed*. London: Penguin, 1981.

Sagi, A., Lamb, M.E., Lewkowicz K.S. *et al.* 'Security of infant–mother, –father and –metaplet among Kibbutz reared Israeli children, in Bretherton, I. and Waters, E. (eds) Growing points of attachment theory and research. *Monographs of the Society for Research in Child Development*, **50**(1–2, serial no. 209), 1985, 257–75.

Sain, S.A. 'Study to investigate particular psychological effects of domestic violence'. Dissertation for BSc Degree. University of Huddersfield, School of Human and Health Sciences: Huddersfield, 1996.

Sainsbury, E. *Social Diagnosis in Casework*. London: Routledge & Kegan Paul, 1970.

Sampson, A., Smith, D., Pearson, G. *et al.* 'Gender issues in inter-agency relations: police, probation and social services', in Abbott, P. and Wallace, C. (eds) *Sex, Gender and Care Work: Research Highlights in Social Work.* London: Jessica Kingsley, 1991.

Sawicki, J. *Disciplining Foucault: Feminism, Power and the Body.* London: Sage. 1991.

Schaffer, H.R. *Making Decisions about Children.* Oxford: Basil Blackwell, 1990.

Schon, D.T. *The Reflective Practitioner.* London: Temple Smith, 1983.

Schutz, A. *The Phenomenology of the Social World.* London: Heinemann, 1972.

Schwartz, A. and Goldiamond, I. *Social Casework: A Behavioural Approach.* New York: Columbia University Press, 1975.

Scott, D. 'How social workers think in action', *British Journal of Social Work,* (in press).

Seligman, M.E.P. *Helplessness: On Depression, Development and Death.* New York: Freeman, 1992.

Sheldon, B. *Behaviour Modification, Theory, Practice and Philosophy.* London: Tavistock, 1982.

Sheldon, B. *Cognitive-Behavioural Therapy, Research, Practice and Philosophy.* London and NewYork: Routledge, 1995.

Sheppard, M. *Care Management and the New Social Work. A Critical Analysis.* London: Whiting & Birch/Social Care Association (Education), 1995.

Sibeon, R. *Towards a New Sociology of Social Work.* Aldershot: Avebury, 1992.

Sinclair, I., Parker, R., Leat, D. *et al. The Kaleidoscope of Care: A Review of Research in Welfare Provision for Elderly People.* London: HMSO for National Institute of Social Work, 1990.

Sinclair, R., Garrett, L. and Berridge, D. *Social Work and Assessment With Adolescents.* London: NCB, 1995.

Skinner, B.F. *Science and Human Behaviour.* New York: Macmillan, 1953.

Skinner, B.F. 'Reinforcement theory', *American Psychologist,* **13**, 1958, 94–9.

Skynner, A.R.C. 'Boundaries', *Social Work Today,* **V**, 1974, 290–1.

Smale, G. and Tuson, G., with Brehal, N. and Marsh, P. *Empowerment, Assessment, Care Management and the Skilled Worker.* London: National Institute for Social Work, 1993.

Smale, G., Tuson, G., Ahmad, B. *et al. Negotiating Care in the Community.* London: HMSO for National Institute for Social Work, 1994.

Social Services Inspectorate. *Getting the Message Across. A Guide to Developing and Communicating Policies, Principles and Procedures on Assessment.* London: HMSO, 1991.

Spence, M.F. 'Finding a healthy path through racism and sexism', *Social Work Education,* **14**(4), 1995, 106–13.

Stanley, L. and Wise, S. 'Method, methodology and epistemology in feminist research process', in Stanley, L. (ed.) *Feminist Praxis: Research, Theory and Epistemology.* London: Routledge, 1991.

Strean, H.F. 'Casework with ego-fragmented parents', *Social Casework,* April, 1968.

Stuart, R.B. 'Behaviour modification: a technology for social change', in Turner, F.J. (ed.) *Social Work Treatment.* New York: Free Press, 1974.

Sugarman, L. *Lifespan Development.* London: Methuen, 1986.

Taylor, K. 'Keeping mum: the paradoxes of gendered power relationships in interviewing', in Burman, E., Aldred, P., Bewley, C. *et al.* (eds) *Challenging Women: Psychology's Exclusions, Feminist Possibilities*. Buckingham: Open University Press, 1996.

Thoburn, J., Lewis, A. and Shemmings, D. *Paternalism or Partnership? Family Involvement in the Child Protection Process*. London: HMSO, 1995.

Thompson, N. *Existentialism and Social Work*. Aldershot: Avebury, 1992.

Thompson, N. *Anti-Discriminatory Practice*. London: Macmillan, 1993.

Thompson, N. *Theory and Practice in Health and Social Welfare*. Buckingham: Open University Press, 1995.

Tunstill, J. 'Local authority policies on children in need', in Gidden, J. (ed.) *The Children Act 1989 and Family Support*. London: HMSO, 1993.

Turner, F.J. (ed.) *Social Work Treatment*. New York: Free Press, 1974.

Violence Against Children Study Group. *Taking Child Abuse Seriously*. London: Unwin Hyman, 1990.

Walford, G. 'A new focus on the powerful', in Walford, G. (ed.) *Researching the Powerful in Education*. London: University College London Press, 1994.

Walker, N. *Crime and Criminology*. Oxford: Oxford Paperbacks, 1987.

Wallerstein, J.S. and Blakeslee, S. *The Good Marriage: How and Why Love Lasts*. London: Bantam, 1996.

Walters, M. *The Invisible Web. Gender Patterns in Family Relationships*. New York: Guildford Press, 1988.

Ward, E. *Father–Daughter Rape*. London: Women's Press, 1984.

Wasserman, S.L. 'Ego psychology', in Turner, F.J. (ed.) *Social Work Treatment*. New York: Free Press, 1974.

Weiss, R.S. *Loneliness: The Experience of Emotional and Social Isolation*. Cambridge, MA: MIT Press, 1973.

Weiss, R.S. 'Attachment in adult life', in Parkes, C. Murray and Stevenson-Hinde, J. (eds) *The Place of Attachment in Human Behaviour*. New York: John Wiley & Sons, 1982.

Weiss, R.S. 'The attachment bond in childhood and adulthood', in Parkes, C. Murray, Stevenson-Hinde, J. and Marris, P. (eds) *Attachment Across the Life Cycle*. London: Routledge, 1991.

Werner, H.D. (ed.) *New Understandings of Human Behaviour*. New York: Association Press, 1970.

Westwood, S. 'Racism, black masculinity and the politics of space', in Hearn, J. and Morgan, D.H.J. (eds) *Men, Masculinities and Social Theory*. London and Winchester: Hyman, 1990, 55–71.

Westwood, S. 'Feckless parents. Masculinities and the British state', in Mac an Ghaill, M. (ed.) *Understanding Masculinities*. Buckingham: Open University Press, 1996.

White, M. 'The externalizing of the problems and the re-authoring of lives and relationships', *Dulwich Centre Newsletter*, Summer: 3–21, 1988.

White, M. 'Deconstruction and therapy', *Dulwich Centre Newsletter*, **3**, 1991.

White, M. Conference on narrative work. Doncaster, 1996.

White, M. and Epston, D. *Narrative Means to Therapeutic Ends*. New York: Norton, 1990.

White, V. 'Commonality and diversity in feminist social work', *British Journal of Social Work*, **XXV**, 1995, 143–56.

Whyte, G. 'Groupthink reconsidered', *Academy of Management Review*, **14**(1), 1989, 40–56.

Whyte, G. 'Decision failures, why they occur and how to prevent them', *Academy of Management Executive*, **5**(3), 1993, 23–31.

Wilgosh, R., Hawkes, D. and Marsh. I. 'Session two and beyond', *Context*, **17**, 1993, 31–3.

Wise, S. 'Feminist ethics in practice', in Hugman, R. and Smith, D. *Ethical Issues in Social Work*. London: Sage, 1995.

Wittgenstein, L. *Remarks on the Philosophy of Psychology*. Oxford: Blackwell, 1980.

Woodrow, K.M., Freidman, G.D., Siegelaub, A.B. *et al.* 'Pain tolerance differences according to age, sex and race', in Weisenbergh, H. (ed.) *Pain: Clinical and Experimental Perspectives*. St Louis, MO: C.V. Mosby, 1975.

Wright, K., Haycox, A. and Leadman, I. *Evaluating Community Care Services for People with Learning Difficulties*. Buckingham: Open University Press, 1994.

Yapko, M. *When Living Hurts: Directives for Treating Depression*. New York: Brunner/Mazel, 1988.

Young, L. *Out of Wedlock*. New York: McGraw-Hill, 1954.

Zeig, J.K. *Ericksonian Psychotherapy*. Volume 1: *Structures*. New York: Brunner/Mazel, 1985.

Index